bread book

bread book

Ideas and Innovations from the Future of Grain, Flour, and Fermentation

Chad Robertson with Jennifer Latham

LORENA JONES BOOKS

An imprint of TEN SPEED PRESS

California | New York

Contents

Introduction

The most rewarding thing about making bread is that the process of learning never ends. Every day is a new study. Scores of factors, including the temperature, ambient humidity, type of grain, and age of the flour, influence how the dough develops. To end up with a consistent loaf, the baker must make hundreds of micro-adjustments daily. Even if a baker were to make only country bread every day for the rest of their life, the process of learning, refining, and thinking about that one dough would never be perfected. Making naturally leavened bread engages a living process that grows and changes each day. When you then consider various styles of bread—baguettes, pan loaves, and slab breads, to name a few—as well as different grains, milling techniques, fermentation times, and non-grain inclusions, the possibilities are infinite.

I have always had a strong drive to learn and innovate—by nature I'm never content when resting—and this has influenced how Tartine operates. Bakeries in general are expected to be consistent and predictable. People want a good cup of coffee and a morning pastry along with fresh hot bread—daily provisions—and we strive impossibly hard to deliver that consistency. But operating the bakery more from my chef's perspective and less from a traditional baker's approach has led us to explore what an open-all-day neighborhood bakery could become. I'm constantly asking myself and our bakers and chefs, How can we make this better? No tenet of what we do goes unexamined. It's always worth scrutinizing the assumptions we make as a team and deciding whether they should be held, adapted, or discarded. This is how Tartine bread came about in the first place: by starting with the idea of a loaf and then building on it in unconventional ways in the context of modern baking while staying deeply rooted in tradition.

The central innovation in recent Tartine bread history has been our renewed and more heightened focus on flour sourcing. I was taught the importance of sourcing good grain and flour by Richard Bourdon, my first mentor in bread baking. At Tartine, we have always used sustainably farmed and milled grains, but several years ago, I decided to dive deeper in my relationships with grain breeders, farmers, and millers. I had been obsessively focused on making bread and the process of fermentation for two decades and then I noticed that my chef friends were having a bit more fun coloring outside the lines of traditional categories of cuisine. It was time for me to apply this same approach to baking.

Six years ago, I started to spend some time at the Bread Lab at Washington State University. I wanted to explore grain varieties and milling techniques with an eye to innovate. There I met grain breeders, farmers, and millers ready for change. We were all asking ourselves what makes grain and flour good. At the Bread Lab, they were looking at different types of grains—both new and ancient

varieties—and selecting for flavor and nutrition versus yield and machinability. Historically, as we've tried to grow more inexpensive food to feed more people, flavor and nutrition have fallen by the wayside, and highly processed grain-based foods have proliferated, leading to all sorts of health and wellness problems. This had to change, and I couldn't wait to collaborate.

Most modern flour comes from a handful of hard red winter wheat varieties that are selected for yield, in the field *and* in the mill. This is starkly different from most of agrarian history, during which people cultivated the grains that naturally thrived in the microclimates of the communities where they lived, milled, and ate. At the turn of the twentieth century, there were 2,000 flour mills in the United States. Now there are about 530. Several hundred years ago, most communities had a central mill, often powered by water, where families could take the grain they grew (wheat, corn, or other grains) to have it milled fresh for them. They would then take it home and bake with it right away. The flour was usually whole grain and was rarely sifted. (Sifting technology to produce white flour is modern, and discarding what's sifted off is a luxury.) Many communities had a baker who made bread weekly in a communal wood-fired oven. Each community had its own recipes—different breads, biscuits, flatbreads, or crispbreads—and they used whichever flour, given the climate, was best suited for their specific recipes. In parts of Europe, such as Scandinavia, you will find crispbreads that work particularly well with the low-gluten rye or soft wheat grains that grow there, and in northern Mexico, you will encounter tender flour tortillas that perfectly highlight the soft local Sonora wheat. This knowledge was passed on by generations of bakers who shared what they had learned from those who came before them.

The Industrial Revolution changed bread completely (along with the structure of communities). Bread started to be made in the same way as a Ford Model T: uniformly and mechanized as much as possible. The grain had to be uniform so it could be harvested by combines and milled by a Rube Goldberg system of tubes, rollers, vacuums, and fans. There was no place in this system for grains that had exquisite flavor but lower protein than was required to make fast-rising bread with commercial yeast, or grains that demonstrated amazing performance for bread baking but had stalks of different heights, which made efficient harvesting on an industrial scale impossible.

Nowadays, most of the wheat cultivated in the United States (along with Canada, Russia, and Kazakhstan) is grown from very few strains of hard red winter wheat. This means that farmers cannot save their own seed and must buy anew each planting season from the large corporations that own the seed patents. Historically, farmers chose the seeds from grains that worked best for them, their miller, and the community bakers. Today, farmers must plant the guaranteed variety to be ensured a full return on the harvest.

There is a new generation of farmers and millers looking to historical models of grain communities for inspiration in the same way that I first looked to historical methods of making bread. They are also using modern technology in innovative ways to get the maximum benefit from ancient techniques. We are both working to create methodologies that are scalable in regional communities and can have a restorative effect on modern food systems. Using ancient techniques and modern technology to empower the artisanal process has become the core value of Tartine's baking.

While farmers and millers are reclaiming historical knowledge about landrace and ancient grains, we, as bakers, are now taking the flours made with those grains and finding the best uses for them. Not every grain is suited to making country bread (in fact, few are). We are working to find opportunities to use these flavorful and nutritious grains, whether that's in pan loaves, flatbreads, pasta, tortillas, pizza, cakes, cookies, or pastries.

How we grow food has become the biggest environmental problem of our generation. What we eat, how we produce it, and how we prepare it will determine the well-being of our world for posterity. It is vitally important to make sustainable agriculture and food systems not only possible but economically attractive. It is just as critical to make good foods with those raw materials and to make them available and affordable to as many people as possible.

Tartine began as a small corner bakery serving the best things we knew how to make to the people in our neighborhood. We are now innovating on a broad scale, reaching toward the deep source of grain breeders, farmers, and millers and to our communities with the hope of delivering a product that has better flavor and nutrition than any of us has ever tasted, while leaving a lasting positive imprint on our regional food system.

After nearly twenty years on our corner in San Francisco's Mission District, the most exciting chapter of Tartine is just beginning.

Glossary of Terms

There are only about twenty terms you need to know to use our recipes fluently. They are words we frequently use as we work together discussing bread and developing new recipes; they represent the foundation of our approach to making bread. Once you memorize them, you'll better understand the science and craft of working with wild yeast, flour, hydration, and fermentation.

Autolyze: A period of rest between initial mixing and hydrating the flours and mixing for development, the autolyze allows flours to absorb hydration, relax, and begin to gently develop gluten. That translates to a shorter active mixing time and gentler mixing. At Tartine, we autolyze a dough for a minimum of 20 minutes, which is just enough time to start to gain the beneficial effect of this rest period. Doughs can be autolyzed with or without leaven or yeast. If you choose to include leaven in the autolyze, the fermentation will begin at the time you combine the flour, water, and leaven or yeast. If you choose to autolyze without leaven or yeast, the fermentation will begin once the leavening agent is added. Doughs can be autolyzed for much longer without leaven (we autolyze slab dough overnight, for example), but most of the hydrating and conditioning effect can be achieved in 20 to 40 minutes. The best reason for a longer autolyze is to make production smoother (to give you time to do something else while the dough is hydrating).

Baker's percentage: In any given recipe, bread bakers measure ingredients against a total flour weight. The flour weight is always 100%; everything else is measured proportional to that. For instance, when we say that a dough is 85% hydration, that means that the water weight is 85% of the total flour weight. This math may seem confusing at first, but once you become fluent, you will be able to understand recipes more deeply and create your own formulas with more predictable results. For more about this, see Introduction to Formulas, page 63.

Bassinage: This French term refers to the addition of hydration after the initial water (or other liquid) is mixed into the dough. At Tartine, we always start our high-hydration doughs with a little less water than we will end up adding. This allows for more dough strength to be built into the initial mixing phase (the more water in the mixture, the more difficult it is for protein strands to form) and permits us to adjust hydration by feel as we go along. For super-hydrated doughs, we always add the final portion at the end. The bassinage also helps you adjust your dough temperature as needed. If your dough is a little cooler than you want it to be, you can add very warm water to warm it up. If your dough is too warm, you can add cold water (I've even been known to add a trickle of ice water on very hot days) to bring down its temperature. In the case of slab bread, which autolyzes overnight and tends to get cool during that rest, I add a large amount of very warm water with the leaven, poolish, and yeast to bring the dough up to a temperature that will facilitate yeast activity.

Booster leaven: This is the leaven from the overnight starter that we feed in the morning before mixing. This leaven is fed with a large amount of seed and then, once it's ripe, is used to feed the leaven that goes into the dough. This booster feeding gives us tons of microbial activity in the final leaven and adds a fresh, creamy, floral aroma and flavor to the final leaven and the dough.

Bulk fermentation: This is the period between the end of mixing and the beginning of cutting the dough. During this time, the dough develops enough strength, gas bubbles, and acidity to hold its shape.

Commercial yeast: This refers to the yeast strain *Saccharomyces cerevisiae*. This is the same yeast often used in commercial alcohol fermentation and is commonly known as either "baker's yeast" or "brewer's yeast." It is the yeast you can purchase in fresh, active dry, or instant form at the store.

Development: The strength and structure of gluten formed by hydrating and agitating flour over time as dough ferments is known as "development." In general, you're looking for enough development that your dough has both strength and extensibility but not so much that it starts to break down. For doughs such as the one for the country bread method, which ferment overnight, we don't like to get maximum development in the mixing phase because some development occurs during bulk fermentation as we give turns, as well as

overnight as the dough rests and continues to slowly rise. Michel Suas, a dear friend and mentor, has often joked that we don't mix our doughs at Tartine, we just "temper" them. For doughs that are baked sooner after mixing than country bread is, such as those with added commercial yeast, I like to get a little more development in the mixing phase.

Dusting flour or work surface flour: You'll find lots of directions in this book to lightly dust your loaves or table with flour for shaping or pre-shaping. Almost any finely milled wheat flour will do for this purpose. You can use a little of your high-extraction bread, all-purpose, or pastry flour, or some more refined flour if you have that available. I don't generally use whole-wheat flour because the larger bran flakes stick to the loaf and make the surface rougher, but in a pinch that, too, would work just fine.

Float test: The float test is a great way to figure out if your leaven or dough is ready to move to the next step, especially when you're just starting out as a bread baker. It works well for testing the readiness of both the starter and the dough. When a batch of raw flour and water has just been mixed, no fermentation has occurred yet and no bubbles appear in the dough. As it starts to ferment, the microbial activity creates carbon dioxide, the bubbles of that carbon dioxide get trapped in the dough, and the dough becomes lighter relative to the water. Instead of being a solid mass, it now has pockets of gas in it. Right after you mix it, the dough is heavier than water. At a certain point, so much gas is trapped in it that it becomes lighter than water. That is just about the right point to use the starter to inoculate your leaven or to divide and pre-shape your dough. This is not completely infallible. I use the float test as a point of reference, but sometimes I like to use the dough just before it fully floats, when it bobs in the water, especially if it's warm in the house and I know fermentation is going to move quickly. If the kitchen is cold or if I know that the dough has been stalling out for the last few days, I may wait 15, or even 30, minutes after the dough passes the float test before I divide it. The float test is not the final arbiter, but it is a great tool. With practice, you'll be able to tell when your starter or dough is ready by other signs, such as how much it has grown, how domed it is, and how it feels when you stretch it, but the float test is always a handy way of gathering information.

High-extraction flour: Flour that has had some of the bran removed in the milling process but retains much of the germs and oils is classified as high-extraction flour. It is slightly sifted, so it is not a whole-wheat flour, but it is not nearly as sifted as a white, or refined, flour. For more about milling, see About Grain and Flour, starting on page 28. Pure white sifted flour contains about 50 percent of the whole grain, while true whole wheat contains 100 percent. High-extraction flour, like the one we use to make our breads and pastries at Tartine, contains between 75 and 90 percent of the grain.

Hydration: This term refers to the amount of water in the dough, which is always expressed as a percentage of the flour in the recipe. However, porridge recipes include an additional amount of hydration that is cooked with the flour or grain until the starch is gelatinized before mixing the base dough. So, technically in porridge doughs you have the basic hydration based on percentage of flour plus an additional hydration that is specific to the porridge. The latter goes in toward the end of the mix after the main hydration has been added and the dough is well developed. (A colleague aptly articulated this approach by noting that we "cheat the math" in our porridge breads at Tartine.)

Leaven: Known as "levain" in French, this is the culture of flour, water, yeasts, and lactobacillus bacteria that inoculates the dough with the proper agents for leavening. In the United States, it's also called "sourdough starter" or "mother." For more information, see the Leaven Primer, starting on page 146.

Naturally leavened: Doughs or breads made using only wild yeast and bacteria, without added commercial yeast, are referred to as "naturally leavened."

Poolish: A mixture of flour, water, and yeast that is allowed to ferment and ripen before being added to the dough, poolish contributes subtle but complex yeasty flavor, increased extensibility, and a gentle leavening or lightening of the dough without introducing fresh commercial yeast.

Porridge bread: This is any bread that has a portion of cooked or scalded broken-down grain added to the dough. This can be whole or rolled grains, such as rolled oats or barley groats. It can also be cooked flour, such as durum flour, buckwheat flour, or einkorn flour. Adding cooked grain gives the dough structure by adding vegetable gels, but it also adds hydration in the form of lots of water trapped in those vegetable gels. It's a great way to incorporate whole grains, especially grains without much or any gluten (like rye). Using scalded grain also adds tenderness and longevity to the bread.

Preferment: Any component of the dough, such as the leaven, poolish, biga, or sponge, that is fermented before the final mixing step is known as a preferment.

Salt: Considering our country bread is just flour, water, and salt, we like to pay equal attention to each of the ingredients. Salt can vary tremendously, from the simple NaCl (sodium chloride) in Morton's table salt to pink mountain-mined salt (as opposed to salt evaporated from saltwater), which contains more than forty different trace minerals. Our general rule of thumb is to use a salt that is refined as little as possible and tastes delicious. If you taste super-refined sodium chloride next to a pink salt or a sea salt from Brittany, France, you will notice a clear difference in flavor. The refined salt tastes a little metallic and one-note, while the salts with a wider variety of minerals have a more subtle and complex taste. The flavor of your salt certainly comes through in the bread, and there are nutritional benefits to consuming a wide variety of trace minerals. Almost any salt will work in these recipes, as long as you measure it by weight. There's a big difference in volume between a fine or a coarse salt, but if measured by weight they'll provide roughly the same salinity (just don't use a very coarse rock salt—that won't dissolve into the dough). I've called for "sea salt" in most of these recipes to differentiate from table salt, but any minimally refined salt will do. I like medium-coarse (similar in grain size to kosher salt) sea salts from Brittany and the Pacific Northwest coast.

Scalded flour (also known as gelatinized flour or porridge): This describes flour that has been heated with two to four times its weight in water so the starch molecules burst and the vegetable gums are released and then gel. Adding scalded flour to bread dough creates a custardy texture and increases the shelf life of the baked bread by adding an extra portion of hydration bound by the gelled starch vegetable gums—essentially a way of cheating the math of traditional dough hydration to give you a crumb that retains moist texture much longer than it would without the addition. It is also a great way to utilize grains that don't have much gluten. For more information, see Scalding Flour, page 44.

Scoring: Cutting into the top of shaped bread dough helps the loaf to fully expand in the oven. If you do not score a loaf, it will not rise to its potential and will likely burst open along the sides. Scoring also determines the final appearance of the loaf, and experienced bakers use different techniques—varying the angle, quantity, and pattern of the scores—to create the look they want. After baking many loaves of bread, you will gain an understanding of how different scores affect the way a loaf expands in the oven. For example, cuts made at a very low angle (almost horizontal) to the dough will create pronounced "ears," or risen edges.

Sourdough: In addition to being used interchangeably for the term *leaven*, "sourdough" also refers to doughs made without the use of commercial yeast. At Tartine, instead of using the term *sourdough*, we tend to use the term *naturally leavened* because it more accurately describes the balanced flavor—acidic and fresh, creamy and floral, with the flavor of the grain still detectable—we are aiming for. This balance is usually much less sour tasting than the classic sourdoughs for which San Francisco became famous.

Recommended Equipment

Bread-making requires a few specialized tools, but most of what you need is probably already in your kitchen. A handful of the recipes in this book call for tools designed for specific tasks, such as a pasta maker, but I have tried to keep those to a minimum. Most of the recipes can be made with the same few trusty everyday pieces.

Tools for Country Bread (and Other Pan and Hearth Loaves)

Baking stone or baking steel: The purpose of a baking stone is to store a lot of heat so that when dough is placed on it to bake, the surface stays very hot instead of being cooled by the dough. This assists with oven spring and crust formation. It serves a similar function as cast iron when a Dutch oven or skillet is used. Baking stones and steels produce a significant difference in baguettes and pizzas, making them fluffier and crisper. The rapid introduction of high heat enables pita bread dough to puff up and create an air pocket inside. Make sure to check the manufacturer's instructions and preheat the stone for as long as necessary. Some stones require up to 1 hour of preheating time.

Bowl: You will need a large bowl for pre-mixing, mixing, and fermenting in bulk (before you divide and shape). I like to use a large, thick clear glass bowl because it makes it easy to mix and turn the dough. Glass is the best material for a couple of reasons: it holds temperature well, keeping your dough nice and warm, and it also allows you to look at the structure of the dough as it develops, giving you a good idea of how fermentation is proceeding. You can actually see the fermentation by watching the bubbles start to form through the glass. Ceramic and clay work well, too, because they also hold their temperature nicely. If you want to use a big metal bowl, remember that metal conducts heat effectively, so you'll need to keep the bowl somewhere it won't cool off (or heat up) too much while fermenting in bulk and to monitor your dough temperature closely.

Bread box: There are lots of ways to store your freshly baked bread. A bread box with a snug-fitting lid is the most sustainable choice. You can store your unwrapped loaf inside the box at room temperature for a few days. To store it longer, many people like to slice the bread once it has cooled, place it in an airtight freezer-proof container, and freeze for up to 2 weeks. With this approach, you can toast a fresh-tasting slice whenever you like.

Bread knife: A serrated or very sharp carbon-steel knife is good for slicing bread. Many of the breads in this book are very moist, with an extreme textural contrast between crust and crumb. A dull knife will crush the crumb, which frustrates the process at best.

Cast-iron double Dutch oven (5 quart): This sturdy pot becomes a completely sealed oven within your oven, trapping heat and steam under ideal conditions for your loaf to rise and your crust and crumb to form properly during the bake. This is the best way we've found to trap steam and mimic the heat of a full-size bread oven with steam injection. I use a Lodge cast-iron double Dutch oven that I reserve only for this purpose. The double Dutch works well because the top doesn't have a handle and is deeper than a regular lid. That means you can cook in both the top and the bottom of the pot. For baking bread, you will be placing the loaf to bake in the shallower top half and covering it with the deeper pot. You can use a Le Crueset or other enameled Dutch oven instead of a double Dutch oven, but it will be more difficult to place the dough in the pot and score it.

Cooling rack: It is important to keep loaves from steaming themselves as they cool, as the crust will get soft if the steam cannot escape. To ensure air circulates freely around loaves, always set them on a cooling rack.

Digital scale: This is one of the most essential tools in any kitchen. Weighing ingredients is much faster, more accurate, and cleaner than measuring with cups and spoons. All the measures for the ingredients for the bread recipes in this book are given by weight for these reasons. Kitchen scales are widely available at kitchen stores and online. Entry-level scales are inexpensive and work just fine for all purposes in this book, but you can also get highly accurate and waterproof scales by spending a little more.

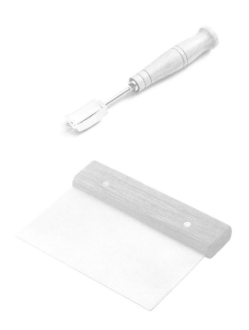

Hot pads or oven mitts: Find pads or mitts that are thick and sturdy, as you'll be baking at very high temperatures and handling the heavy top and bottom of a double Dutch oven.

Kitchen thermometer: A probe thermometer is essential for checking the temperature of your dough as it is fermenting and the internal temperature of pan loaves to determine whether they are finished baking, especially when you are just beginning to learn the process. An infrared thermometer is not essential, but it is handy to now the temperature of your baking surface, as ovens vary. I also use it to measure the temperature of my Dutch oven and my baking stone to make sure they are sufficiently heated for baking.

Kitchen towels and linen couche: Clean kitchen towels are handy for covering doughs to keep them warm while they proof and to protect them from drafts that can cause a skin to develop on the surface. They are also useful for lining proofing baskets and placing baguettes to proof. The classic French ones we use at Tartine are made of tightly woven, undyed, stiff linen—called a "couche"—but any clean, tightly woven, untreated linens will work.

Lame: A lame is a blade with a handle that bakers use to score their loaves. You can change the blade often so you are always scoring with a very sharp edge. The thinnest blades are best, as they have less "drag," enabling a clean and precise score. We use very thin double-edge blades, which are available at kitchen and baking supply stores. If you don't have a lame, you can use scissors or a very sharp knife, though it is hard to get the right angle and depth to get a good ear on your loaf with anything but a lame.

Metal bench knife: This is basically a rectangle of stainless steel with a wooden handle attached along one of the long sides. It is an extension of my hand when I'm cutting and pre-shaping dough. I use it just that way, holding it in my right hand to steer and scoop dough while guiding with my left. It's great for mixing eggs into flour for pasta dough and for picking up and moving pieces of dough when

making flatbread or tortillas. It's also useful for scraping the work surface clean after the dough has been shaped and put away.

Pitcher: I use a small Pyrex measuring pitcher to perform float tests, dampen my fingers, and add water as I mix. This tool is indispensable in the dough-mixing process and also very handy in other areas of the kitchen.

Plastic bowl scraper: This is a stiff yet flexible piece of plastic that fits in your hand and is curved on one edge and straight on the other. It's handy for getting dough out of bowls and for scraping bits of dough off your hands and off the sides of the bowl after mixing or turning dough.

Proofing basket: The baskets we use at Tartine are made of woven wicker and are lined with a piece of undyed linen sewn in place. The wicker is woven with just enough space in the weave to allow the linen to breathe as wet doughs rise. There

are lots of different styles of proofing baskets, made from a variety of materials. Because the dough relaxes in the basket overnight, the shape of the basket will influence the final shape of the loaf. We avoid putting our loaves directly into any basket without a liner, as the dough is too wet and proofs too long to come away from the basket without sticking. You can use any clean, tightly woven material as a liner; just drape it into the basket, covering the bottom and sides, and flour it well. At Tartine, we use a long, oval-shaped basket for our country batards and a round basket for our porridge and whole-grain hearth loaves. For home use, I'd recommend getting two 9-inch round proofing baskets. These will work just as well for country dough as for any other hearth loaf. Having two allows you to bake two loaves at once, which most of our hearth bread recipes yield (one for you and one for your neighbors). The dimensions of this basket match the dimensions of the 5-quart double Dutch oven perfectly. If you do not have a proofing basket, a bowl will work. Look for one about 9 inches in diameter and line it with a clean, tightly woven cloth.

Spray bottle: A clean, food-grade spray bottle with a very-fine spray nozzle, used only for water, is handy for introducing steam to a hot oven when you're baking baguettes, slab bread, or pan loaves.

Work surface: You will hear me refer to a "work surface" repeatedly in this book. Almost all the recipes require some table or counter space to mix, knead, divide, and shape dough. If you are a committed baker, it makes sense to have a wooden butcher block–topped area for performing these tasks. Wood is the best material for dough, as it does not conduct heat very well, and thus won't chill your dough too much, and the texture of wood is compatible for kneading and shaping. If you are working with limited space in your kitchen, you could purchase a large cutting board to go on top of a counter or a table when you need it. Make sure the surface that your dough comes into contact with has not been treated with any substance that is not food safe.

Other Tools

Enameled cast-iron Dutch oven: Many of the savory nonbread recipes in this book are for broth, beans, and braises that are best made in a Dutch oven. I use an enameled cast-iron one for this purpose, as the cast-iron one that I use for bread is a little more difficult to care for and is often in service at the same time. This is one of the most universally useful pieces in the kitchen.

Pasta extruder: This is the device you'll use to make spaghetti, bucatini, macaroni, fusilli, or any other extruded pasta. At home, I use an extruder that attaches to my KitchenAid mixer, but there are a wide variety of machines available for this purpose. Some are attachments, like mine, that use the motor of a stand mixer to power them; others are freestanding.

Pasta-rolling machine: I use an Atlas hand-cranked machine to sheet my pasta at home. There are electric-powered models and stand-mixer attachments on the market that also work well. You can use a rolling pin, but you'll need extra elbow grease. The Atlas is what you'll use for making wide, flat egg noodles.

Peels: A baker's peel is a thin piece of wood that is used to transfer a piece of dough ready to be baked onto the hot baking surface. A baguette peel is roughly the shape of a baguette. It has no handle; you just grasp it by its edge. A pizza peel is nearly square and has a long handle for maneuvering the pizza off the peel and into and out of the oven. Peels are found at baking and kitchen supply stores.

Skillet: I like to use a 10-inch cast-iron skillet for toasting buns and rolls, cooking tortillas, and griddling sandwiches. Make sure yours is properly seasoned so eggs and other delicate ingredients don't stick. Instructions on how to season a skillet can be found on the pan's packaging and online; I like to use flax oil to season mine. Many recipes in this book call for sautéed or seared vegetables or wilted greens. I like to use a 10-inch nonstick skillet for these purposes, but if you have a well-seasoned cast-iron skillet, it will also work.

Timer: In this book, you will be regularly instructed to let the dough rest for a few minutes or half an hour. It is easiest to keep track of these intervals (and bake times) with a kitchen timer.

Tortilla press: I use the press to pre-shape my tortillas and then I finish them by hand with a rolling pin. You can use a rolling pin for the whole process, but the tortilla press speeds things along quite a lot.

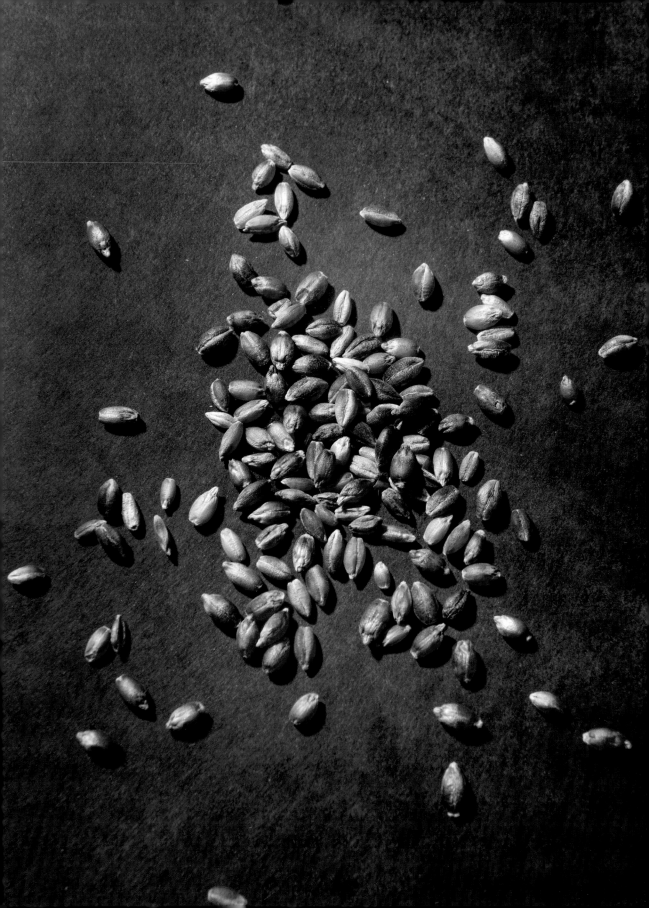

About Grain and Flour

The cultivation of reliable food sources, including grains, has been considered one of the biggest technological innovations of humankind, ushering in the shift from hunter-gatherer societies to modern civilized culture as we know it. It is widely understood by historians and archaeologists that people have been consuming grains for much of human history. Consequently, bread has been a cornerstone of sustenance for families and communities for millennia, nourishing generations across the world.

Wheat is a cereal grain in the grass family. The seeds of the wheat plant are edible for humans, more so when they are crushed, hydrated, fermented, and baked into bread. There are a tremendous number of different types of wheat. Some, like einkorn and emmer, are relatively unchanged from the wild grasses that still grow in the Fertile Crescent (the birthplace of grain cultivation). Some, such as Øland wheat in Scandinavia and Sonora in Mexico, have evolved slowly along with the regional cuisine, so the distinctive local breads and the flour they are made from are well suited to each other. Still others, such as the Turkish Red varieties grown for commodity milling across much of the United States, have been bred for qualities such as uniform height of seed head and maximal yield per acre.

A wheat berry is made up of three basic components: the bran, the germ, and the endosperm. The bran, which is made mostly of insoluble fiber and some vitamins, is the outer hull that protects the seed. The germ contains all the information for a new plant to grow—the "germ" of the new plant. It is made of oils, vitamins, and enzymes. It is often the first part of the grain to be sifted off during flour production because the oils go rancid quickly compared with the other parts of the wheat berry. The endosperm is made of the starch and protein that will feed the young plant as it starts to sprout. The endosperm makes up about 80 percent of the wheat berry. If you think of a wheat berry as an egg, the bran is the shell, the endosperm is the white of the egg, and the germ is the yolk.

A raw wheat berry contains a tremendous amount of nutrition, but not in an ideal form for people to digest. Ruminant animals, such as cows and goats, have evolved to eat grasses (wheat, rice, barley, rye, and oats are all in the grass family). They chew the leaves and berries several times and have four stomachs to ferment and break them down. Humans must perform the crushing and fermenting steps outside their bodies to access the best nutritional potential of the grain.

As humans became more adept at consuming grains, the crushing, fermenting, and baking became more refined. If you simply crush grain, add water, wait for the mixture to ferment, and then bake it, you will get some form of bread. The properties of grain—ample starch available for yeast and bacteria to consume (ferment) and stretchy protein to trap the gasses that are a by-product of that fermentation— mean that at its most basic level, bread-making almost happens by itself. It takes the baker to shepherd it along to the next steps when it's ready. Hence, the best bread comes from bakers who are skilled in choosing when to move on to the next stage of the process.

Protein content is one of the most relevant aspects of grain makeup. Gluten *is* protein (though not the only protein found in grain). The webs of gluten that are formed when wheat flour is hydrated, agitated, and fermented trap gas bubbles to form the beautiful open crumb we love to see when we cut into a loaf.

Higher-protein wheat flour contains more gluten. The more gluten there is in the flour, the stronger the dough will be. As a general rule, higher-protein flours (12 to 14 percent) are better for bread baking, especially if you are looking for a fluffy loaf with an open crumb. Lower-protein flours (8 to 10 percent) are often used for making cakes and pastries, in which lower protein results in a more tender crumb. All-purpose flours, which contain 10 to 12 percent protein, are usually somewhere in the middle. That's not the whole story, however. In wheat, gluten itself is made up of two constituent proteins, glutenin and gliadin. Glutenin has more strength and plasticity, while gliadin contributes to the extensibility of dough. Two different flours may have the same protein percentage, but if one has a higher ratio of gliadin to glutenin, it will be much more extensible and viscous. Another flour at the same protein percentage with a higher proportion of gliadin will feel much stronger and more elastic. That's why you can't always know how a flour will perform by only looking at protein percentage.

A baker will come across several different categories of wheat when making bread. The most common will be winter/spring, hard/soft, and red/white. The seasonal designation for wheat refers to when the farmer plants it. In milder climates, a farmer might sow wheat in the fall so it overwinters in the ground. The seed lies dormant until the weather warms up, when it then grows into a plant. This is winter wheat. Spring wheat is sown in the spring and sprouts soon after planting. The same variety can be a winter or spring wheat, depending on when it is planted, but more often different varieties are recognized to be better suited for one of the two seasons. The winter/spring designation of the grain has a little influence on the baking properties of the flour, though not nearly as much as the strain of wheat or other growing factors, such as irrigation and fertilization.

The terms *hard* and *soft* are the biggest indicator to a baker of how the flour will perform. Hard wheats have a higher protein content than soft wheats. Often hard wheats are used to make bread flour, and soft wheats are used to make pastry flour. All-purpose flour can be made with either or with a blend of the two.

Red or white wheat refers to the color of the kernel (there are also amber, purple, black, and blue wheats, but for classification purposes most of our common-use wheats are either red or white). The same components that give red wheat its color also give it a nutty, sometimes slightly tannic flavor. White wheats tend to taste rich and creamy. The difference between a red-wheat flour and a white-wheat flour often can't be seen if the flour is sifted, unlike with whole-grain flours, where the distinctions are much more apparent. Although a loaf made with whole-grain white wheat can have the lighter color of one made with sifted flour, it will have much more flavor, fiber, and higher nutritional value.

The term *sifting* refers to how much of the bran and germ are left in the flour after milling. Stone-milled whole-grain flour has all the bran, germ, and endosperm of the wheat berries. White flour has had almost all of the bran and germ removed and is primarily composed of the endosperm of the grain. The sifted-off bran of commercial whole-wheat flour is usually put back in, but not the germ, as it can spoil. High-extraction flour (see page 20) has had some of the largest pieces of bran sifted off, but almost all of the germ and the oils (and some of the finer bran) are retained. Since the bran and the germ contain dietary fiber, B vitamins, antioxidants, and minerals such as zinc, iron, and magnesium, whole-grain and high-extraction flours are much more healthful.

The answer to the question, What makes good wheat *good*? depends on whom you are asking. A commodity farmer who is looking for the highest yield per acre and crops with reliable protein content will want a wheat that is consistent, hardy, and predictable. A community farmer who has an ongoing relationship with a miller and maybe even a baker might want to plant a specialty wheat that is particularly flavorful but won't behave exactly the same or may yield a little less from crop to crop. If the baker is looking for grain that has more flavor and better properties for a particular type of baked good, then the farmer has incentive to plant that grain.

It's also critical to consider the growing and harvesting practices that make wheat harmful to the land and human health. Commodity wheat is grown in a monoculture farming style, which depletes and exhausts the soil and, because of the lack of biodiversity, draws pests, which are handled with herbicides and pesticides to ensure the highest yield per acre. The majority of commercial wheat farmers and agribusiness producers in the United States spray their crops with Roundup (glyphosate) right before harvesting, which kills the stalks and dries them out, making them easier to thresh. The pesticide remains in the grain throughout milling, so traces of glyphosate are present in the flour. US government agricultural agencies have long held that glyphosate is safe for human consumption, but in 2015, the World Health Organization (WHO) classified it as a "probable human carcinogen" after considering peer-reviewed studies by researchers around the world who found a pattern of association between exposure to glyphosate and non-Hodgkin's lymphoma and other cancers.

It is also important to consider the holistic picture of how the wheat is grown. Throughout the agricultural cycle, farmers make many choices that have a tremendous effect on our environment. Is crop rotation being practiced to naturally replenish the soil and deter pests and disease? Is the crop being irrigated in a region prone to drought? There are many factors to consider, but the more proximal you are to your miller and farmer, the easier it is to make an informed choice.

The miller is the essential middle link in the chain between the farmer and the baker. There are several different ways to mill flour, but the most common ways to do so at scale are either with a roller mill or a stone mill. A roller mill crushes wheat berries between two rollers. In large operations, the berries pass through a whole series of rollers and sifters, with the rollers getting closer together and bran and germ being sifted away as the berries are ground. The great majority of flour (and all large-scale commercial flour) is milled this way. Even commercial whole-grain flour is milled this way: all the components of the grain are separated until only the white flour that comes from the endosperm is left and then, as noted earlier, the bran is added back before packaging.

Stone mills are an ancient technology. They employ two stones (natural or composite): one stationary and one rotating. The grain is fed between the stones and crushed as grooves in the stones move against each other. All of the parts of the grain are ground together into the flour. Stone mills can be as big as a train car or small enough to fit on a tabletop.

At Tartine, we have partnered with miller Kevin Morse at Cairnspring Mills in Skagit Valley, Washington, who employs a combination of old and new technology in a way that echoes my own ethos. He uses a roller mill to first crack the grain so it can be ground more finely when he then passes it through a stone mill. His is the most beautiful flour I've ever baked with—soft and fine yet incredibly flavorful and nutritious. It's high-extraction flour that essentially has the baking qualities of white flour, which means we get the flavor and nutritional value of an almost soft whole-grain flour along with the aesthetic qualities afforded by using sifted white flour.

Now you understand why the answer to the question of what makes flour good depends on who's asking. If you're a large commercial bakery trying to get flour to turn into bread as quickly and as cheaply as possible, you want the grain that is going to give you the most predictable performance at the lowest cost. If you're an artisan baker or a home baker making recipes that take some skill, attention, and adaptability, you are more likely to be able to make tiny adjustments as you go along to account for variations in flour and to prioritize flavor and performance over predictability. Also, if you're making small batches of different baked goods, you may want to buy modest amounts of flours that are more suited to those recipes. For example, buy a soft white wheat flour for cakes or a hard red spring flour for bread. The resulting baked good will have more flavor and more of the qualities you're looking for— tenderness in a cake or an open, creamy crumb in a bread.

There are two ways to approach baking with heirloom or landrace grains (varieties that have been improved through the use of traditional agricultural methods). You can start with a desired product and choose the flour that you think has the right properties for that product (say, hard red spring wheat, like Yecora Rojo, for bread). Or you can start with a flour, make a simple recipe or two to get a feel for what its properties are, and then extrapolate which kinds of baked goods those properties might best be suited for. This is how the einkorn flatbread recipe in this book developed. I had baked with einkorn enough that I had a feel for it, meaning I'd observed its soft, delicate gluten structure and graham-crackery sweetness. Those characteristics made me think of a soft, pillowy flatbread, and that's how our einkorn flatbread was born. This approach is something like the inventive process of a cook who goes to the farmers' market and creates a dish based on whatever beautiful produce inspires them.

Baking with small-batch and heirloom grains takes more time, attention, and practice. Flours made from these grains just aren't as predictable, so sometimes you need to make adjustments along the way, try a recipe a few times, or try the flour in a few recipes of differing styles. But the results and discoveries are worth the extra time you invest. Finding the perfect flour to match what you're baking results in a sublime product, certainly greater than the sum of its parts.

How to Choose a Flour

If you'd like to try flours besides what's on the grocery-chain shelf, the best place to start is with small regional millers who have relationships with the farmers growing regional specialties. Start as locally as possible and then explore farther afield. Over the past few years, thousands of people have discovered their own regional grains and mills. The rich diversity in grain and milling that is building around the country is inspiring to all. Lots of heirloom grains are best suited to particular microclimates. Millers who are milling small batches of these flours are less likely to be distributing broadly. You're also more likely to get fresh flour if you buy from a local mill (if you're buying stone-ground flour with the germ retained, you'll want it as fresh as possible).

The subject of freshness in flour is often debated by bakers. Fresher flour is sometimes thought to be harder to work with because it's less predictable. Commercial flour is deliberately oxidized, either through chemical agents (such as bleach) or by long storage before sale. The uniformity of commercial flour is desirable for large commercial systems that require precise predictability, but it is not necessary for human-powered operations where small adjustments are the norm. The performance variations of fresh flour are also much less noticeable in doughs that are highly hydrated and gently mixed. For me, any small variations in performance are secondary to the marked increase in flavor achieved from using fresh-milled flour with the germ retained.

When choosing flour, consider a few aspects. You'll want to factor the performance you're looking for. What characteristics are you looking for in a bread? Do you need a strong flour? A stretchy one? Is there a regional history associated with the flour you are using? Sonora wheat, for example, evolved concurrently with flour tortillas to become perfectly suited to each other. If you're using a grain that traditionally grows in Denmark, you may want to look and see what is traditionally baked there. Flavor is another consideration. You may want a strong, nutty red wheat flavor in a rustic country loaf, whereas a mellower, creamier white wheat may be more appropriate for a bun.

Sometimes you may want to use a blend of flours. We almost always use a blend for the country dough at the bakery. Yecora Rojo is our cornerstone bread flour, but it is so strong that if we don't blend it with something softer and more extensible, the crumb can be a little tight and chewy. We usually combine it with 10 to 30 percent of a more extensible flour, such as spelt or Sequoia, to balance the super-strength of the Yecora Rojo.

You may also want to consider intentional sourcing, which takes a bit of work. If you are able to find a local mill and can trace the grain back to a farm, it's worth researching how the grain is grown. Throughout the agricultural cycle, farmers make many choices that have a tremendous effect on our environment. To qualify for certification, organic grains are grown with a high level of care. Supporting farmers who are making responsible choices will make these farming practices economically viable and sow positive outcomes for generations.

How to Troubleshoot and Adjust

There are a few things you can do to achieve better results when you're working with a flour that you're unfamiliar with.

First, go slowly with hydration. It's always better to start a little dry than a little wet—adding water is easier than adding flour. Remember, French bread is often as low as 65 percent hydration because European flours are generally lower in protein and thus too weak to handle high hydration. When in doubt, lower the hydration and add water slowly as you mix (when instructed to do so).

Second, mix slowly and rest often. Sometimes, especially with flours that are high in gliadin (the extensible protein), a dough will feel very strong while you are mixing it and then quickly become slack as it rests. If you mix for a minute and then let it rest for a minute, you'll be able to tell whether you want to add more water or not as you finish mixing.

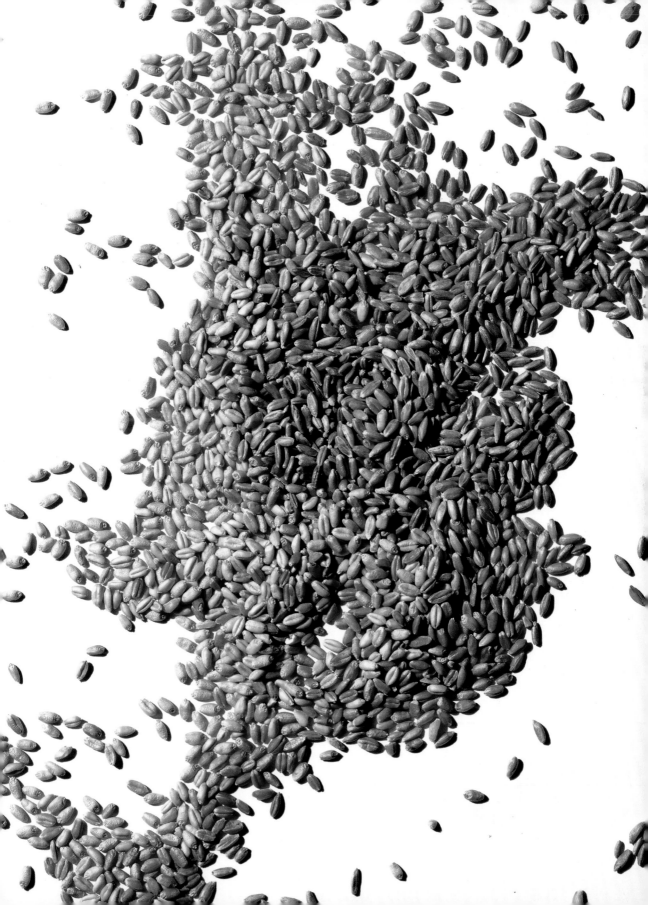

Third, be forgiving with your expectations. Working with a new flour is a learning process, and that means that things will not always go the way you expect them to. Try something, learn from it—whether it's the lesson you expected or not—and take that learning into your next bake. Many of the key innovations that we've made at Tartine over the years have been drawn from observing and building on things we never expected. The process is worth it. As friend and mentor Alan Scott wrote in *The Bread Builders*, "The skillful baker who produces delicious, light whole-grain loaves offers his customers a wonderful gift: a pleasant way to better health."

Grain Guide

Here are some of my favorite grains, with a brief description of our experience baking with them and how we like to use them. This is by no means an exhaustive list; in fact, it is only a very small fraction of the multitude of grains grown across the world. It is also important to remember that this is somewhat subjective. My experience with Sequoia, for instance, may be different from someone else's, especially considering the variability of grains from crop to crop. I happen to really love the flavor of Sequoia, but I also love the flavor of natto, Japan's textural, fermented soybean, and that is not always for everyone. Taste is necessarily subjective.

Cara club: Called "club" because the seed head of the plant is rounded like a club, Cara club wheat is very low in protein and makes the best-ever biscuits, piecrusts, and crumbles. We also blend it in buns, where we want a particularly melting texture, but it is too soft and weak for hearth loaves.

Durum: Durum is, in fact, a family of wheats with many varieties within the type, including Blue Beard durum, a particularly beautiful grass. Durum wheat was bred around 10,000 BCE in the Middle East and Ethiopia by selecting strains of emmer wheat for color and protein qualities. The word *durum* means "hard" in Latin, and it is indeed the hardest wheat—so hard that it must go through extra milling to become fine enough for flour. Very high in protein but low in gluten, a dough mixed from 100 percent durum flour is much more plastic than elastic—think pasta dough rather than bread dough. While semolina flour and couscous are made from durum wheat, bread is almost never made entirely from it, and when it is, it is dense and sometimes gummy.

Buckwheat: Despite its name, buckwheat is not actually a wheat. It's part of a group of plants known as pseudocereals whose seeds are used in a similar way to those of wheats. Notably, pseudocereals aren't grasses and don't contain gluten. Amaranth, chia, and quinoa are also in this group. Buckwheat is rich in minerals—iron, magnesium, manganese—and contains compounds that regulate blood sugar. It has a strong flavor, which I like best when combined with other grains. Because buckwheat doesn't contain gluten, combining it with other grains also helps give it structure.

Edison: A landrace grain, Edison was developed by retired Bellingham Technical College professor Merrill Lewis for Northwest climates and was improved by the Bread Lab at Washington State University. It is a hard white wheat with a beautiful pale gold color and a creamy, buttery flavor. We use a portion of high-extraction (T85) Edison wheat in our pain de mie and in our buns. It looks and acts like a refined white flour but carries some of the wheat's bran and germ. The whole-grain version is also wonderful for adding softness to breads and pastries.

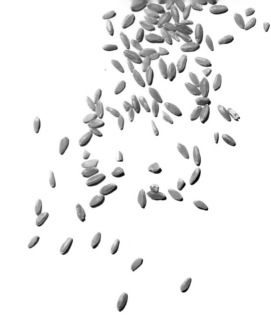

Einkorn: The oldest domesticated wheat, einkorn still grows wild in Turkey, one of the regions where humans first cultivated crops. The wheat berry is tiny, golden, and sweet. Einkorn makes wonderful pastries or bread if achieving an open crumb is not a consideration.

Emmer: This is another ancient grain, also known as farro. Emmer is low in gluten, and we often use it cooked and mixed into the dough for porridge breads.

Kamut: The trademarked name of a strain of Khorasan wheat, Kamut is an ancient golden durum wheat. The name "Khorasan" actually refers to a historical region in what is now northeastern Iran, southern Turkmenistan, and northern Afghanistan. Kamut has a very large golden wheat berry and makes a strong, vibrantly yellow flour with a very sweet flavor. I love to use it for crackers and crispbreads.

Rye: Part of the same botanical family as wheat (Poaceae) but from a different subfamily (along with rice and barley), rye contains some gluten, but the primary source of structure in rye bread is vegetable gums and gelled starch. The process for making rye bread is very different from how wheat bread is made, and one flour cannot be substituted for the other, though they are often combined to make some exceptional breads and pastries.

Sequoia: A hard red winter wheat with a protein content of about 11.5 percent, Sequoia is an excellent all-purpose flour and is also good for blending with Yecora Rojo for country bread. Sequoia berries are a bold red and have a corresponding bold, nutty flavor.

Sonora: A soft white wheat native to northern Mexico, Sonora has a sweet, mellow, creamy flavor and a soft, delicate gluten profile. It is ideal for tortillas and biscuits.

Spelt: A member of the farro family, spelt has an extensible quality and relaxes more during rest than other wheats. As a result, it is best to take extra care when mixing doughs with spelt to not add too much hydration. Spelt can be found in both whole-grain form (whole spelt wheat) and in a sifted, or "white flour," version.

Yecora Rojo: Very high in protein—almost 14 percent—and very strong, Yecora Rojo is a staple in our bakery kitchen. It goes into our country bread and is the basis for lots of other breads. It was originally developed as a cross between Sonora wheat and a red wheat in collaboration between the Mexican Ministry of Agriculture and the International Maize and Wheat Improvement Center. Yecora is the name of a town in the Mexican state of Sonora, and Rojo refers to trigo rojo, or red wheat.

Scalding Flour

Scalding flour has a long history in German and Scandinavian bread baking and a more recent one in Hokkaido milk bread and Tangzhong bread. Heating a slurry of grain and water causes the starch molecules in the grain to burst and gelatinize. It's a good way to use flours that don't have strong gluten structure, such as rye flour, because the gelled starch does the work of building strength and structure in the bread. This is the same principle behind our porridge breads. The gelatinized starch that makes oat porridge so creamy also makes the crumb of the bread creamy. Scalding is a good way to get whole grains or whole-grain flours incorporated into breads while still maintaining a light, soft crumb. Scalded flour also contributes to the longevity of bread by trapping more moisture than would otherwise be possible. When we say "porridge," we are generally referring to any broken-down grain cooked in water, whether that's rolled grains, cracked grains, or milled flour.

Different grains take different amounts of water to scald. The ideal consistency for scalded flour is a thick paste. Both coarse milled polenta and rolled barley flakes take a lot of water—a 3:1 ratio (3 parts barley to 1 part water, and sometimes even a little more water)—to get that consistency. I find that whole-wheat flour works best with a 2:1 ratio (although some people use as much as 4:1). When you're scalding flour for a dough, you can always adjust as you go, adding a little more water as you cook if the flour-water mixture seems too stiff.

The process of preparing scalded flour is the same as making cream of wheat (or cooking oatmeal), which was a regular and beloved breakfast in my house when I was a kid. First, put the water into a wide saucepan with the heat off. Then add whatever flour you're going to use and whisk or stir the flour and water together well until there are no lumps. Then turn on the heat to medium. Stir the mixture continually as it cooks to avoid clumping. The mixture will start off loose, like a slurry, and become stiffer as it gelatinizes, and the color of the flour will deepen. It's important to make sure the flour is cooked all the way before you remove it from the heat. If it is undercooked, it will have a loosening effect on the dough. If it is fully gelatinized, it will have a strengthening effect on the dough. You will get dramatically different results from the same formula if you use undercooked scald or fully cooked scald. It is ready when it has become a thick, smooth paste and registers at least 160°F on your kitchen thermometer. If your mixture does end up clumpy, you can always put it into a stand mixer fitted with the paddle attachment and paddle it until it is smooth.

Once the flour is cooked, you will need to let it cool a bit before you add it to a dough. The easiest way to do this is to spread it thinly on a sheet pan and use it just when it cools off to room temperature.

You can add as little as 5 percent scalded flour to a dough, which will give it increased moisture, longevity, and tenderness, or as much as 50 percent, which will make it very delicate, moist, and custardy. You can make scalded flour in batches and store it in an airtight container in the refrigerator for up to 1 week.

Recipes in this book calling for scalded flour list the weight and percentage of the prepared scald in the formula. This is important because the weight of the gelatinized flour differs from the separate weights of the uncooked flour and water. I usually make a little more scald than I think I'll need, knowing I'll lose some water weight to steam during the cooking process and that some will inevitably stick to the pan.

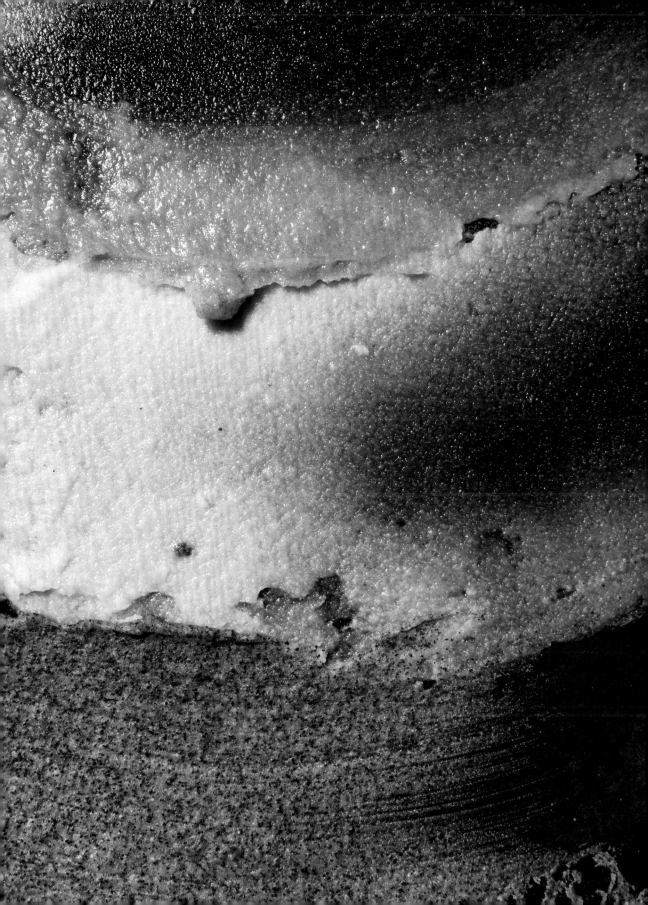

Leaven Primer

The culture of microorganisms that will ferment a flour-water mixture and raise dough goes by many names. At Tartine, we call it "starter" or "leaven." We use the word *starter* to refer to the small amount of culture that is regularly refreshed or "fed" with water and flour to maintain a mix of healthy microbes in the right balance. Other terms for this culture are *sourdough starter* or *mother*. We use the word *leaven* to refer to the particular amount, known as the preferment, that goes into the dough. Leaven can be a noun, meaning the mixture of flour, water, and microorganisms, or a verb, meaning to raise a dough. **Throughout this book, I will be using "starter" to refer to the culture that you are feeding once or twice a day to keep it alive—but not putting directly into the dough—and "leaven" for the culture you will be feeding the night before or just a few hours before mixing it into the dough to raise it.**

How bakers choose to feed and handle the starter and the leaven can vary greatly, depending on what they want to get out of them. At Tartine, we feed our starter frequently and keep it warm, aiming to cultivate a young, fresh leaven with enough wild yeast and leavening power, which we define as being populated with sufficient yeast and bacteria to raise the dough but not enough to develop a too-sour flavor. This now-signature style of young leaven was developed out of circumstantial necessity many years ago when I was working alone in Point Reyes Station, a small town north of San Francisco, sleeping split shifts and building a fire in the oven seven days a week. That technique has been refined and more or less standardized by the Tartine family over many years. When we feed the starter

these days, we discard all but a small amount, which we call "the seed," and then mix in equal parts flour and water.

Once you have a healthy starter going and have some practice feeding it, you can experiment with how much and how often to feed it so it is optimized for your baking schedule and your particular baking conditions. With practice, you will begin to see the direct relationship between the character of a starter or a leaven and the character of the final bread. Many people "taste" the starter and/or leaven to assess its readiness. I've always gathered much more information from smelling than from tasting; try both and develop your own preference.

I love the daily rhythm of feeding a starter. Once you have been doing it for some time, you do not need to pull out the scale and a fresh jar for every feeding. It becomes natural to scoop out all but a pinch of the starter—the discard—and then "feed" the pinch by stirring in fresh warm water and enough flour until the consistency feels right—like a thick batter. I use the same jar until the sides get crusty, and then I transfer the pinch to a clean jar and feed the starter in that jar, moving to a new jar once again when that jar becomes crusty. After feeding, I tuck the jar into a warm spot until the next morning and repeat the process each morning thereafter. If I'm starting a feeding cycle to work up to baking, on the two days before I plan to bake, I retain a slightly larger amount of seed for the morning feedings, and I repeat the feeding cycle after dinner. The fresh scent of a young starter is one of my favorite aromas.

On dough-mixing days (and sometimes the night before, as indicated in the dough methods), I make up the leaven, using a portion of starter. I like to supercharge that process by making what I call a "booster" leaven. Early in the morning, I take a large pinch of seed from the starter, place it in a bowl, feed it with water and flour, and then let it rest for about two hours. When the mixture has aerated enough that I know it's active, or it has passed the float test (see page 19), I will use this booster leaven to feed my primary leaven, which will raise my dough.

Before we started working with very fresh high-extraction flours at Tartine, we always fed the starter with a fifty-fifty blend of refined bread flour and whole-wheat flour. This blend gave us the right balance of nutrients to feed the starter without feeding it so much of the good brown stuff that it fermented too fast, making it difficult to pinpoint the right time to use it (before it got too sour). Now that we are primarily using fresh high-extraction flour, we no longer need to blend in much, if any, whole-wheat flour. If you have access to fresh flour with some bran and germ still in it, it is a good choice for feeding a starter. Trust your senses as much or more than a timer when experimenting with different flours, as the availability of nutrients in the flour can make a big difference in the time it takes for a leaven to become active.

It is possible, of course, to obtain some starter from a friend who already has an active culture and to use that to start your own. It usually takes at least a few days for a starter to stabilize after being moved to a new environment. Our starter acted erratically for weeks when we just moved it from one end of the Mission District in San Francisco, where our original bakery was, to a newer location down the street. Considering that it takes about the same amount of time to establish your own starter as it does to acclimate one acquired from a friend, and that starting one yourself will give you some good skills for monitoring fermentation, I highly recommend starting your own. I don't believe there is anything inherently special about starters from one place or person, though they are different and distinct. (And if your starter has a great story, by all means stick with it.) It will always adapt to your hands, your feeding schedule, your flours, and your particular environment wherever you are— I've tested this all over the world and found it to be true.

Starting a Starter

Establishing a starter from scratch is fairly straightforward. The yeast and bacteria needed for a starter exist naturally on the wheat, on the baker's hands, and in the air. To start a starter, you simply need to create an environment with optimal living conditions for the right microorganisms. Primarily, these microorganisms need food. By mixing together flour and water, you are unlocking the starches in the grain that the yeast and bacteria can eat. Once that food has been consumed, they need fresh food. When you take a small amount of an existing starter in which most of the nutrients have been consumed and there is a high concentration of microorganisms—we describe such starter as "spent"—and introduce a new mixture of flour and water, you are supplying fresh food to those microorganisms in the mature starter. One by-product of that feeding and metabolism is carbon dioxide gas, which bubbles up and becomes trapped in the gluten web in the culture (and later, in the dough), causing visible bubbles. When these bubbles are trapped in dough as it is baked, they create the lacy crumb that distinguishes leavened bread from a cracker or porridge. This process also creates acids, which give sourdough bread its sour flavor and play an important part in conditioning the gluten. In addition to being fed, the microbes need to be kept warm and have some oxygen available.

Make Your Own Starter

Mix the starter.

Pour 300g warm (80° to 85°F) water into a large, widemouthed jar. Add 300g high-extraction flour (or 150g each bread flour and whole-grain flour). Mix with your hand until the flour and water are combined and no dry clumps remain. Cover the jar loosely with a clean kitchen towel or a lid placed slightly askew. Oxygen is an important component in the fermentation process, so don't seal it off. Let the container stand at warm room temperature until bubbles form on the surface and the mixture begins to smell tangy. This can take as few as 24 hours and up to 5 days.

This first step of learning to gauge fermentation will help you develop the skills you need to refine your dough management later on. Fermentation will start and progress much faster if you can maintain a warm environment for the culture. It is a good idea to stir the culture occasionally with your hand between feedings to introduce more oxygen, redistribute any existing pockets of increased fermentation into areas of unfermented flour, and check the temperature to make sure it is warm.

Being able to detect and track fermentation is probably the most important part of perfecting your starter and dough. Fermentation is closely tied to temperature, so it is impossible to gauge when a starter or a dough is ready by time alone, as temperature will greatly affect how long it takes for a starter or dough to ripen. Fermentation often starts off slowly and then seems to increase as more and more microorganisms proliferate. Here are the basic signs of fermentation to keep in mind.

Aroma: Unfermented flour and water smells like wheat, or pancake batter. It will smell earthy and grainy, and not at all tangy, creamy, or alcoholic. It's a good idea to smell your starter right after you mix it so that you have a frame of reference. As it ferments, it will start to smell like fresh fruit and then increasingly tangy. Overripe leaven smells like rotten fruit or alcohol.

Bubbles: As the starter or dough ferments, the metabolic activity of the microorganisms creates gas bubbles that become trapped in the flour-water mixture. Even if your starter isn't rising yet, you will see these bubbles around the edge of your mixture. When you're initially creating your starter, these bubbles around the edge are a great sign that you have some fermentation and can feed again. As your starter establishes more of the right microorganisms, these bubbles will become more prolific and predictable, causing your starter (and your dough) to rise.

Liquid on top: Sometimes, especially as you are just beginning a starter, some liquid will separate from the mixture and settle on the top. This is normal and is a good sign that fermentation is occurring. Just pour off and discard the liquid and then feed your starter. Even if you don't see any bubbles, a layer of accumulated liquid is a great indicator that your starter is ready to be fed.

Feed the starter.

Transfer 30g of the starter to a clean container and discard the remainder or reserve for another project (see page 55 for more about using discarded starter). Add 150g high-extraction bread flour or a 50-50 blend of bread flour and whole-wheat flour and 150g warm (80° to 85°F) water. Mix with your hand to combine; it should be the consistency of pancake batter. Repeat this feeding process once every 24 hours at the same time of day, always retaining just 30g of the starter (the seed) and discarding the remainder or, if it still smells appealing, using it for another purpose, such as flavoring pasta, tortillas, or cakes or other baked goods. The starter used for country-style breads needs to be at a fairly specific point in its life cycle in order to ferment and raise the dough properly. But recipes that don't rely on the leaven to, well, leaven them, instead using it for flavor and digestibility, are much more forgiving of a wide range in its ripeness. Cover the container with a clean towel, and let the mixture stand at warm room temperature after each feeding. The starter should start to rise and fall consistently throughout the day after a few days of feedings. As the starter develops, its smell will change from ripe and sour to sweet and pleasantly fermented (like yogurt). Once this sweet lactic character is established and the regular rise and fall is predictable—after a few days to a week—it's time to prepare the leaven for dough.

Prepare the leaven.

In preparation for baking, we feed the culture a few extra times so the yeast and bacteria are healthy and the leaven will be super-saturated with the right balance of yeast and bacteria. We find that this feeding schedule gives our bread the characteristic loft and flavors of a Tartine loaf. Different bakers have very different feeding schedules and formulas for their leaven, which is part of what gives each baker his or her own signature style of bread, despite using the same three ingredients (flour, water, and salt). Our schedule is designed to give our dough the flavor and texture we like.

This process is a variation on the technique that that I used to use and reflects the evolution of the actual schedule we use at the bakery. The feeding schedules in my previous books still work, so feel free to choose what is best for your schedule and experiment with different timelines.

Two days before you want to make bread, feed the mature starter twice daily: once in the morning and once in the evening. On the day you want to mix your bread dough, first thing in the morning, take a large portion of your starter, place it in a bowl, and feed it twice within the next few hours. For the first feeding: In a bowl, mix together 150g flour, 150g warm (86° to 90°F) water, and 120g starter. When mixed, the target temperature for this leaven is about 85°F. Sometimes you may have to use very warm or even hot water to achieve this temperature, especially if your flour, bowl, or kitchen is cold. We call this initial step the booster leaven feeding. Place the booster leaven in a warm place and let ferment for about 2 hours, stirring it once at the 1-hour mark. Once it has risen and fermentation is evident, perform the float test. To do so, fill a small pitcher or cup with cold, clean water. Wet your hands to prevent the leaven from sticking to your fingers. Gently pinch off about 1 Tbsp of the leaven, handling it minimally so as not to deflate the air bubbles, and carefully place it in the water. It should bob or float on the surface, not sink to the bottom. If it hovers or rises slowly, you can still use it, but your bulk fermentation may take a little longer than it would if you used a riper leaven.

As soon as the leaven ripens and passes the float test, after about 2 hours, feed the leaven again. For the second feeding, which produces your primary leaven, combine 300g flour, 300g warm (86° to 90°F) water, and 120g of the booster leaven in a new mixing bowl and set in a warm place to ripen and reach 85°F, about 2 hours. As soon as the leaven is ripe and passes the float test, use it in your dough. Discard any leftover booster leaven or retain for other uses (see page 55).

How to Build a Gluten-Free Starter

It is relatively easy to convert a wheat-based starter to a gluten-free one. First, blend equal parts teff flour and brown rice flour in a big bin with an airtight lid. This will be the flour you use to feed the starter. Teff ferments very easily—almost too quickly—so it makes a great base for gluten-free sourdough. The brown rice flour tempers the fast-fermenting teff and adds a nice, earthy flavor base.

To establish the starter, in a small bowl or jar, put 90g warm (86° to 90°F) water, 5g wheat-based starter, and 100g teff–brown rice flour blend. Mix well with your hand and let ferment overnight at room temperature (about 75°F).

The next morning, in a clean container, put 90g warm (86° to 90°F) water, 10g ripe teff–brown rice starter, and 100g teff–brown rice blend and mix with your hand. Let sit at room temperature for the duration of the day. Repeat in the evening.

You will see evidence of fermentation as this starter ripens, though it will look and smell a little different from a wheat-based starter.

The teff–brown rice starter will rise higher in the jar and develop bubbles, it usually smells a little sharper, and the texture will be looser because no gluten is forming to hold it together.

If you don't have a wheat-based starter to seed your gluten-free starter and/or want to start a teff–brown rice starter from scratch, you can do so by following the directions for starting a wheat-based starter, but instead of using equal parts flour and water when you feed, use 90 percent of the flour weight for the water amount. Because there is no gluten in the teff–brown rice flour blend to help bind the starter, the 1:1 ratio of wheat flour to water doesn't work with the teff–brown rice blend, which would yield a starter that is too wet and loose. So, for instance, when the instructions say to mix 150g water and 150g wheat flour, instead mix 135g water and 150g teff–brown rice flour blend (135 is 90 percent of 150). Continue as instructed for the wheat flour starter, letting the gluten-free starter sit until fermentation is evident. Feed every time the starter rises and falls until it is rising and falling predictably.

Sample Starter and Leaven Schedule for One Week with One Mix Day on Saturday

1x	**Monday:**	Feed starter once in the morning.
1x	**Tuesday:**	Feed starter once in the morning.
1x	**Wednesday:**	Feed starter once in the morning
2x	**Thursday:**	Feed starter twice—once in the morning and once in the evening.
2x	**Friday:**	Feed starter twice—once in the morning and once in the evening.
Leaven	**Saturday:**	Use a large amount of starter (seed) to make and then feed your leaven at about 7:00 a.m. and at 9:00 a.m. The first cycle creates your booster leaven and the subsequent feeding produces the primary leaven that will raise and flavor your dough. To start the week's feeding cycle again for the next weekend's baking, the leftover leaven from the feedings will be your starter to feed on Sunday.
Bake	**Sunday:**	Bake your loaves. Feed starter once in the morning.

About Discard Starter and Leaven

Whenever you are feeding a starter or a leaven, you are always discarding an amount of the culture. New flour and water need to be introduced in order to keep the microorganisms alive, thus the by-products of old flour and water that have already been metabolized need to be removed. It's almost like feeding (and cleaning up after) a pet. This is inevitable and unavoidable—unless you plan to bake something every time you feed your starter.

That being said, I understand why people often lament throwing away handfuls of the beautiful starter they've so carefully tended. With this in mind, a number of recipes in this book call for starter or leaven you might otherwise discard.

There are several great reasons to use leaven in dough besides to raise it. Leaven improves flavor, adding complexity and acidity. It improves the digestibility of any dough by adding some portion of fermented flour, which is easier on the stomach than fresh, unfermented flour. In this book, leaven is added to tortillas, crackers, and pasta, to name a few non-risen doughs. The leaven or starter that you are using for all doughs does not need the specific leavening power that leaven for country dough does. The country bread method needs a young, fresh leaven right at its peak to get the very specific flavor, crumb, and texture I'm seeking. Pasta does not need those same leavening properties; the purpose of adding the leaven to pasta dough is to achieve complexity in flavor and improve digestibility and nutritional value. This can be accomplished by adding a more sour leaven than is used for country bread dough, either one that hasn't been refreshed within 24 hours or one that has peaked and started to fall. Sour starter is also a great addition to cakes and cookies—its subtle acidity a perfect foil for the sweet. Generally, I like to add starter to cakes and cookies both for flavor and to increase digestibility. Mixing in a small percentage—a tablespoon or two—with the wet ingredients won't change the recipe much. But if you add more than that, you'll need to decrease the other wet ingredients by the same amount to account for the extra moisture contributed by the starter.

If you are wondering whether to use discarded starter or very ripe or discarded leaven for a recipe, the best way to decide is to use your senses. If it smells good and you think you would like to eat something that smells like that, then you can use it to bake. You can even taste the leaven if you think that will help you gauge whether you want to use it. If you have fed the starter using a small amount of seed, as you would for a feeding schedule of once every 24 hours, you could probably use it within 24 hours of its ripening. A leaven that uses a larger amount of starter, like a booster leaven, should probably be used within 12 hours of ripening. If you like, you can hold the leaven in the fridge for a few hours or up to a few days until you are ready to use it for this purpose.

For the recipes in this book, I have specified whether it is important for the leaven to be optimal for the dough to rise or whether you can use any leaven or starter that still smells good.

Guide to Leaven by Recipe

There are basically three types of leaven used in this book. Country bread leaven is leaven that is fed with a booster and used at its peak to maximize the open crumb. Peak leaven is leaven that is used at its peak but doesn't require a booster. It's the leaven used in recipes where the flavor and leavening properties are important, but we're not necessarily trying to get the wildly open crumb of country bread. Then there are recipes that can use a discard leaven—any starter or leaven that is past its peak—which will have become more sour and spent than we would want for a leavened dough but that works great for adding fermentation and flavor to nonleavened doughs. Here's a quick reference to which kind of leaven is used for each of the forms of bread in this book.

LEAVEN TYPE	BREAD
Country bread leaven	Country Bread
Peak leaven	Rustic Baguettes
Peak leaven	Slab Breads
Peak leaven	Kids' Bread
Peak leaven	Einkorn Flatbreads
Peak leaven	Sweet Potato Buns
Peak leaven	Mission Rolls
Country bread leaven	Spiced Scalded Rye Bread
Peak leaven	Seeded-Sprouted Barley Vegan Bread
Peak gluten-free leaven	Seeded Multigrain Gluten-Free Bread
Any discard leaven	Rye Crispbreads
Any discard leaven	Sonora Flour Tortillas
Peak leaven	Pizza Dough
Any discard leaven	Fermented Pasta

A Few Words about Dough Temperature

It's very important to keep doughs warm as they are rising and proofing. In general, we keep yeasted doughs a little cooler than naturally leavened doughs. Even at the cooler temperature, the yeasted doughs will ferment a little faster simply because of their higher concentration of yeast. Here's a cheat sheet to the specific temperatures and temperature ranges I'll reference throughout the dough formulas and methods.

USE	DESCRIPTION	TEMPERATURE
For general use	Very cold water	40°F
For general use	Cold water	60°F
For general use	Cool water	70°F
For yeasted doughs	Room-temperature water	72° to 75°F
For naturally leavened doughs	Room-temperature dough	75°F
	Warm water	85° to 90°F
	Warm dough temperature	82° to 85°F
	Warm ambient temperature	82° to 85°F

Poolish

Some of the recipes in this book call for "poolish." This is a preferment—the equivalent of the leaven—that is made with commercial yeast instead of wild yeast culture. A poolish will be bubbly, light, and active and have a yeasty aroma. Sometimes I like the properties of commercial yeast; there is something pleasant about the aroma, light texture, and thin crisp crust it produces in bread, especially slab breads (inspired by classic French baguettes, which are traditionally very yeasty). I find using a poolish is a good way to get those properties, but always in combination with a natural leaven.

If you are feeding a poolish and natural starter or leaven, always feed the natural yeast mixture first and wash your hands very well after feeding the poolish. If you feed a poolish made with commercial yeast and then feed a natural yeast leaven, the commercial yeast will remain on your hands and can throw off the balance of your natural leaven. The natural leaven will eventually come back into balance but can be unpredictable for a few days if this happens.

When making a poolish, the yeast is measured by volume because most scales don't measure fractions of a gram, which is required for this amount of yeast. Measuring less than ⅛ tsp is tricky, so the instructions for making poolish are based on that aspect. As a result, the instructions here produce more poolish than you'll need for most recipes and you may end up discarding a little poolish or keeping some in the refrigerator for another use. It will last about 24 hours when refrigerated.

To make a poolish, in a large bowl combine 200g room-temperature (about 75°F) water, ⅛ tsp instant yeast, and 200g high-extraction bread flour, mixing well with your hand. Set aside at room temperature for 3 to 4 hours or overnight in the refrigerator. The poolish is ready once it has more than doubled in volume and is very bubbly.

How to Adjust Your Starter Feeding Schedule

If you know that you are going to be unable to feed your starter for some time, or if you don't plan to bake for a while, there are a few ways to store your starter. My favorite is to dry it out to a very stiff consistency by changing the flour-to-water ratio. In this form, fermentation will slow down, and the starter will be much more portable. (I've flown all over the world with starter in this form, often landing twelve hours later and moving right into the next fresh feeding in my hotel room.) You can also refrigerate this stiff starter, and it will last for several weeks.

To dry out your starter to store it, feed it with 50g room-temperature water (about 75°F), 100g high-extraction flour, and 10g starter. This will be too stiff to mix in a jar like you do the liquid starter. I like to combine the ingredients as much as I can in a small bowl, then knead them on my work surface until a stiff ball forms. Once everything has come together, transfer the ball to a small canning jar or other airtight container and either place it in the refrigerator or take it with you.

To revive the starter after storage, let it sit at warm room temperature until it smells sour. It will soften up somewhat as it ferments. Once it smells sour, give it a few successive feedings (see page 53) and use it as you would your liquid starter.

If you are going to be unable to feed your starter for an undetermined amount of time and want to store it indefinitely, you can dry it out completely and make starter "flakes." To make the flakes, spread some ripe liquid starter on a parchment paper–lined sheet pan. Turn on your oven for a few minutes at 150°F, just until it is barely warm, and then turn it off. Place the sheet pan in the oven and leave it overnight with the oven door cracked. In the morning, you will have dry flakes of starter. You can store these at room temperature for a few days, in the refrigerator for a few weeks, or in the freezer for a few months. To revive your starter, combine 100g warm water (about 85°F), 100g flour, and 20g starter flakes and then proceed with the starter instructions on page 52.

Starter Troubleshooting

Sometimes, a starter can become "stuck," especially as you're just getting it going. The answer is almost always to have patience. Here are some of the most common scenarios and recommendations for what to do.

The starter is clearly fermenting (smells sour, has bubbles) but is not rising.

You have activity. That's great! Give it another feeding and keep it warm. Sometimes you have the right yeasts and bacteria, but they are in the wrong balance. They will always eventually achieve the right balance if you just wait for signs of fermentation and then start feeding. It may take a week (or more!) of regular feeding to achieve balance. Don't get stuck on a particular schedule in the beginning; just feed your starter when you see clear signs of fermentation.

I don't see any signs of fermentation. The starter still smells like fresh flour (pancake batter) and is not sour at all.

Just be patient. Stir it with your hand to introduce some oxygen and possibly some important microorganisms from your skin. Keep it in a warm spot. Cool climates will slow the fermentation exponentially.

The starter was rising and falling, but now it has stopped.

Sometimes the starter will seem to backslide as you get it going. This is totally normal while the yeast and bacteria find equilibrium. As long as you just keep feeding your starter when you see clear signs of fermentation— primarily when it smells sour—it will become predictable and stable.

I missed a few feedings, and now my starter has become gray and runny.

That's okay, starters are remarkably resilient. All the yeasts and bacteria are still there, you just need to give them some flour, water, and oxygen to bring them back to life. Pour off any liquid that has collected on the surface, peel back any gray or crusty layer from the top (the gray is just the color of the oxidized flour when it has been exposed to air for too long), and get a pinch of the starter from underneath to use for feeding.

Introduction to Formulas

Instead of referring to recipes when we make bread, we primarily use formulas. The main difference is that a formula is based on ratios and percentages instead of teaspoons, cups, or other volume measurements. This allows a baker to clearly see the relationships among ingredients and to scale batch sizes easily and reliably. To develop a formula, we use specific arithmetic called "baker's math" to factor the percentages of each ingredient. In this system, all the ingredients are measured against the total flour weight. It can seem opaque and confusing at first, but once you have a good grasp of baker's math, you can look at any formula and have a general idea of what it will produce. In time, you will be able to wield baker's math to create your own formulas.

The most important thing to keep in mind about baker's math is that everything is relative to the total flour amount, which is always 100%. Any time a formula refers to the percentage of another ingredient, it is in relation to the flour weight of 100%. If a formula refers to a dough as being "85% hydration," that means the water weight is 85% of the flour weight. If you have 2.5% salt, then salt is 2.5% of the total flour weight. If you are using only one type of flour, say, bread flour, that means you have 100% bread flour. If you are blending flours, for example, using half whole-wheat and half bread flour, that means you have 50% whole-wheat and 50% bread flour and the total flour percentage is still 100%.

This is easiest to see in the country bread dough formula. I have deliberately structured the formula so the numbers reflect the percentages and, since the flour weight is exactly 1 kilogram, or 1,000 grams, and all of the rest of the numbers are measured against that flour number, you can easily see how the percentage is reflected in the amount of flour in grams.

INGREDIENT	QUANTITY	BAKER'S %
Water	750g	75%
High-extraction wheat flour	1,000g	100%
Leaven	200g	20%
Bassinage	100g	10%
Salt	25g	2.5%

Total percentage: 207.5%
Total dough: 2,075g
Total flour: 1,000g
Total loaves: 2
Weight per loaf: 1,038g

Notice that the water, which is 75% of the flour weight, is 750g of that total 1,000g (1kg) flour. If you wanted to add an ingredient, say, scalded flour or porridge, without changing anything else, you could add 35% cooked oat porridge, for example, which would be 350g (35% of 1,000g flour). This would also give you a little more dough, since you would be adding that to the rest of the ingredients.

Most of the recipes don't have numbers that are this even. In this case, I started with 1,000g flour because I knew that would give me roughly two 1kg loaves. Notice that the total dough is actually the only number that isn't even. That is the result of working the formula backward from the flour amount.

Usually when I build a formula, I need to figure out the total dough weight. I know each tortilla will weigh 60g, for example. And say I want to make 12 tortillas. I'm starting with the total dough amount of 720g (that's 60g multiplied by 12 pieces).

```
Weight per piece: 60g
Total pieces: 12
Total dough: 720g
```

Now here's the kind of magical part: I need the total flour weight so I can calculate all of the rest of the ingredients in relation to it. In order to get that number, I simply divide the total dough weight by the total percentage. So, total dough ÷ total percentage = total flour. You have to factor that as a percentage, and place the decimal point accordingly, to the left of the last two digits.

INGREDIENT	QUANTITY	BAKER'S %
Sonora wheat flour	750g	100%
Lard	1,000g	25%
Water	200g	50%
Leaven	100g	15%
Salt	25g	3%

```
Total dough: 720g
Total percentage: 193%
Total flour: 373g
```

Tortilla calculation would be: 720 ÷ 1.93 = 373. Now you have that foundational number, 373g, to calculate the rest of the formula.

The lard is 25% of 373g, or 93g. The water is 50% of 373g, or 187g, and so on.

INGREDIENT	QUANTITY	BAKER'S %
Sonora wheat flour	373g	100%
Lard	93g	25%
Water	187g	50%
Leaven	56g	15%
Salt	11g	3%

The more you do these calculations, the easier it becomes, and the more you are able to tell what a dough will be like after baking just from looking at the formula.

Country
Bread

My first real exposure to what we call "country bread" in the United States was in Europe, where the version that migrated west originated. It was a super-wet, long-fermented dough and was traditionally baked in a wood-fired oven. The loaves were amply coated in flour so they didn't stick to their baskets during the long fermentation and then were baked when the oven was very hot, giving them a dark, blistered crust. They emerged from the oven to land on an ancient wooden table, where they looked like a pile of river stones. The loaves were baked in the evening so people could have hot bread for dinner. This became my paradigm of bread.

Nowadays, I always go back to the question my dear friend, mentor, and collaborator Chris Bianco often asks: "What makes good food *good*?" I did not have that exact prompt in my head back when I started, but I was always asking myself some iteration of that question. I had learned from a few mentors, each of whom had different techniques and factors that they considered key elements of bread-making. They all believed in nutrition, digestibility, and flavor, but each had taken a slightly different path to turn their techniques and philosophies into final loaves. I began to approach bread-making as a study, finding the most important qualities of bread that I wanted to focus on and amplify.

Classic European country bread is defined by a few factors. It's made with at least a portion of whole grain such as a little rye, depending on where in Europe it's baked. Country bread is always naturally leavened. The loaves have a rustic appearance, varying slightly from loaf to loaf and day to day. Oftentimes they are baked in wood-burning ovens, whether communal or professional (such as Poilâne's bread, an iconic loaf from France). Traditionally, the grain was stone-milled and often it still is. It is always long fermented, either by using a very small bit of leaven or by taking advantage of refrigeration and extending that final rise to develop more flavor and create longer keeping qualities. The longer the rise, the longer it takes for the bread to go stale. With the use of commercial yeast, the dough rises faster, but the bread goes stale very quickly.

Country bread keeps for a full week of slicing and eating and even longer when dried into croutons or bread crumbs. We like to eat the bread fresh on the first and second day, toast it on the third through seventh days, and then make croutons. Add the bread crumbs to soup or sauces to thicken them. Traditionally, country bread never goes to waste.

The mixing of the dough is also very important. Country bread is mixed gently and slowly for a few minutes at a time with frequent periods of rest. This approach gradually facilitates the physical process that coaxes the flour into becoming dough. Vigorous kneading forces the gluten to form quickly but results in bread that is both less tender and less long-lasting.

For the first ten years or so at Tartine, I was focused primarily on fermentation and, while I was still sourcing carefully, I wasn't emphasizing whole-grain flours. By the time we started to build a new bakery in San Francisco, after having baked at the same corner location for so long, I was getting a little bored with our original country bread. I had seen many developments in grains, milling, and bread baking over that time, so I wanted to try to make a more wholesome, whole-food country bread that still had the same distinguishing qualities—the light texture and dark, shattering crust—that people really appreciated in our country bread.

My first attempts toward evolving our country bread came from adding inclusions, such as porridge in the form of cooked whole or rolled grains or cracked and fermented grains. Those developments were what my second bread book, *Tartine Book No. 3*, documented. Conferring with bakers across Europe as I worked out the ideas and recipes for that book was a wonderfully creative and energizing experience that has informed the way I ideate and innovate ever since.

Historically, bakeries have not been known for innovation, primarily because customers typically want the same thing every day. I had originally trained as a chef, however, so I always had one foot in the kitchen and one in the bakery. Both perspectives have been equally important sources of inspiration for my creative process.

As I traveled and researched, I was always generously granted entry into other chefs' kitchens. I helped them set up bread programs, and through that experience, I got to use wheats and other grains that I had never used before. I knew a little bit about how to optimize a soft Swedish or Danish wheat, so I could show them that they had beautiful flour to work with but just had to treat it differently. In return, I gained tons of inspiration from seeing how those chefs sourced and used their regional ingredients and also their techniques and overall creative approach to making food.

Once I got back to the States, and after my previous bread book had gone off to press, I was firmly set on the next evolution of country bread being based on the grain breeders and farmers and on evaluating different milling technologies. I wanted to reexamine some of the myths and superstitions about flour and to research what makes good grain good and what makes good milling good.

Ultimately, this led me and my team to Kevin Morse and Tom Hunton and Cairnspring Mills in Washington state and Camas Country Mill in Oregon. We started to spend time with them and quickly realized we had come upon a rare find: skilled, dedicated people with a strong vision for both growing grain in some of the richest soil in the world and for building food systems that benefit the farmer, environment, and community. We were able to partner with Kevin and Tom and pay the farmers in advance for the grain, which was the kind of collaboration seen in both the coffee and wine business (in the best-case scenarios) but still unheard-of in grain cultivation and milling.

Because of the revolutionary way that Morse mills at Cairnspring we were able to get a very high-extraction flour that has a granulation more like that of white flour. It means we are able to bake with a fresh-milled, high-percentage whole-grain flour and get a lot of the same qualities, such as the volume and open-cell structure, that you get from using refined white flour. The cornerstone qualities of country bread are present, but the flavor and nutrition are dramatically improved. We became friends with our farmers and millers, closing the loop in sourcing. Now our bakers and millers call one another all the time to talk about grain varieties, planting times, milling techniques, their dogs, and the weather.

At the same time that we were starting to work with these beautiful flours, we were also beginning to tackle the problem of getting more of this good bread to more people. When I was starting out as a baker in my early twenties, scaling was never a priority. I wanted to learn from the best. I wanted to travel to France and learn from my mentor's mentor. Any time I could find a small batch of grain, it was thrilling to me. I wanted to emulate legendary Parisian baker Lionel Poilâne's model: a single person making each loaf from beginning to end. I still think it's very romantic, and the experience formed my foundation. But with that approach, you're chasing an ideal that's very deliberately self-limiting. Of course, there's nothing wrong with that, but I always thought of the bread I was making as a staple food. Ultimately, I wanted to take something that is elemental and elevate it without making it rarefied.

One of the best parts about working in this industry for decades is realizing the opportunity to reach more people.

Focusing on that has enabled us to create systems that extend beyond our little corner of the industry to help make professional baking and everyone's communities better. That's the goal: to get more good bread to more people. In a parallel universe in Europe, my friend Apollonia Poilâne, Lionel's daughter, has done just that.

Maybe the greatest benefit of being in this community of bakers and chefs is the opportunity to collaborate. Even the most driven and experienced person can accomplish only so much alone. When you have ten people working together well as a team, you have ten times more magic. We are making the best bread we have ever made *and* there are more Tartine-influenced bakers around the world making exceptional bread.

Any time you are making something that is fermented and has just three ingredients, the way that you make it better is by searching out the best-quality ingredients to source and then properly applying the best technique and timing. The flours we are using at Tartine are available online to home bakers, but look to your community and see what you can find locally or regionally. The recipe for country dough here has been written to give you some ideas about how to adjust and be flexible to the differences in different flours. I encourage you to experiment, practice, and seek out other inquisitive bakers with whom you can confer and collaborate.

Country
Bread
Method

Makes two 1kg loaves

INGREDIENT	QUANTITY	BAKER'S %
Leaven	200g	20%
Water	750g	75%
High-extraction wheat flour	1,000g	100%
Warm (86° to 90°F) bassinage	100g	10%
Salt	25g	2.5%
White rice flour	for dusting the baskets	

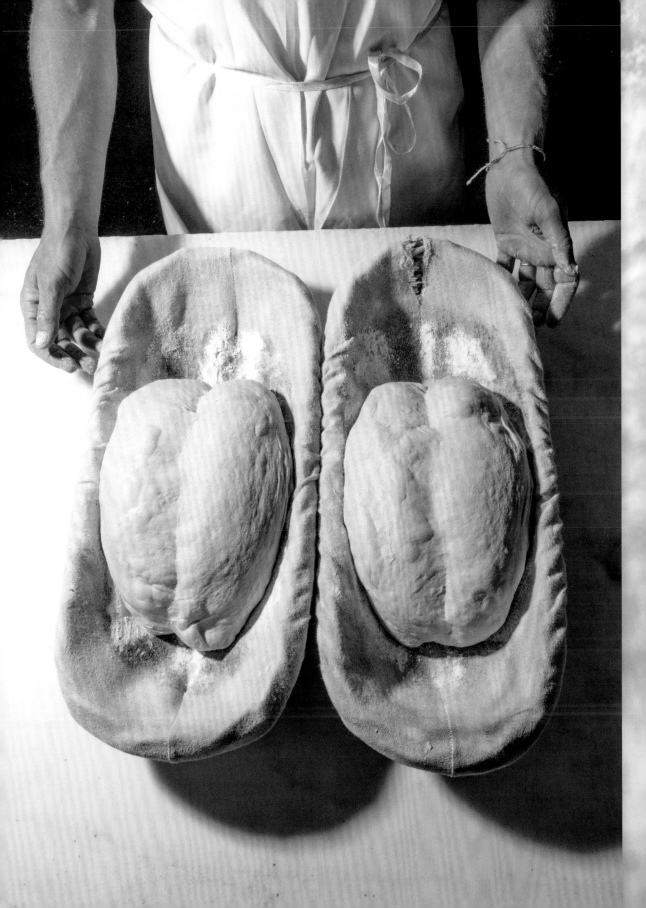

Prepare the leaven.

Prepare the leaven as directed on page 46. The leaven is ready for bread-making when it looks bubbly and tastes slightly tangy but also slightly creamy (like yogurt). Unready leaven tastes like raw pancake batter. Overripe leaven tastes very sour or boozy.

If you are unsure if your leaven is ready, you can perform a float test. To do so, fill a small pitcher or cup with cold, clean water. Wet your hands to prevent the leaven from sticking to your fingers. Gently pinch off about 1 Tbsp of the leaven, handling it minimally so as not to deflate the air bubbles, and carefully place it in the water. It should bob or float on the surface, not sink to the bottom. If it hovers or rises slowly, you can still use it, but your bulk fermentation may take a little longer than it would if you used a riper leaven.

Measure the water.

You are aiming for a final dough temperature of 82° to 85°F. You will need to adjust the temperature of the water to achieve that dough temperature. Consider the ambient temperature of the room, the temperature of your bowl, and the temperature of the flour.

If the weather is warm and you are using a clay bowl that doesn't conduct heat very well and your flour has been sitting out on a warm countertop, you should use tepid water to achieve optimal dough temperature.

If it is wintertime and your kitchen is drafty and you are using a cold metal bowl and flour that has been kept in a cool pantry, you should use hot water.

This is the kind of thing that you will get better at with practice. A few degrees' difference in dough temperature can lead to a difference of an hour or more in bulk fermentation time. A dough that stays at 83°F all the way through bulk fermentation usually takes about 3 hours to bulk ferment. A dough that is 78°F and cools off to 76°F during bulk fermentation can take more than 5 hours to bulk ferment. It is a good idea to have a kitchen thermometer handy, but you should also practice being patient, using your senses, and getting a feel for the right temperatures in the context of the conditions.

Add the water to a large mixing bowl.

Pre-mix the dough.

There are two options: (1) autolyze (the baker's term for the initial rest between the hydration of the flour and the mixing to develop it) with leaven or (2) autolyze without leaven. Either way, make note of the time when you add the leaven. The introduction of the leaven to the dough is what starts fermentation and determines the beginning of the bulk fermentation time.

To autolyze with leaven, add the leaven to the water. Add the flour and mix with your hands until no dry clumps remain. Cover with a clean kitchen towel and autolyze for 20 to 40 minutes. When autolyzing with leaven, do not let the mixture rest longer than 40 minutes, because you don't want it to start fermenting before you have fully mixed the dough.

To autolyze without leaven, add the flour to the water and mix by hand until no dry clumps remain. Cover with a clean kitchen towel and let rest in a warm place for at least 20 minutes or up to 2 hours. Add the leaven when you are ready to start mixing. Sometimes autolyzing without leaven makes your production schedule easier; you can put the flour-water mixture aside while you do something else and then return to mix the dough later. Also, higher-extraction flours often soften and become more extensible with a long autolyze, making them easier to mix, handle, and shape.

The Ideal Country Loaf

Feels light for its size.

Has a lacy, irregularly open crumb.

Has an ear that opens wide and is tall and thin.

Is tender but not gummy.

Retains its tender texture for three or more days.

Has a range of dark caramel colors on the outside; is light blond inside the ear, with a very dark brown, almost black-eyeliner color on the edge of the ear.

Is not burned on the bottom and has no burnt smell.

Mix the dough.

After the autolyze resting period, turn the dough in the bowl by gently lifting and stretching up the sides and folding them into the middle. Repeat this action for 3 minutes to build strong gluten bonds in the dough, an important step before a final addition of bassinage (water), which will stress those bonds. If the dough starts to tear or shred while you are stretching it, stop right away and let the dough relax for 2 minutes before continuing. It should feel more cohesive and supple when you resume mixing. After mixing for 3 minutes, let the dough rest for 3 minutes.

Turn the dough in the bowl again for 3 minutes, trickling in the bassinage while you lift, stretch, and fold the dough. You can squeeze the water into the dough to help the dough absorb it. Don't feel that you have to use all of the bassinage (or even any of it). You want to add enough water that the dough feels soft and extensible—when I am getting it right, I always think it feels marshmallowy at this point—but not so much that the dough gets waterlogged or starts to fall apart. You also want to be conservative with how much water you add if you are unfamiliar with handling high-hydration bread dough, which is sticky and delicate. If you are making country bread for the first time, you probably want to add only minimal bassinage, if any, so you can get comfortable handling the dough.

Developing a feel for the correct hydration is one of the finer points of bread-making expertise. The more water you add, the softer, more custardy, and more open your crumb will be—to a point. Add too much water, and your loaf will be gummy and/or go flat. Remember that different flours and weather conditions can lead to very different results with the same recipe. That's why it is more important to learn to get a feel for the texture of the dough than it is to measure exactly the same amount of water every time.

This becomes even more relevant when you are working with fresh-milled and heirloom flours, which can vary quite a lot in the amount of water required when making country bread. A country loaf made with Edison flour that is 87% hydration would probably be completely flat, as that flour doesn't have the strength to hold that much water, whereas 87% hydration might not be enough to make a Yecora Rojo–based country loaf open and soft. The water amounts given in this formula are for a typical high-extraction, high-protein wheat flour.

After turning the dough and adding the bassinage (if needed), let it rest for 3 minutes.

All of the water should have been absorbed by the dough, and it should feel cohesive and strong. If not, give the dough a few more turns. Add the salt and turn the dough for a few minutes until the salt is completely incorporated. The dough will feel smooth, supple, and strong. If the dough seems stiff, you can add a bit more bassinage during this final mixing stage. Let the dough rest for 3 minutes.

Turn the dough during its bulk fermentation.

Loosely cover the dough with a clean kitchen towel and let rest in a warm (82° to 85°F), draft-free place for about 3 hours from the time you added the leaven to the dough. Every 30 minutes, wet your hands and give the dough several series of turns in the bowl, using the same gentle lifting, stretching, and folding technique you used when mixing the dough. This builds strong gluten bonds in the dough without deflating it. The last turn should be a gentle one, turning the dough just until it has all been gently folded over once; the mass should hold its shape in the bowl. This first rise, also called the bulk fermentation or bulk rise, is a crucial time for the dough to develop strength and depth of flavor.

This rise is highly temperature-sensitive. At home, you will want to create a cozy microclimate for your dough. You can use your turned-off oven as a makeshift proofing box by putting a small pot of just-boiled water in the oven near the dough, which will raise the ambient temperature and humidity in the oven. An inverted cardboard box can also be used as a proofing box of sorts. As noted, you need a constant dough temperature of between 82° and 85°F to accomplish the bulk fermentation in 3 hours, starting from the time you mixed in the leaven.

If the temperature is cooler, this first rise will take longer. You don't want it to be too much warmer or cooler, not only because you want your fermentation times to be somewhat predictable but also because at higher or lower temperatures you are cultivating a different stratus of microorganisms and a different pH. These variations will cause differences in flavor, dough strength, and crumb character. Other recipes use these variations to elicit certain characteristics in breads, but between 82° and 85°F is the ideal temperature range for our country bread.

When the dough has finished its first rise, it will look domed and feel elastic, billowy, and bubbly. A well-developed dough will have increased in volume by about one-third. You can check the dough's readiness with a float test: If a small piece of dough bobs or floats when gently placed in a pitcher of cool water, your dough is ready for the next stage. If it sinks, the dough needs additional time to bulk ferment. One of the most challenging parts of making bread is being patient until the dough has fermented sufficiently. If you start shaping the loaves too early, the dough will not have enough strength, and the bread will turn out flat and dense. The dough also needs time for some of the starches in the flour to convert to sugars, which will give the baked loaves that beautiful burnished range of caramel colors.

Pre-shape the dough.

Transfer the dough to a clean, unfloured work surface. Lightly flour the top of the dough and use a bench knife to cut into two equal pieces. The dough should sit on the work surface, sticking to it, with the lightly floured side on top. Using barely floured hands and the bench knife, work each piece of dough into a round shape, creating some taut tension on the surface without causing any rips. Use as little flour as possible—just enough so you can handle the dough. Using too much flour will prevent the loaf from holding its shape as you build tension. Use decisive yet gentle force when handling the dough and *try to shape it in as few movements as possible*. If it starts tearing, stop and let rest for a few minutes.

Let the rounds rest, uncovered and tucked closely together, to keep the dough mass as warm as possible as the rounds rest on the work surface for 20 to 30 minutes. During this stage, called the bench rest, the dough will relax and spread into a thick mound. At the end of this rest, the dough edge should look plump, not tapered. If the edge is tapered or the dough flattens too fast or too much, the dough did not develop enough strength during the first rise. You can correct this by shaping each round a second time and letting them rest on the work surface for another 20 to 30 minutes. The second pre-shape is essentially an extra turn, like you would do in the bowl.

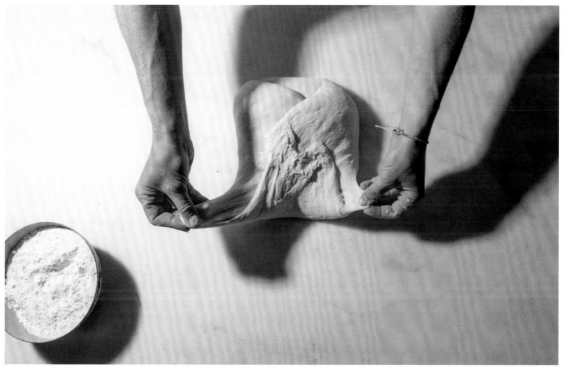

Finish shaping the loaves.

Generously flour the top of the dough rounds. Gently flip the first one over, taking care to maintain the round shape and all the aeration. The floured side is now on the bottom, and the top, now facing up, is unfloured. To form the final loaf shape, start by folding the third of the dough closest to you up and over the middle third of the round. Then use your right hand to gently stretch out the dough on the right side and fold it over the center. Use your left hand to do the same stretch-and-fold action with the left side. Finally, stretch out the third of the dough farthest from you and fold this flap toward the center, over the previous folds, creating a neat rectangular package with the edges at the top and bottom being slightly narrower than the length of the sides. Using just the tips of your fingers and grabbing the thinnest portion of dough possible, stitch the edges of the sides together in a few places to make your rectangle a little more oblong and to create an even, strong tension along the sides of the loaf. Grabbing the top edge very gently, roll the whole package lengthwise toward you until the seam is on the bottom. Let the shaped loaf rest while you repeat the shaping with the second round.

Let rise before baking.

Line two proofing baskets or medium bowls with clean kitchen towels and lightly flour the towels with rice flour. Using your bench knife as an extension of your dominant hand, and working quickly so the dough doesn't stick to your hands, transfer each shaped loaf to a basket, placing it smooth-side down and seam facing up (the bottom of the loaf is now on top and will become the bottom again when you tip it out to bake). Cover with a clean kitchen towel and let rest in a warm (82° to 85°F), draft-free place for about 3 hours. Alternatively, you can choose to delay the final rise by placing the dough loaves in their baskets, covered with a kitchen towel to keep the tops from drying out, in the refrigerator for up to 12 hours. The cool environment will slow the fermentation and create more complex and mildly acidic flavors in the dough.

Bake the loaves.

Thirty to 40 minutes before you are ready to bake, place a cast-iron double Dutch oven in the oven and preheat the oven to 500°F. If you do not have a double Dutch oven, see page 23 for an alternative.

If you are baking the loaves after they have risen in the refrigerator, there's no need to let them come to room temperature before baking; they can go straight from refrigerator to preheated oven. However, if they look a little smaller in the baskets than you hoped they would, you can take them out of the refrigerator when you begin preheating the oven and let them rise a bit more before baking.

Dust the top surface of one of the loaves with flour. Put on oven mitts and, using extreme caution, very carefully remove the shallow lid of the preheated Dutch oven and place it, upside down, on the stove top. Leave the deep pot in the oven. Invert the loaf in one basket onto the upside-down lid. Don't worry if the dough sticks to the kitchen towel; just gently separate them and remember to use a little more flour next time.

Use a lame, razor blade, or sharp scissors to score the top of the loaf, being careful not to burn your forearms. I suggest a simple square pattern of four cuts. Cutting or scoring a loaf helps it to expand fully in the oven. If you do not score a loaf, it will not rise to its potential and will likely burst open along the sides. Scoring also determines the final appearance of the loaf, and experienced bakers use different techniques—varying the angle, quantity, and pattern of the scores—to create the look they want. After baking many loaves of bread, you will gain an understanding of how different scores affect the way a loaf expands in the oven. For example, cuts made at a very low angle (almost horizontal) to the dough will create pronounced "ears," or risen edges.

Put on oven mitts again and carefully remove the deep pot from the oven, invert, and place it over the loaf and lid. You now have an upside-down Dutch oven with the loaf inside—a little bread oven that will go inside your oven. Return the Dutch oven to the oven. Immediately decrease the oven temperature to 450°F. Bake the loaf for 20 minutes.

Remove the cast-iron bread oven from the oven. Carefully remove the top part of the Dutch oven (the pot piece, which you are using as a lid), opening it away from you and releasing a cloud of very hot steam. Return the lid and loaf to the oven and continue baking uncovered, until the crust is a burnished, dark golden brown, 20 to 25 minutes. Don't be afraid to continue baking the loaf until it turns a dark, rich color. The bread is done baking when it has a deeply caramelized, crackling crust. The edges of the ears might even be nearly black. The loaf should feel light for its size and will sound hollow when tapped on the bottom.

Transfer the bread to a cooling rack to cool. (If you don't have a cooling rack, prop up the bread on its side so air can circulate around the bottom.) To bake the second loaf, increase the oven temperature to 500°F. Wipe out the lid and pot with a dry kitchen towel, close up, and return to the oven to reheat for 10 minutes. Then repeat the scoring and baking process with the second loaf.

Let the loaves cool to room temperature before slicing. Using a bread knife, slice the bread with a gentle sawing motion. Store in a bread box at room temperature for up to 3 days. To store longer, slice the bread once it has cooled, place in an airtight freezer-proof container, and freeze for up to 2 weeks. To refresh, toast directly from the freezer.

Croutons and Bread Crumbs

Make days- or week-old bread into croutons or bread crumbs. For croutons, tear the bread into bite-size pieces. Toss with extra-virgin olive oil to coat. Transfer to a sheet pan and bake at 350°F for 10 minutes, until golden brown. Alternatively, don't toss the bread with olive oil and instead add a couple tablespoons oil to a cast-iron skillet over medium-high heat. Add the bread and fry until golden brown on all sides.

To make bread crumbs, crisp slices in a toaster or on a sheet pan in a 375°F oven for about 5 minutes. Tear the toasted slices into pieces. Pulverize the pieces in a food processor.

Store croutons and bread crumbs in an airtight container at room temperature for up to 3 days.

Pan con Tomate

This one I've done before, but not quite like this. With this iteration I've simply intensified the main qualities that have always made this beloved Spanish preparation one of my favorite ways to eat bread. It's still very simple, basic, and traditional. Thankfully, tomato season here in California lasts for months. The demi-sec tomatoes and shavings of bottarga (pressed and dried gray mullet roe) take this tomato toast to the next level.

Makes 4 servings

2 lb ripe tomatoes (such as Early Girl or Brandywine), each about 6 oz

Finely grated zest and juice of ½ orange

1 small shallot, grated or finely chopped

½ tsp fine sea salt

Good-quality extra-virgin olive oil for drizzling and brushing

6 sprigs thyme

7 garlic cloves

4 slices country bread (page 74)

4 sprigs basil

2-oz piece bottarga

On the large holes of a box grater, grate the flesh of half of the tomatoes; discard the stem ends and skins. Transfer the grated tomatoes to a bowl and stir in the orange zest and juice, shallot, and salt. Cover and let marinate at room temperature for 1 hour.

Meanwhile, preheat the oven to 300°F. Cut the remaining tomatoes crosswise into 1-inch-thick slices. Arrange the slices in a single layer on a sheet pan and drizzle generously with oil. Add the thyme and 6 of the garlic cloves, scattering them over the tomatoes. Roast the tomatoes until they are wrinkly and reduced, about 50 minutes.

Set a large cast-iron skillet or griddle over medium-high heat until very hot. Meanwhile, lightly brush the bread slices on both sides with oil. Working in batches, place the bread slices in the hot pan and toast, turning once, until both sides have a good crust of caramelization and char, about 3 minutes on each side.

Rub the remaining 1 garlic clove across one side of each toasted bread slice and set the warm toasts on a serving plate. Spoon the grated tomato over the top, using enough to cover each toast completely. Arrange the warm roasted tomato slices on top of the grated tomato. Garnish each toast with torn basil leaves and, using a fine-rasp grater, grate the bottarga generously over the top. Serve immediately.

Chickpea Stew

Here, simplicity of method belies complex and satisfying layers of flavor. This is generally the way I eat these days: beans, bread, strong broth, greens, and tinned fish with some aromatics and warming harissa—quick to put together, nutrient dense, and inexpensive.

Makes 4 servings

1 Tbsp good-quality extra-virgin olive oil

4 shallots, sliced

1 tsp harissa powder, plus more as needed

Fine sea salt

2 oz dinosaur kale, stemmed, and leaves coarsely chopped

3 cups chicken stock or chicken bone broth

1 cup drained cooked chickpeas

3½ oz days-old country bread (page 74), torn into bite-size pieces and toasted until golden brown

2 oz tuna confit in oil, drained

¾ cup loosely packed mixed fresh herb leaves (such as cilantro, flat-leaf parsley, mint, and fennel fronds)

Set a Dutch oven or other large, heavy pot over medium heat. When the pot is warm, add the oil and shallots and cook, stirring, until the shallots are translucent, about 3 minutes. Add the harissa powder and a sprinkle of salt, then stir in the kale and cook, stirring occasionally, until wilted, about 5 minutes.

Pour in the stock and bring to a simmer. Add the chickpeas, return to a simmer, and cook for 10 minutes, until heated through and the flavors have blended. Mix in the bread, then taste and adjust with more harissa powder and salt if needed.

Portion the stew into four bowls. Flake the tuna and arrange on top of the bowls, dividing it evenly, and then finish with a generous topping of the herbs. Serve immediately.

Bread Soup

Basically, this is a vegetable-and-broth soup with lots of garlic and the addition of day-old bread that's toasted. I tend to use a concentrated bone broth simmered with kombu, dried mushrooms, and sometimes a bit of dried fish as the base—a homestyle technique that I picked up from our Tartine chef team in Seoul. In the United States, we've never had much imagination when it comes to days-old bread. Whenever I make this soup, both to celebrate our bounty of produce and to make use of an ingredient that would otherwise go to waste, I'm reminded of how nourishing and restorative humble dishes can be.

Makes 4 servings

¼ cup good-quality extra-virgin olive oil, plus more for drizzling

1 small yellow onion, cut into ½-inch cubes

Fine sea salt

8 garlic cloves, sliced

6 petite rainbow carrots, peeled and cut into ½-inch-thick slices

2 small summer squashes (such as patty pan or zucchini), cut into ½-inch-thick slices

1 head Treviso radicchio

4 cups chicken stock or chicken bone broth

Finely grated zest and juice of 1 lemon

6 sprigs thyme, leaves pulled from stems

10 ½ oz days-old country bread (page 74), torn into bite-size pieces and toasted until golden brown

Set a Dutch oven or other large, heavy pot over medium heat. When the pot is warm, add the oil, onion, and a light sprinkle of salt and cook, stirring, until the onion is translucent, 5 to 7 minutes. Add the garlic and cook, stirring, until fragrant but not brown, 2 to 3 minutes. Increase the heat to medium-high, add the carrots, and cook, stirring occasionally, until they start to soften, 10 to 12 minutes. Add the squashes, sprinkle lightly with salt, and cook the vegetables, stirring, until they start to caramelize around the edges, about 10 minutes.

Once you begin cooking the vegetables, preheat the oven to 375°F. Trim off the bottom stem end of the radicchio and separate the head into individual leaves. Spread out the leaves on a sheet pan, toss them with a drizzle of oil, and sprinkle with a few pinches of salt. Roast until wilted but not browned, 5 to 7 minutes. Set aside until ready to serve.

When the vegetables have started to caramelize, pour in the stock and bring to a simmer. Add the lemon zest and juice, the thyme, and another sprinkle of salt.

Divide the bread among four individual bowls, layering it with the radicchio leaves. Ladle the broth and vegetables over the bread and radicchio and serve immediately.

Ribollita

Continuing the variations on a theme here, this is essentially another bread soup but a drier version that is closer to what many of us would think of as a moist and creamy bread stuffing. The kombu, mushrooms, and tomatoes create a very rich umami. Serve this as a hearty base or side dish to pretty much anything, from fresh or tinned fish to roasted chicken or lamb.

Makes 4 servings

1 (3 by 6-inch) piece dried kombu

6 cups water

5 oz dried shiitake mushrooms

Good-quality extra-virgin olive oil for searing

9 oz fresh maitake (hen-of-the-woods) mushrooms, cleaned, trimmed of any woody stems, and torn into bite-size pieces

9 oz chanterelle mushrooms, cleaned and left whole if small or cut into 1½-inch pieces

2 yellow onions, cut into ½-inch cubes

9 oz petite rainbow carrots, peeled and cut into ½-inch-thick slices

Sea salt

9 oz Swiss chard, coarsely chopped

2 cups canned crushed tomatoes (preferably Bianco DiNapoli)

6 oz days-old country bread (page 74), torn into ½-inch pieces

Minced chives, organic garlic flowers and/or cucumber blossoms for garnish (optional)

Use kitchen scissors to snip small slits in the kombu to help release its flavor. Combine the water and kombu in a medium pot over medium heat. Bring to a gentle simmer, about 180°F; do not let the water boil. Add the shiitakes, turn down the heat to low, and simmer very gently for 30 minutes. Strain the liquid, discarding the kombu and shiitakes. There should be about 5 cups mushroom broth.

Set a Dutch oven or other large, heavy pot over medium-high heat. When the pot is warm, pour in a few tablespoons oil. When the oil is hot, add as many maitake mushroom pieces as will fit in a single layer with a little room around each piece—you want them to sear, not steam—and cook until browned, 8 to 10 minutes. Transfer the seared mushrooms to a plate. Continue cooking the remaining maitake and then the chanterelles in batches the same way until you have seared and transferred all the fresh mushrooms.

Turn down the heat to medium, add the onions to the pot, and cook, stirring occasionally, until caramelized, 5 to 7 minutes. Add the carrots and cook, stirring occasionally, until caramelized around the edges, 7 to 10 minutes. Sprinkle lightly with salt, then add the chard and cook until the leaves wilt, about 5 minutes. Add the tomatoes and bring to a simmer.

CONTINUED

Once the soup is simmering, return the seared mushrooms to the pot. Pour in the mushroom broth, add the bread, and simmer for about 10 minutes. Turn off the heat and let the soup rest for at least 10 minutes or up to 30 minutes before serving. The soup should be quite thick, like a porridge. Ladle into deep bowls, then garnish with chives, garlic flowers and/or cucumber blossoms, if desired. Serve immediately.

Store any leftover soup in an airtight container in the refrigerator for up to 1 week. To reheat, gently warm over medium-low heat.

Caramelized Shallot Soup with Black Garlic Aioli and Nettle Pesto Toast

Onion soup is always about the broth, alliums, and cheese—the flavorful sum punching way above the modest weight. In this recipe, we concentrate on the first two elements by creating a rich brown beef bone broth and layering in extra allium umami via the black garlic and shallots. I like to include some deep green with nettle pesto, which adds flavor and nutrition.

Makes 4 servings

Beef Broth

5 lb beef bones

2 large carrots

2 leeks

1 Tbsp black peppercorns

1 bay leaf

3 garlic cloves

6 qt cold water

1 Tbsp tomato paste

Nettle Pesto

1 bunch fresh nettles

¼ cup good-quality
extra-virgin olive oil

1 oz good-quality parmesan
cheese, grated

Pinch of sea salt

Zest of 1 lemon

1 Tbsp cold water

Black Garlic Aioli

3 black garlic cloves

1 cup aioli (page 113)

Caramelized Shallot Soup

4 sweet yellow onions

½ cup olive oil

2 bunches thyme

4 garlic cloves

Salt

24 to 30 whole shallots,
sliced lengthwise

¼ cup unsalted butter

4 slices country bread (page 74)

12 slices Gruyere or other melting cheese

1 small bunch garlic chive blossoms
(or other organic edible flowers)

2 bunches garlic chives, finely chopped

To make the broth: Preheat the oven to 450°F. Spread the beef bones on a sheet pan and roast for 20 minutes, until the edges and marrow show some caramelization. While the bones are roasting, chop the carrots into 1-inch pieces. Cut the leeks, including the green parts, into ½-inch pieces, and wash thoroughly. Place the roasted bones in a stockpot with the carrots, leeks, peppercorns, bay leaf, and garlic. Add the water. Turn the heat to medium and bring the stock to a simmer. Turn the heat to low and stir in the tomato paste. Cover and simmer for 8 hours.

Strain the liquid and discard the solids. Let the broth cool. Measure out 2 qt and store the remainder in an airtight container in the refrigerator for up to 1 week or in the freezer for up to 1 month.

To make the pesto: Wearing gloves or using tongs, pick or snip the nettle leaves and buds from the stems. Discard the toughest part of the stems, and coarsely chop the more tender stems. Bring a pot of water to a rolling boil. While the water is coming to a boil, prepare an ice bath by filling a mixing bowl with ice water. Set a fine-mesh strainer over another pot. Submerge the leaves in the boiling water for roughly 60 seconds, until they turn bright green. Pour the nettles and water through the fine-mesh strainer and transfer the nettles to the ice water bath. (The nettle-cooking liquid will be bright green. This is nettle tea, which is both delicious and healthful. I recommend drinking it hot or iced.

CONTINUED

Once the nettles are cooled, strain them from the ice water and transfer to the jar of a blender. Add the oil, parmesan, sea salt, lemon zest, and cold water and blend until smooth. The pesto can be made ahead and stored in an airtight container in the refrigerator for up to 1 week.

To make the aioli: Place the black garlic in a mortar and pestle. Pound until the garlic forms a paste. Add about 1 Tbsp of the aioli and combine, using the pestle. Scrape the garlic and aioli paste into a small bowl. Add the remaining aioli and stir well to combine. The aioli can be made ahead and stored in an airtight container in the refrigerator for up to 1 week.

To make the soup: Cut the onions into 1-inch cubes. Set a 10-inch cast-iron skillet over medium-high heat. Add 2 Tbsp of the oil and tilt the pan to coat the bottom. Place half of the onions in a single layer in the skillet. Don't crowd the skillet—it's better to cook them in two batches so they caramelize instead of steaming. Cook the onions, turning them only after they have caramelized on the underside. Cook until completely caramelized and then transfer to a bowl and repeat with another 2 Tbsp oil and the remaining onions. Set aside the skillet, but don't clean it; you'll use it for the shallots.

Place the caramelized onions in a clean stockpot, along with the thyme and garlic. Pour in the reserved beef broth, turn the heat to medium, and bring the soup to a simmer. Simmer for 45 minutes, then season with salt and taste. Strain out the solids, using a fine-mesh strainer. Discard the solids and reserve the liquid.

While the soup is simmering, set the cast-iron skillet over medium-high heat. Add a splash of the beef broth to the skillet to deglaze the pan and, using a wooden spoon, scrape up any bits and then pour the deglazing liquid back into the beef-onion soup. Add 2 Tbsp oil to the skillet and add half of the shallots in a single layer in the skillet. Cook the shallots, turning them only after they have caramelized on the underside. Cook until completely caramelized and then transfer to a bowl and repeat with another 2 Tbsp oil and the remaining shallots. Let the shallots aside until ready to serve.

Using the fine-mesh strainer, strain the broth and discard the solids. Return the broth to the pot and keep warm over low heat.

Set a 10-inch cast-iron skillet over medium-high heat. Preheat the oven on the broiler setting. Add the butter to the pan, let melt, and then place two slices of bread in the pan. Griddle the bread until brown on the bottom, then turn over. Top with 6 slices of the cheese. Transfer to a sheet pan and repeat with the remaining slices of bread and cheese. Place the sheet pan under the broiler until the cheese is melted and starting to brown around the edges. Spread ¼ cup aioli over each slice. Spread ¼ cup of the nettle pesto over the aioli. Garnish with the garlic chive blossoms.

Divide the shallots equally among four soup bowls. Pour an equal amount of broth into each bowl. Garnish the bowls with the garlic chives and serve with the toasts on the side or set in the bowls.

Baguettes

The baguette is a surprisingly variable bread. Essentially, it is a long, skinny, lean, and crusty loaf. But within that seemingly strict framework, there is a whole lot of room for interpretation.

At the bakery, we use commercial yeast, natural leaven, and yeasted poolish preferment to make relatively classic baguettes that look more or less like what you might expect to find in a Paris boulangerie: long, tapered, and golden blond. In reality, there is a wide range of variation in Paris baguettes, even though most Americans (myself included) have a preset notion of what defines the classic. For our rustic baguettes, we slow down the fermentation to allow more flavor to develop and add precooked durum porridge for sweetness and moisture.

Developing this baguette variation was a bit of a tightrope walk because our goal was to make the best version of a traditional baguette while also putting a deliberate, recognizable Tartine spin on it. We added some toasted corn flour, which has a sweet popcornlike aroma that comes through in the baked loaves. We use it more like a spice than flour in this recipe, which is why you don't see it included in the total flour percentage. A note about the leaven in this formula: you'll want to use a peak leaven.

There's nothing quite like tearing off a hot, crusty chunk of baguette, warm from the oven, and eating it out of hand, spread with fresh cultured butter; a young, creamy cheese; aioli; or (my favorite) tempered Stilton blue cheese. Simple sandwiches—whether served fresh or hot-pressed—are also wonderful on this baguette. The tender crumb and thin, crisp crust are the perfect vehicle for fillings and spreads.

Rustic
Baguettes
Method

Makes two 500g baguettes

INGREDIENT	QUANTITY	BAKER'S %
Poolish	69g	15%
Leaven	69g	15%
Toasted corn flour	5g	1%
Scalded whole-grain durum flour	32g	7%
Warm (85° to 90°F) water	324g	70%
Whole-grain spelt flour	46g	10%
High-extraction wheat flour	417g	90%
Salt	14g	3%
Instant yeast	3g	7%
Warm (85° to 90°F) bassinage	23g	5%

Prepare the poolish.

As directed on page 59, prepare the poolish 3 to 4 hours before you plan to mix the dough. Alternatively, prepare the poolish the night before, covering loosely with a kitchen towel, and refrigerating overnight to ripen.

Prepare the leaven.

Prepare the leaven as directed on page 46. This dough requires a young, fresh leaven (you can also use a booster leaven) for the right flavor and rise. The leaven is ready for bread-making when it looks bubbly and tastes slightly tangy but also slightly creamy (like yogurt). Unready leaven tastes like raw pancake batter. Overripe leaven tastes very sour or boozy.

If you are unsure if your leaven is ready, you can perform a float test. To do so, fill a small pitcher or cup with cold, clean water. Wet your hands to prevent the leaven from sticking to your fingers. Gently pinch off about 1 Tbsp of the leaven, handling it minimally so as not to deflate the air bubbles, and carefully place it in the water. It should bob or float on the surface, not sink to the bottom. If it hovers or rises slowly, you can still use it, but your bulk fermentation may take a little longer than it would if you used a riper leaven.

Toast the corn flour.

Preheat the oven to 350°F. Spread the corn flour in a very thin layer across a sheet pan and toast until fragrant, 5 to 7 minutes. Be careful not to toast it too darkly, or it will become bitter. (In this recipe, the toasted corn flour is used as a seasoning and thus is not factored in to the 100% flour quantity.) Set aside to cool.

Scald the durum flour.

Once the leaven passes the float test, it's time to scald the durum flour. Measure 60g cold water and 30g durum flour into a small saucepan and whisk together until well mixed. (This will yield a little more than the required 32g for the recipe, but some will inevitably get stuck to the spatula and pan.) Place the slurry over medium heat and cook, whisking constantly, until the mixture starts to thicken, then switch to a heat-resistant rubber spatula and stir continuously until it darkens and becomes a stiff paste, 3 to 5 minutes (it should register at least 160°F on a kitchen thermometer.) Transfer the gelatinized flour to a sheet pan and spread it out to cool until just warm to the touch (85°F) while you start mixing the dough. (For more on scalding flour, see page 44.)

Pre-mix the dough.

In the bowl of a stand mixer fitted with the dough-hook attachment, combine the water, leaven, poolish, spelt flour, wheat flour, and corn flour. Mix on low speed, stopping the machine to scrape down the sides of the bowl with a rubber spatula as needed, until all the ingredients are well incorporated, about 3 minutes. (Alternatively, you can mix this dough by hand in a large bowl.) Cover the bowl with a clean kitchen towel and let the dough autolyze (rest) for 20 minutes.

Finish mixing the dough.

Add the salt and yeast to the dough and mix on low speed for about 3 minutes to develop the gluten and dough structure. Let the dough rest for a few minutes, then add the scalded durum flour and mix for 2 minutes. Feel the dough. If it feels stiff, add some or all of the bassinage until the dough feels supple, strong, and stretchy, and mix on low speed for another 3 minutes.

Let the dough rest.

Loosely cover the dough with a clean kitchen towel and let rest in a warm (82° to 85°F), draft-free place for about 3 hours. It should almost double in volume.

Preheat the oven.

Place a baking stone or steel or a sheet pan on the middle rack of the oven and preheat the oven to 475°F.

Pre-shape the dough.

Very lightly flour a clean work surface. Transfer the dough to the surface and use a bench knife to cut into two equal pieces. Working with one piece at a time, gently shape it into a rectangle about 6 by 3 inches, with the long sides positioned perpendicular to your chest. Let the dough rectangles rest on the work surface for 20 minutes.

Prepare the couche.

Generously flour a linen couche (see page 24) or thick, tightly woven kitchen towel.

Finish shaping the baguettes.

Lightly flour the tops of the pre-shaped dough rectangles. Using a bench knife, loosen each rectangle from the work surface, lift it up, and turn it over so the floured side is now resting on the work surface. Gently grasp the long edge of dough farthest from you, fold about 1 inch of it toward you, and press down on the folded part. Repeat the process, again folding about 1 inch of the far edge toward you and pressing down on the folded part. Continue folding in this way until you have rolled the entire rectangle into a log. It should be about 10 inches long and about 3 inches in diameter.

Do not seal the seam by pinching it; instead, sprinkle the seam with flour and place the baguette seam-side down on the couche. Shape the second baguette the same way and add it, seam-side down, to the couche. Create high folds in the couche, accordion-style, between and on either side of the loaves, so the loaves are supporting each other but are not touching. Fold the ends of the couche up and over the baguettes to cradle them and help them hold their shape.

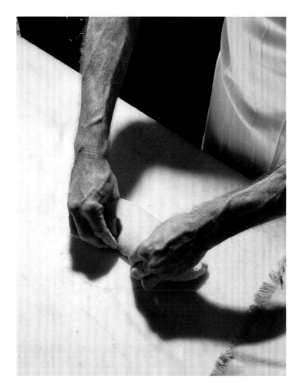

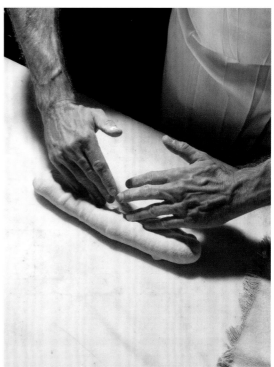

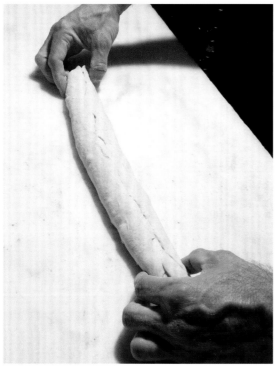

Let rise before baking.

Let the shaped baguettes rest in the couche in a warm place (ideally 82° to 85°F), for 30 to 60 minutes. After this final rise, when you gently press the dough with a fingertip, it should spring back slowly. If it springs back quickly, it has not risen enough and is not yet ready to bake. In this case, let the dough rest a little longer until it springs back slowly to the touch. One of the trickiest aspects of making this bread is being sure the dough has had enough time to finish rising before you bake it. If the ambient temperature is cooler, say, below 75°F or even colder, it can take much longer to finish proofing.

Bake the baguettes.

Lightly flour a baguette peel. Fill a clean, food-grade spray bottle with water. To transfer the baguettes from the couche to the peel, place the peel right next to a baguette and use the couche to rock the baguette onto it. Make sure once the baguette rolls onto the peel its seam is facing up. Repeat with the second baguette. You can score the loaves shallowly, but there's no need to do so; the seams will open beautifully while they bake.

Keeping the seams facing up, slide the baguettes onto the preheated baking surface in the oven. Spray the sides and bottom of the oven with water, then quickly close the oven door and bake for 2 minutes. Repeat spraying the sides and bottom of the oven, again quickly close the oven door, and then bake the baguettes until they have a caramel-brown crust, about 40 minutes.

Transfer the baguettes to a cooling rack to cool slightly before serving warm. Or let cool to room temperature before slicing. Using a bread knife, slice the baguettes with a gentle sawing motion. Store the sliced loaf wrapped in cloth or paper in a bread box at room temperature for up to 3 days. After the first day, I tend to toast to refresh. This bread can be sliced in half horizontally and frozen. Toast directly from the freezer under a very hot broiler and serve immediately.

Clams in Broth

Combine baguette slices just off the grill with fresh clams, dense layers of green herbs, briny clam broth, some aioli, and a glass of dry rosé and you have the ingredients for a memorable summer afternoon with friends and family.

Makes 4 servings

Aioli

1 garlic clove, coarsely chopped

Grated zest and juice of 1 lemon

Pinch of sea salt

1 egg yolk

1 cup good-quality extra-virgin olive oil

2 lb clams (such as littleneck, Manila, or similar), scrubbed

2 limes, cut in half

1 Tbsp good-quality extra-virgin olive oil

1 Tbsp unsalted butter

1 shallot, thinly sliced

2 garlic cloves, thinly sliced

1 sprig thyme

Pinch of crushed red pepper flakes

Juice of 1 lemon

Juice of 1 blood orange

½ cup dry white wine

1 serrano chile, thinly sliced

4 stems mint, basil, or cilantro or a combination, leaves pulled from steps

4 slices rustic baguette (page 102), toasted

To make the aioli: Put the garlic, lemon zest, and salt in a mortar and pound to a paste with the pestle. Add the egg yolk and ½ tsp of the lemon juice and stir the mixture vigorously against the walls of the mortar. When the mixture is smooth, add a few drops of the oil and stir until the oil is incorporated. Continue adding the oil, a few drops at a time, stirring well after each addition. After a few additions, the mixture should be creamy, smooth, and opaque. Now, while stirring constantly, add the oil in a slow drizzle until all is incorporated and the mixture is thick and creamy. Taste and adjust with more lemon juice if needed. Transfer to an airtight container and store in the refrigerator for up to 3 days.

Soak the clams in cold water to cover for 20 minutes and then drain. In a cast-iron skillet over high heat, place the limes cut-side down and griddle until seared. Set aside.

In a large, heavy pot over medium-low heat, melt the oil and butter. Add the shallot, garlic, thyme, and pepper flakes and sauté for 2 minutes. Add the clams, lemon juice, orange juice, and wine and cover. Turn the heat to high and cook for 5 to 8 minutes, checking after 5 minutes to see if the clams have opened. If nearly all of the clams have opened, remove the pot from the heat. If not, re-cover and cook for 1 to 3 minutes longer, until the rest of the clams have opened. Remove and discard any unopened clams.

Divide the clams among four bowls and ladle the broth over. Garnish with the serrano and herb leaves. Serve each with the grilled lime, bread, and aioli on the side.

Anchovy Toast

Two of the bread services that I've had in restaurants and liked the most over the years involved really good anchovies. At Manfreds in Copenhagen, their excellent house-baked bread was served with cultured butter and a tin of anchovies, which effortlessly complemented every other dish on the menu. Mission Chinese (the original, in San Francisco) served hot, naturally leavened flatbreads from a wood-burning oven with fresh kefir butter and its whey, a tin of best-quality anchovies, fermented chiles, and, if it was a special night, a glass ramekin of caviar. I've also always been partial to the classic French-afternoon wine pairing of radishes and butter. The idea for this recipe was a simple merging of all three. I like to make the butter very green with lots of spicy watercress. Smashing the radishes and quickly fermenting them in the classic Chinese style with a touch of ginger–chile oil links the flavors well without overpowering any of them.

Makes 4 servings

Salted Radishes

2 lb radishes (same variety or mixed)

1 tsp salt, plus 1 pinch

1 tsp granulated sugar, plus 1 pinch

2 Tbsp rice vinegar

2 tsp sesame oil

2 tsp soy sauce

1 Tbsp good-quality extra-virgin olive oil

3 large garlic cloves, finely minced

1½ Tbsp finely minced ginger

1½ tsp chile oil

Watercress Butter

3 cups watercress leaves

1 cup spinach leaves

1 shallot, finely diced

¾ cup cultured butter, at cool room temperature

Juice of 1 lemon

Pinch of salt

8 slices rustic baguette (page 102)

5-oz can anchovies

CONTINUED

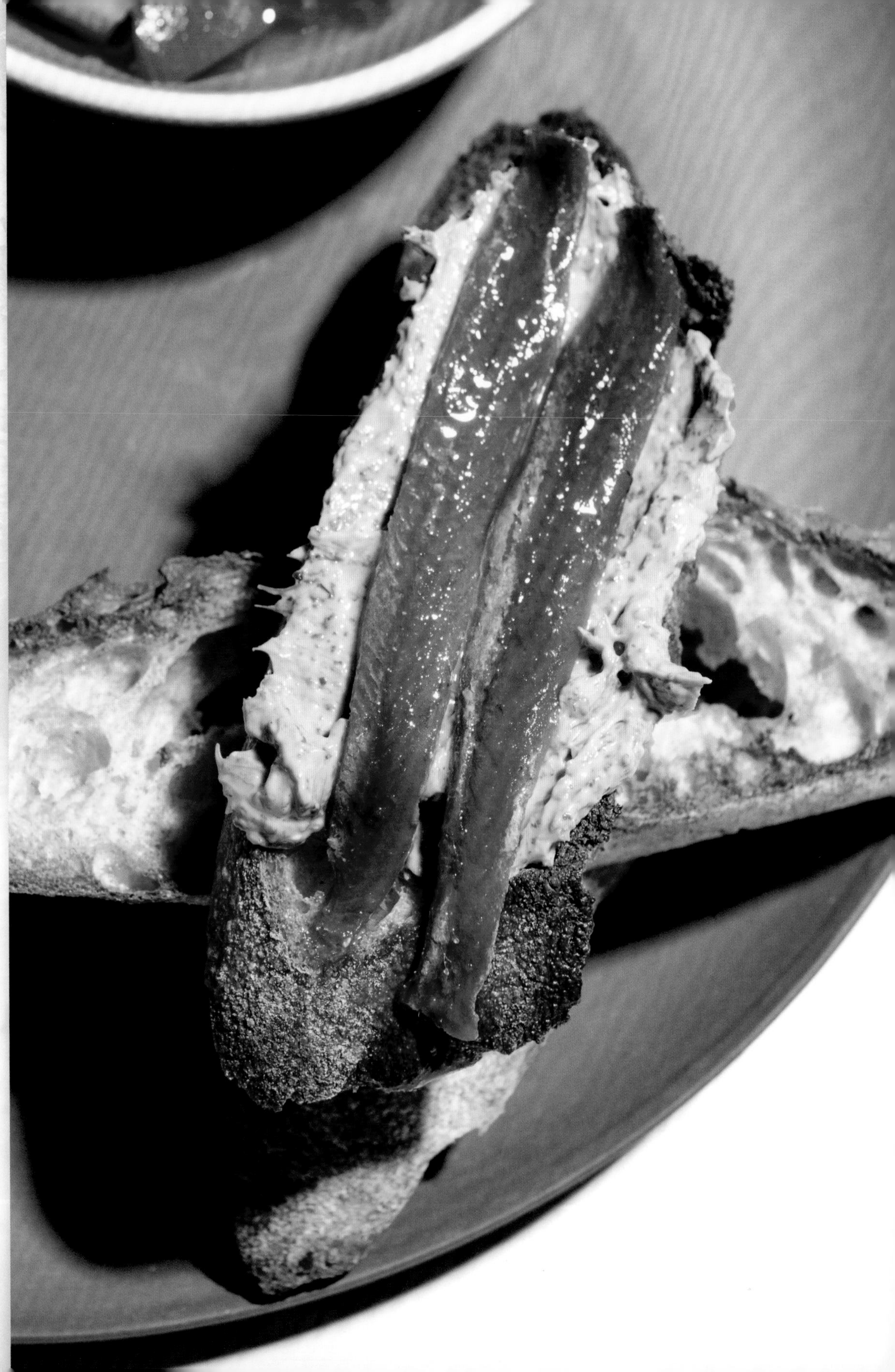

To make the radishes: Rinse, dry, and cut the radishes in half lengthwise.

Using the side of the knife blade, carefully smash the radishes into small chunks. Place the radishes in strainer set over a bowl. Distribute the 1 tsp salt and 1 tsp sugar over the radishes and gently massage. Set aside to drain for 30 minutes or up to 5 hours in refrigerator.

In a small bowl whisk together the vinegar, sesame oil, soy sauce, 1 pinch of salt, and 1 pinch sugar. To make a dressing, shake the strainer to remove any remaining liquid from the radishes and transfer them to a serving bowl. Add the olive oil and toss to combine, then add the dressing and garlic and continue tossing. In a separate small bowl, stir the ginger into the chile oil. Spoon the ginger–chile oil over the radishes.

To make the butter: In the bowl of a food processor, puree the watercress and spinach. Add the shallot and butter and process until well blended. Squeeze in the lemon juice and pulse to incorporate. Transfer to a bowl and stir in the salt.

Toast the bread slices. Spread generously with the watercress butter. Top each slice with two anchovy fillets. Enjoy with the radishes spooned over.

Slab
Breads

The characteristics that we strive for in our country bread (pages 74) happen to make the bread imperfect for some sandwiches (for some people). The very open crumb structure we achieve when we're on our game isn't the ideal architecture for holding oozy elements, like jam, mustard, and mayo. We wanted to make a bread with a wildly open crumb that would also work well for melty, creamy, saucy sandwiches, so we turned our country bread format on its side. Instead of making a loaf and slicing it as usual, we made a thin-crusted flatbread and sliced it horizontally, keeping the crust intact along the top and bottom. Of course, it's been done many times before, but we definitely owned our own style here, and it's become one of my favorites.

The dough is based on our classic baguette dough: it's leavened and flavored with poolish and leaven along with a little commercial yeast. But for slab bread, we add a portion of scalded flour. Usually it is made from durum wheat flour, but we have also used scalded rye flour, barley, Rouge de Bordeaux, einkorn, and Edison, among others. Each will give you a different flavor profile, but they all result in a fluffy flatbread with a craggy moonscape of a crumb. For our core slab bread dough, we use high-extraction wheat flour for our main flour, while the scalded durum flour gives the finished bread a beautiful golden color and an earthy, sweet flavor.

Another technique that makes our slab dough unique is the length of the autolyze, or rest period, after the flour and water are mixed together. We started doing an overnight autolyze for a practical reason: to give the dough a head start for our team of morning bakers. It turns out that an overnight autolyze also creates additional strength and super-extensibility in the dough and is particularly beneficial for whole grains.

At Tartine, we use this slab dough in several different forms: baked into flat focaccia-like bread that we split horizontally for sandwiches; studded with olives and shaped into fougasse, a slab shape that gets cut and stretched apart to resemble leaves or ladders with lots of crust; or topped with ingredients to make a square, baker's-style pan pizza. You can also vary the flours you use for the scalded porridge addition to the dough to alter the flavor and color. I love fougasse laced with preserved lemon and thyme or other fresh herbs. In the winter, we make scalded-rye flatbreads topped with bresaola, crème fraîche, and orange zest. And during summer, we make scalded–Sonora wheat flatbreads topped with fresh corn, soft goat cheese, herb salad, and allium blossoms. There is a lot of room for creativity with this dough.

Slab
Breads
Method

Makes two 4 by 6-inch slabs

INGREDIENT	QUANTITY	BAKER'S %
Poolish	180g	50%
High-extraction wheat flour	360g	100%
Cold (60°F) water	216g	60%
Leaven	90g	25%
Scalded whole-grain durum flour	216g	60%
Instant yeast	1g	0.25%
Sea salt	12g	3.25%
Warm (85° to 90°F) bassinage	90g	25%
Extra-virgin olive oil	36g	10%

Prepare the poolish.

The night before you want to mix the dough, prepare an overnight poolish by following the directions on page 59. Store in the refrigerator until ready to use.

Autolyze the flour.

In the bowl of a stand mixer fitted with the dough hook attachment, combine the high-extraction flour and cold water and mix on medium speed until well mixed and smooth, about 8 minutes. Lightly oil the top surface of the dough, cover the bowl with a clean kitchen towel, and autolyze (rest) at room temperature overnight.

Prepare the leaven.

The next morning, prepare the leaven as directed on page 46. This dough requires a young, fresh leaven (but not a booster leaven) for the right flavor and rise. The leaven is ready for bread-making when it looks bubbly and tastes slightly tangy but also slightly creamy (like yogurt). Unready leaven tastes like raw pancake batter. Overripe leaven tastes very sour or boozy.

If you are unsure if your leaven is ready, you can perform a float test. To do so, fill a small pitcher or cup with cold, clean water. Wet your hands to prevent the leaven from sticking to your fingers. Gently pinch off about 1 Tbsp of the leaven, handling it minimally so as not to deflate the air bubbles, and carefully place it in the water. It should bob or float on the surface, not sink to the bottom. If it hovers or rises slowly, you can still use it, but your bulk fermentation may take a little longer than it would if you used a riper leaven.

Scald the durum flour.

Once the leaven passes the float test, it's time to scald the durum flour. Measure 400g cold water and 200g durum flour into a medium saucepan and whisk together until well mixed. (This will yield a little more than the required 216g for the recipe, but some will inevitably get stuck to the spatula and pan.) Place the slurry over medium heat and cook, whisking constantly, until the mixture starts to thicken, then switch to a heat-resistant rubber spatula and stir continuously until it darkens and becomes a stiff paste, 3 to 5 minutes total (it should register at least 160°F on a kitchen thermometer). Transfer the gelatinized flour to a sheet pan and spread it out to cool until just warm to the touch (85°F) while you start mixing the dough. (For more on scalding flour, see page 44.)

Mix the dough.

In the bowl of a stand mixer fitted with the dough-hook attachment, combine the leaven, poolish, and autolyzed flour and mix on medium speed until incorporated, 2 to 3 minutes. On low speed, add the yeast and salt and then slowly add the bassinage and continue to mix until well combined, about 5 minutes. Add one-third of the scalded flour, followed by half of the oil, and mix for 1 to 2 minutes. Add another one-third of the scalded flour and the remaining oil and mix for another 1 to 2 minutes. Then add the remaining scalded flour and continue mixing on low speed until the dough is elastic and smooth, 3 to 4 minutes.

Turn the dough during its bulk fermentation.

Loosely cover the dough with a clean kitchen towel and let rest in a warm (82° to 85°F), draft-free place for about 2 hours. Every 30 minutes, wet your hands and give the dough several series of turns in the bowl, gently lifting and stretching the sides and folding them into the middle to build strong gluten bonds in the dough without deflating it. The last turn should be a gentle one, turning the dough just until it has all been gently folded over once; the mass should hold its shape in the bowl. This first rise, also called the bulk fermentation or bulk rise, is a crucial time for the dough to develop strength and depth of flavor.

When the dough has finished rising, it will feel airy and fluffy. You can check the dough's readiness with a float test: If a small piece of dough bobs or floats when gently placed in a pitcher of cool water, your dough is ready for the next stage. If it sinks, the dough needs additional time to bulk ferment.

Preheat the oven.

About 30 minutes before the dough finishes rising, place a baking stone or steel or a sheet pan on the middle rack of the oven and preheat the oven to 500°F.

Pre-shape the dough and let rest.

Transfer the dough to a clean, unfloured work surface. Lightly flour the top of the dough and use a bench knife to cut into two equal pieces. Using lightly floured hands and the bench knife, work each piece of dough into a rough rectangle. Lightly flour each dough rectangle and let rest, placed a few inches apart, on the work surface for 20 minutes.

Finish shaping the slabs.

Generously flour a linen couche or thick, tightly woven kitchen towel. Use the bench knife to lift one piece of dough onto the cloth and gently shape into a 4 by 6-inch rectangle, handling the dough as little as possible. Repeat with the second piece of dough, placing the slabs about 2 inches apart on the couche and then pulling them alongside each other, separated by a fold of the couche. Cover the slabs with a clean kitchen towel and let rest for 45 to 60 minutes, until very fluffy and large. When you gently press the dough with a fingertip, it should spring back very slowly. If it springs back quickly, let it rise a little longer.

Bake the slabs.

Generously flour a baker's peel. Working with one slab at a time, gently invert the shaped dough onto the generously floured peel. Slide the slab onto the preheated baking surface in the oven and bake until golden brown, about 20 minutes. Transfer the slab to a cooling rack to cool. Allow the oven and baking surface to reheat for 5 to 10 minutes before baking the second slab.

Store in a paper bag or a bread box at room temperature for a couple of days. If using more than a day after baking, griddle or toast to use. To store longer, place in an airtight freezer-proof container and freeze for up to 2 weeks. Refresh straight from the freezer in a 400°F oven for 10 to 15 minutes.

Olive Fougasse

After pre-shaping the slab bread dough into rough rectangles and letting the rectangles rest on the work surface for 20 minutes, turn each rectangle so the long side is perpendicular to your chest. Evenly scatter ¾ cup pitted olives (I like green Cerignola, but any, or a blend, will do) onto the left half of each rectangle, then lift the right half of the rectangle and fold it over the left half, as if closing a book you've just finished. Pinch to seal the dough along the top, left, and bottom edges. Gently lift the dough onto a generously floured peel or the backside of a sheet pan. Using a lame or sharp knife, cut shallow diagonal slashes on the left and right halves of the dough, making about three slashes per side in a pattern reminiscent of leaf veins. Using your fingers, gently stretch open the cuts to create some space. Bake as directed for slab bread. Because this shape is so crusty, it doesn't hold or refresh as well as loaves with more crumb. I recommend eating this one the same day it is baked. (Freshly baked warm fougasse is one of our bakers' favorite snacks.)

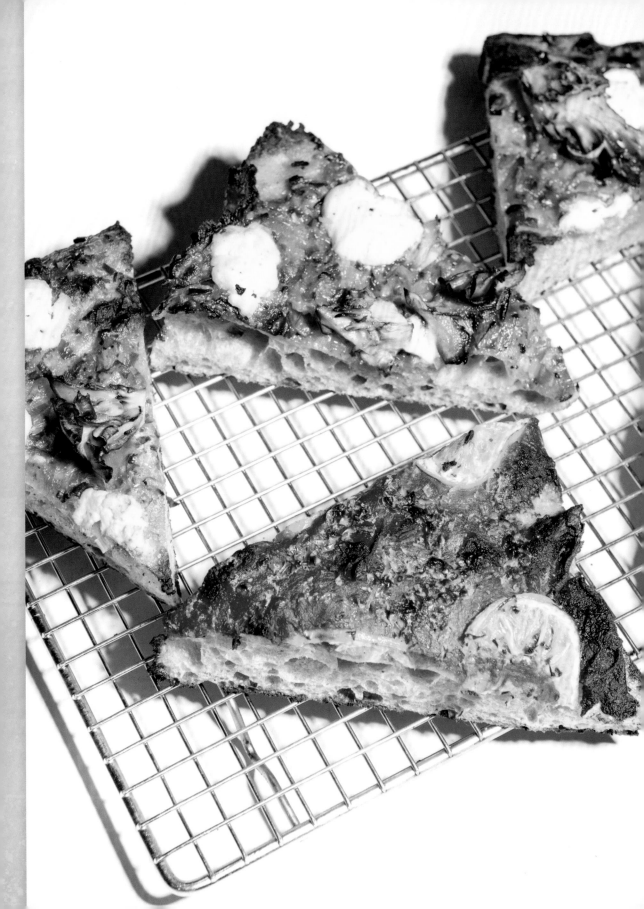

Topped Flatbread

Make sure all your chosen toppings are ready to go before you finish shaping the slab bread dough. If you're using tomatoes, strain them before you begin shaping your dough. Once you've flipped the dough onto a generously floured peel, use your hands to stretch the dough to a 5 by 8-inch rectangle. Spread a very thin layer of crushed tomatoes across the dough. (Using too much tomato will make for soggy flatbread.) Slide the dough onto the preheated baking surface and bake as directed for slab bread. Remove the flatbread from the oven and immediately top with shaved Parmesan and torn fresh basil. Serve right away.

Red Sauce, Lemon Zest, and Lemon Slice-
Topped Flatbread

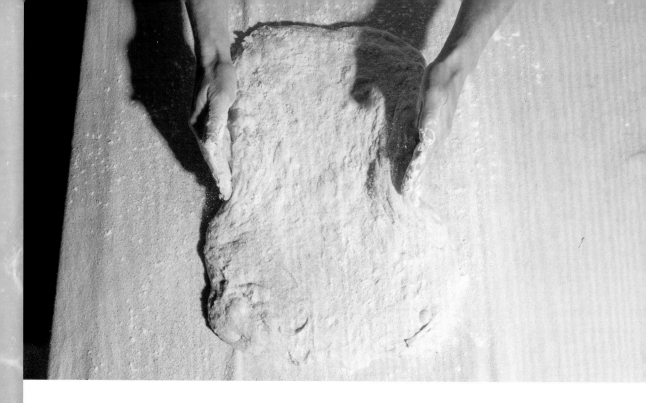

English Muffins

Follow the directions for slab bread through the bulk rise. Lay a linen couche or thick, tightly woven kitchen towel flat across a sheet pan. Generously flour the cloth and sprinkle with cornmeal. Turn the dough out onto the prepared cloth and gently pat it until it is 1 inch thick. Using a 4-inch round biscuit cutter or cookie cutter, cut the dough into twelve rounds. Remove and discard the dough scraps. Gently cover the rounds with the edges of the couche and refrigerate for about 45 minutes.

About 30 minutes before the dough finishes chilling, place a baking stone or steel or a sheet pan on the middle rack of the oven and preheat the oven to 450°F. Working with three or four rounds at a time, use a metal spatula to transfer the rounds from the couche to the preheated baking surface. Bake until browned on the bottom, 5 to 7 minutes, then flip and bake until both sides are well browned, 5 to 7 minutes longer. The rounds should rise quite a bit while baking. Let cool just slightly on a cooling rack before eating. Repeat to bake the remaining rounds.

Let leftover muffins cool completely, then store in an airtight container at room temperature or cut in half horizontally, place in an airtight container, and freeze for up to 1 month. Toast straight from the freezer.

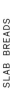

French Bread Pizza

One of our favorite ways to use slab bread at Tartine is to split it horizontally, top it like a French bread pizza, and place it under the broiler or in a hot oven until the whole thing is crispy on the outside and hot and gooey on the inside. If you have kids, well, you're welcome. They'll think pizza is for dinner and you can actually craft something healthful, building on a long-fermented, whole-grain porridge slab bread. Get creative with the toppings for this one. Because it is sturdier than a thin-crust pizza, you can cover it with tomato sauce, cheese, broccoli, and sausage for a classic combo, or go with béchamel, squash, preserved lemon, and herbs for a white pizza. Generally, I like to add as much green— chard, spinach, collards—as I can get away with. Once you layer the sauce and vegetables on top, just bake it until it's crispy, melty, and caramelized. This bread is retro-engineered for this treatment and fully optimized for the "second bake."

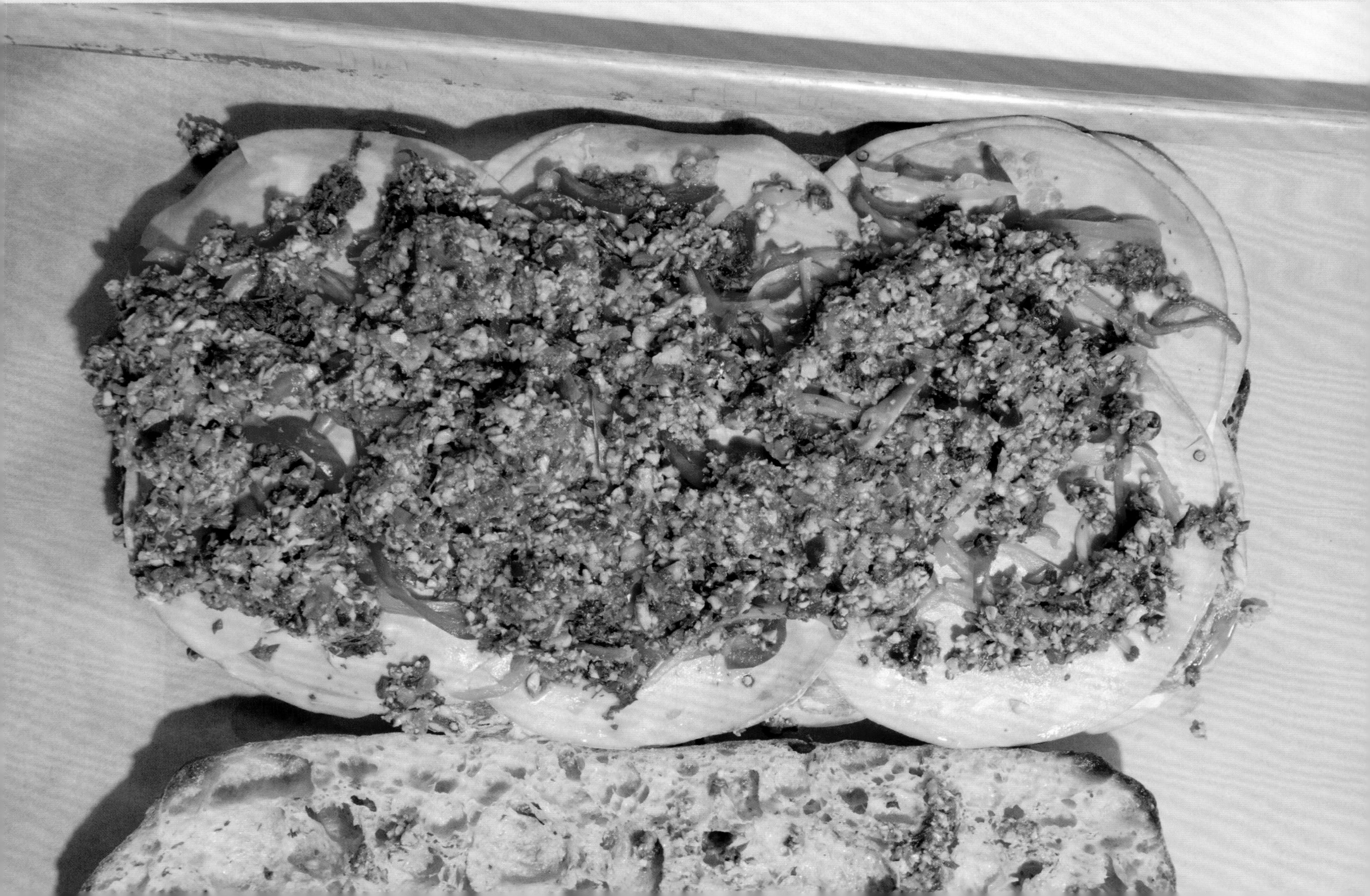

Soaked Slab Sandwiches

The way we most often use slab bread at Tartine is to make a really juicy sandwich—the kind that gets better after it has been chilling in the fridge for most of the day. It is part of a widespread juicy sandwich tradition, with many examples found around the world. A few years ago, when we had the honor and pleasure of collaborating with my dear friend, and inspiration (and sometimes vegan), chef Brooks Headley, we made some extra-juicy vegan sandwiches, letting them marinate overnight and then griddling them hot to serve. Here's one meaty version that I really like. Be creative with the makeup of the sandwich—just make sure it's really juicy.

Makes 4 servings

6 Tbsp good-quality extra-virgin olive oil

6 Tbsp red wine vinegar

6 sprigs thyme, leaves pulled from stems

6 sprigs marjoram, leaves pulled from stems

Fine sea salt and freshly ground black pepper

1 cup mixed pitted green and black olives

2 small olive oil-packed anchovy fillets

1 slab bread (page 122)

12 oz thinly sliced mortadella

8 oz provolone cheese, sliced

4-oz jar pickled red peppers, drained and cut into ¼-inch-wide slices

In a jar with a tight-fitting lid, combine the oil, vinegar, thyme, marjoram, and a pinch each of salt and black pepper. Close the jar and shake vigorously to emulsify this vinaigrette.

Pile the olives and anchovies on a cutting board and chop them together until finely chopped and well combined.

Slice the slab bread in half horizontally and place the halves cut-side up. Spread the olive-anchovy mixture across the bottom half of the loaf. Top with the mortadella, followed by the provolone and red peppers.

Pour about half of the vinaigrette evenly over the meat and cheese and pour the remainder evenly over the top half of the bread. Close the sandwich with the top half, tightly wrap the whole thing in wax paper, and chill in the refrigerator for at least 4 hours or up to overnight.

Unwrap the sandwich and cut it crosswise into quarters. The sandwiches can be eaten chilled or warm. To heat, place a large skillet over high heat. Once it's hot, arrange the sandwich quarters in the pan, and heat until the bottoms are browned, then flip and heat until the other side is browned and they are warmed through.

Sprouted Lentil and Purple Barley Tempeh Sandwiches

A staple of Java, tempeh is traditionally made by first soaking and boiling soybeans and then draining them, spreading them out, and inoculating them with *Rhizopus oligosporus* (a fungus) or with a piece of tempeh from a previous batch. They are then left to ferment, during which time they form a solid sheet, which is cut into smaller pieces for use. Although soybean tempeh is the best-known type, any dried bean or grain can be used to make tempeh. And if you are short of time, you can substitute store-bought for this recipe.

Makes 4 sandwiches

Tempeh

1 cup dried French lentils

1 cup whole-grain purple barley

3 Tbsp brown rice flour

2 Tbsp rice vinegar

1 tsp tempeh starter (*Rhizopus oligosporus*), or 1 oz tempeh from a previous batch (no more than a few days old), crumbled

Assorted Quick Pickles

1 large carrot, peeled and cut into ⅓-inch-wide by 3-inch-long sticks

2 sweet red peppers (such as Lipstick or Corno di Toro), stemmed, seeded, and cut into ⅓-inch-wide slices

8 oz green beans (such as Blue Lake), trimmed and sliced on the diagonal into ⅓-inch lengths

1 red onion, cut into ⅓-inch-thick slices

1 cup apple cider vinegar

1 cup water

½ cup loosely packed raw sugar (such as Demerara or turbinado)

¼ cup sea salt

1 Tbsp coriander seeds

1 Tbsp fennel seeds

Olive-Caper Vinaigrette

¾ cup good-quality extra-virgin olive oil

¾ cup sherry vinegar

2 large shallots, finely diced

2 Tbsp drained capers

¼ cup Cerignola olives, pitted and finely chopped

4 sprigs thyme, leaves pulled from stems and chopped

4 sprigs oregano, leaves pulled from stems and chopped

Finely grated zest of 1 lemon

Tare marinade (page 199)

1 Tbsp peanut or other vegetable oil

2 slab breads (page 122)

2 handfuls watercress

CONTINUED

To make the tempeh: Rinse the lentils well, then put them into a 1-qt canning jar and add cold water to cover by several inches. Rinse the barley well, put it into a separate 1-qt canning jar, and add cold water to cover by several inches. Let the lentils and barley soak at room temperature for 12 hours.

After 12 hours, drain the lentils and rinse well again, rubbing them and rinsing away any loose hulls, then return them to the jar. Drain and rinse the barley the same way and return it to its jar. Cover the mouth of each canning jar with cheesecloth and secure with a rubber band. Place the jars upside down on a cooling rack set over a sheet pan so the lentils and barley continue to drain and have good air circulation as they sprout. Let sprout at room temperature for 12 hours.

After 12 hours, the sprouts can be used immediately, or they can be stored in the jars in the refrigerator for up to 2 days.

Place the barley sprouts in a medium saucepan and add water to cover by 1 inch. Set over medium-low heat, bring to a low simmer, and cook until slightly tender but still fairly firm to the bite (you don't want them to be mushy at all), about 20 minutes. Drain the sprouts, spread them on a sheet pan, and let cool and dry for 20 to 30 minutes.

In a medium bowl, combine the lentil and barley sprouts, flour, vinegar, and tempeh starter. Using your hand, mix together all the ingredients, making sure everything is very well blended. Transfer the mixture to a 9-inch square glass baking dish and press it evenly into the bottom. It should not be more than 1 inch high. Cover the dish with cheesecloth and secure with string or a large rubber band. It is important the covering not be airtight, as oxygen is a critical element in the fermentation process.

You need to keep the tempeh in a very specific temperature range. If it is too hot or too cold, the right fungus will not grow and undesirable microbes can be introduced. It must stay between 85° and 90°F for 24 hours, and then between 60° and 75°F for another 24 hours. A home dehydrator is a great way to maintain these temperatures. You can also use an oven set to the lowest temperature (150° to 200°F) with the door cracked, a yogurt maker, an Instant Pot on the yogurt setting, or a dough proofer for the first 24 hours. If you are unable to maintain the temperature of your fermenting zone, use an ambient thermometer to keep track as you adjust locations.

After 48 hours, the tempeh will be ready. It will have a slightly funky smell, but *if it has any colorful mold growing on it or if it smells unpleasant, it should not be consumed.* If you're not using it immediately, it can be kept in an airtight container in the refrigerator for up to 5 days.

To make the pickles: Pack the carrot, red peppers, green beans, and onion into a 2-qt canning or other heatproof jar. In a medium saucepan over medium heat, combine the vinegar, water, sugar, salt, coriander seeds, and fennel seeds and bring to a boil, stirring to dissolve the sugar and salt. Remove from the heat and carefully pour the boiling pickling liquid over the vegetables, immersing them completely. Let sit, uncovered, until completely cool. Cover tightly and store in the refrigerator for at least 24 hours before using. The pickles will keep for up to 2 weeks.

To make the vinaigrette: In a 1-qt jar with a tight-fitting lid, combine the olive oil, vinegar, shallots, capers, olives, thyme, oregano, and lemon zest. Cover the jar and shake vigorously to emulsify. Let sit for at least 1 hour before using. It will keep in the refrigerator for up to 1 week.

Transfer four 4 by 3-inch rectangles of tempeh to a baking dish and place in a single layer in the dish. Cover the tempeh with the tare marinade, then cover the dish and refrigerate for 24 hours.

Remove the tempeh from the marinade and pat dry with paper towels. Set a large skillet over medium-high heat. When the skillet is warm, add the peanut oil. When the oil is hot, add the tempeh pieces and sear, turning once, until well browned on both sides, about 5 minutes on each side.

Cut each slab bread in half vertically. You should have four 4 by 3-inch pieces. Slice each piece in half horizontally and place the halves cut-side up on a work surface.

Dress the bottom halves of the bread with some of the vinaigrette. Place a seared tempeh rectangle on each bottom half. Top the tempeh with some pickles, then cover with the watercress. Drizzle a little more of the vinaigrette over the watercress, then close the sandwiches with the top halves. Serve immediately or place in an airtight container, refrigerate, and serve up to 24 hours later.

Kids' Bread

We all have memories of eating soft sandwiches when we were kids, whether it was peanut butter and jelly packed for beach picnics, grilled cheese alongside tomato soup with Grandpa, or a perfect ham, mayonnaise, and tomato sandwich in a school lunch box.

Unfortunately, most commercial grocery-store sliced bread is made with artificial colorings, flavorings, preservatives, additives, and vital wheat gluten to achieve a pillowy texture and long shelf life. The wheat is stripped of nutrients and minerals and is almost always grown and harvested using harmful chemical pesticides and herbicides. We wanted to make a bread that had the same desirable characteristics as the grocery-store bread—the softness and longevity—but use responsibly sourced and milled whole grains and careful techniques instead of additives.

In order to achieve the same texture and longevity as a bread with chemical stabilizers and preservatives, we use two techniques that are cornerstones of Tartine bread-making: First, we use natural leaven and poolish to raise the dough slowly. This sets up the dough to undergo a long, slow fermentation, much like the country bread. We wanted a little bit of that yeasty flavor and texture, but by using it second generation in the form of a poolish instead of adding it directly, we are able to keep the bread on much the same schedule as the country bread. We slow the fermentation down overnight without stopping it completely, which encourages flavor and texture to develop over time. Second, we add gelatinized flour, as we do for the slab bread and the scalded rye bread. The starches in gelatinized flour give the dough a very tender and moist crumb that lasts for days and add the flavor, fiber, and nutrients of whole grain.

The bones of this recipe can be used to make lots of variations on a soft sandwich bread. Since this bread is baked in a loaf pan, there is more leeway with the flours you can use than is possible with hearth loaves. That's because the pan supports the loaf as it bakes, so the gluten doesn't need to be as strong. Nor are you looking for the open crumb of a hearth loaf that's only possible with high-performing gluten flour. Pain de mie is a very popular, very white soft bread that is traditionally baked in a loaf pan with a removable sliding lid, which turns out a perfectly square loaf (with no domed top). We don't use such a pan for our version, but this recipe is well suited to a lidded pan if you want to try using one. Many wheats, such as Sonora, Rouge de Bordeaux, and spelt, have wonderful flavor but tend to make hearth loaves (loaves not baked in a pan) bake up flat. They would be great blended with other flours in this loaf, however. A high proportion of whole grain also works well here and there is a lot of room to play around with the scalded grain. Porridges, such as oat, barley, and rye (or some blend of those), work beautifully. Brown rice–koji porridge kids' bread is a favorite of ours. As with the slab bread, a variety of flours can be scalded; einkorn is used here, but durum would work and so would rye. Toasted and scalded buckwheat groats would also be delicious. As you get familiar with some of the landrace wheats and non-wheat grains available to you, this bread is a great way to get to know them even better.

Kids' Bread Method

Makes two 8½ by 4½-inch loaves

INGREDIENT	QUANTITY	BAKER'S %
Poolish	132g	20%
Leaven	185g	28%
Scalded whole-grain einkorn flour	331g	50%
Warm (85° to 90°F) water	106g	16%
Buttermilk	199g	30%
Honey	46g	7%
Barley malt syrup	20g	3%
High-extraction white wheat flour (such as Edison)	331g	50%
High-extraction red wheat flour (such as Yecora Rojo)	199g	30%
Whole-wheat flour	132g	20%
Buttermilk powder	33g	5%
Salt	20g	3%
Unsalted butter, at room temperature, cut into 1-inch pieces	66g	10%

Prepare the poolish.

As directed on page 59, prepare the poolish 3 to 4 hours before you plan to mix the dough. Alternatively, prepare the poolish the night before, covering loosely with a kitchen towel, and refrigerating overnight to ripen.

Prepare the leaven.

On the morning you're ready to mix, prepare the leaven as directed on page 46. This dough requires a young, fresh leaven (but not a booster leaven) for the right flavor and rise. The leaven is ready for bread-making when it looks bubbly and tastes slightly tangy but also slightly creamy (like yogurt). Unready leaven tastes like raw pancake batter. Overripe leaven tastes very sour or boozy.

If you are unsure if your leaven is ready, you can perform a float test. To do so, fill a small pitcher or cup with cold, clean water. Wet your hands to prevent the leaven from sticking to your fingers. Gently pinch off about 1 Tbsp of the leaven, handling it minimally so as not to deflate the air bubbles, and carefully place it in the water. It should bob or float on the surface, not sink to the bottom. If it hovers or rises slowly, you can still use it, but your bulk fermentation may take a little longer than it would if you used a riper leaven.

Scald the einkorn flour.

Once the leaven passes the float test, it's time to scald the einkorn flour. Measure 250g cold water and 125g einkorn flour into a medium saucepan and whisk together until well mixed. (This will yield a little more than the required 331g for the recipe, but some will inevitably get stuck to the spatula and pan.) Place the slurry over medium heat and cook, whisking constantly, until the mixture starts to thicken, then switch to a heat-resistant rubber spatula and stir continuously until it darkens and becomes a stiff paste, 3 to 5 minutes total. (It should register at least 160°F on a kitchen thermometer). Transfer the gelatinized flour to a sheet pan and spread it out to cool until just warm to the touch (85°F) while you start mixing the dough. (For more on scalding flour, see page 44.)

Pre-mix the dough.

In the bowl of a stand mixer fitted with the dough-hook attachment, combine the water, buttermilk, poolish, leaven, honey, and barley malt syrup. In a large bowl, stir together the high-extraction white wheat flour, high-extraction red wheat flour, whole-wheat flour, and buttermilk powder. Add the flour mixture to the liquids in the mixer bowl and mix on low speed, stopping the machine to scrape down the sides of the bowl with a rubber spatula as needed, until all ingredients are well incorporated, about 2 minutes. Cover the bowl with a clean kitchen towel and let the dough autolyze (rest) for 20 to 30 minutes.

Finish mixing the dough.

Add the salt to the dough and mix on medium speed for 3 minutes to develop the gluten. Re-cover with the towel and let rest for 3 minutes. Mix on medium speed for 3 minutes more, then continue mixing while slowly adding the butter, one piece at a time, waiting until each addition is incorporated before adding the next piece. When all the butter has been incorporated, the dough will form a smooth, elastic, cohesive ball. If it is still sticky and tearing, rest for 3 minutes, then mix for another 1 to 2 minutes, until smooth. Add half of the scalded flour and mix on medium speed until incorporated. Then add the remaining scalded flour and continue to mix until completely incorporated.

Let the dough rest.

Loosely cover the dough with a clean kitchen towel and let rest in a warm (82° to 85°F), draft-free place for about 3 hours. Every hour, turn the dough in the bowl a few times by gently lifting and stretching up the sides and folding them into the middle. The dough is ready to be shaped when it passes the float test: If a small piece of dough bobs or floats when gently placed in a pitcher of cool water, it's ready for the next stage, If it sinks, it needs additional time to bulk ferment.

Pre-shape the dough.

Transfer the dough to a clean, unfloured work surface. Lightly flour the dough and use a bench knife to cut into two equal pieces. Using lightly floured hands and the bench knife, work each piece of dough into a round, creating some taut tension on the surface without causing any rips. Lightly flour each dough round, cover with a clean kitchen towel, and let rest on the work surface for 20 to 30 minutes, until the dough has visibly relaxed a little bit (although this one won't relax as much as country bread dough does). While the dough rests, butter two 8 ½ by 4 ½-inch loaf pans.

Finish shaping the loaves and let rise overnight.

Working with one round at a time, start by gently flipping the dough, taking care to maintain the round shape and all the aeration. The floured side is now on the bottom, and the top, now facing up, is unfloured. Stretch out the top one-third of dough farthest away from you and fold it over the middle third of the round. Repeat the same action two or three times until you have created an oblong loaf about the length of the loaf pan. Place the dough, seam-side down, into one of the prepared pans. Repeat the process to shape the second loaf. Loosely cover the loaves with a slightly damp kitchen towel and let rest at room temperature for 20 minutes. Then transfer the loaves, loosely covered with the kitchen towel, to the refrigerator to rise slowly overnight.

Bake the loaves.

The following day, when you are ready to bake, remove the pans from the refrigerator and let the dough come to room temperature while you preheat the oven to 425°F.

Use a lame or sharp scissors to score the top of each loaf. Cutting or scoring prevents the loaves from bursting and large bubbles from developing under the crust during baking. Bake the loaves, rotating the pans front to back after about 20 minutes to promote even baking, until the tops are dark golden brown and the sides that have risen above the rims of the pans feel set when pressed gently, about 45 minutes. You can use an instant-read thermometer to test for doneness: the loaves are finished baking when their internal temperature is 210°F.

Let the loaves cool in their pans on cooling racks for 10 minutes, then turn them out onto the racks and let cool completely before slicing. Using a bread knife, slice with a gentle sawing motion. Store in a bread box at room temperature for up to 3 days. To store longer, slice the bread once it has cooled, place in an airtight freezer-proof container, and freeze for up to 2 weeks. To refresh, toast directly from the freezer.

BLTs

In California, we are thankful to have access to exceptional local fruits and vegetables year-round. The state is also home to some of the most talented and dedicated ranchers, butchers, and cheese makers in the world. Here, we combine late-summer dry-farmed tomatoes, lettuce, salty smoky bacon, mayo, and freshly baked rustic kids' bread to make a sublime version of the very American classic.

Makes 4 sandwiches

Tomato Jam

2 pints cherry tomatoes, cut in half

2 Tbsp apple cider vinegar

1 Tbsp grated ginger

1 Tbsp chopped fresh tarragon

2 Tbsp diced shallot

1 Tbsp dark brown sugar

1½ tsp smoked Spanish paprika

¼ tsp crushed red pepper flakes

Tarragon Aioli

⅔ cup tarragon leaves

1 large garlic clove

1½ Tbsp lemon juice

1 tsp olive oil

1 tsp salt

1 cup plus 10 Tbsp mayonnaise (or aioli, page 113)

12 thick slices smoked bacon

8 slices kids' bread (page 156), toasted

6 large ripe tomatoes, cut into ½-inch-thick slices

1 head Little Gem lettuce, leaves washed and patted dry

To make the jam: Combine the tomatoes, vinegar, ginger, tarragon, shallot, brown sugar, paprika, and pepper flakes in a sauce pot over medium-high heat and bring to a boil, stirring occasionally to prevent it from scorching. Turn down the heat to medium-low and simmer for 2 hours, until thickened to jamlike consistency. Set aside to cool.

To make the aioli: In the jar of a blender, combine the tarragon, garlic, lemon juice, olive oil, and salt and blend until smooth. Transfer the tarragon mixture to a small bowl and fold in the mayonnaise.

Set a cast-iron skillet over high heat. Add the bacon in a single layer and cook (in batches if necessary) until the edges are crisp and brown and the centers of the slices are still soft. Transfer the cooked bacon to a plate and continue cooking the remaining slices. Drain the bacon fat from the skillet and return to the heat. Place four slices of bread in the hot pan and toast until browned on the underside, about 3 minutes. Flip the slices and toast until browned on the second side, about 3 minutes. Transfer the bread to individual plates and repeat with the remaining slices.

Slather the bottom bread halves of each sandwich with tomato jam and the top halves with aioli. On the bottom halves, place a layer of tomatoes. Add three bacon slices to each sandwich. Cover the bacon with the lettuce leaves. Close the sandwiches and serve immediately.

Tarragon-Sorrel Egg Salad Toasts

We love this soft bread for simple one- or two-ingredient sandwiches—everything from peanut butter and bananas to cucumbers and cream cheese. This bread is a great vehicle for re-creating your favorite childhood sandwich or for dressing up with cured salmon. I could eat egg salad every day, always adding greens where I can.

Makes 2 sandwiches

4 medium-hard boiled
(7 ½-minute) eggs, peeled
and chopped

1 shallot, minced

2 sprigs tarragon, leaves pulled
from stems and finely chopped

5 sprigs chervil, leaves pulled
from stems and finely chopped

3 sprigs dill, fronds pulled from
stems and finely chopped

3 stems sorrel, leaves pulled
from stems and finely chopped

10 sprigs flat-leaf parsley,
leaves pulled from stems and
finely chopped

3 garlic cloves, minced

2 Calabrian chiles, minced

1 ½ cups good-quality
extra-virgin olive oil

Fine sea salt

4 slices kids' bread (page 156)

2 to 4 oz caviar

Chives, minced

In a medium bowl, combine the eggs, shallot, tarragon, chervil, dill, sorrel, parsley, garlic, chiles, and olive oil. Add salt and taste.

Toast the bread slices. Trim off the crusts and cut the bread on the diagonal into triangles. Spoon the egg salad over the toasts, distributing it evenly. Spoon caviar over the egg salad and garnish with the chives. Serve immediately.

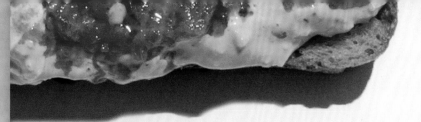

Open-Face Sandwiches on Kids' Bread

chicken liver mousse and blackberry jam

whole-grain mustard and liverwurst

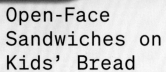

grilled pineapple and aioli

green herb and/or
watercress compound butter
and prosciutto cotto

salmon lox with
butter and caviar

green egg salad and
Calabrian chile

chocolate-hazelnut spread,
nut butter, and bananas

Flatbreads

I first worked with einkorn grain at Boulangerie Savoyarde, in the village of École in the Auvergne-Rhône Alps of southeastern France, with Patrick LePort many years ago. Einkorn is a small spelt and believed to be the first wheat cultivated by humans (thus its name in German translates to "one grain"). It is especially soft and tender with a graham cracker–like sweetness. We use einkorn flour in doughnuts, shortbreads, and pâte sucrée, for example, and it is very well suited to those uses. It doesn't lend itself to country bread, however. Its gluten character is almost the opposite of the strong and stretchy qualities we get from Yecora Rojo flour or the similar high-protein bread flours. I wanted to create a bread that showed off the soft and sweet characteristics of einkorn, and this is the dough that came from that exploration.

This base dough recipe can be handled in different ways to create various styles of flatbread. At its simplest, it can be a soft, tandoor-style flatbread. When it is baked hot and quickly, it splits and puffs up like pita.

My favorite way to use this dough is to quick-laminate it with butter by stretching it super-thin, spreading soft butter on it, rolling it up, curling it into a pinwheel, and then rolling it out. This creates tiny butter pockets that disappear in the oven, leaving soft flakes of dough that are tender on the inside and beautifully crispy and caramelized around the dark edges.

Einkorn
Flatbreads
Method

Makes 12 flatbreads

INGREDIENT	QUANTITY	BAKER'S %
Leaven	96g	20%
Warm (85° to 90°F) water	263g	55%
High-extraction wheat flour	239g	50%
Whole-grain einkorn flour	239g	50%
Whole-milk plain yogurt	96g	20%
Extra-virgin olive oil	15g	3%
Sea salt	15g	3%
Unsalted butter, at room temperature	13 Tbsp	

Prepare the leaven.

Prepare the leaven as directed on page 46. The leaven is ready for bread-making when it looks bubbly and tastes slightly tangy but also slightly creamy (like yogurt). Unready leaven tastes like raw pancake batter. Overripe leaven tastes very sour or boozy.

If you are unsure if your leaven is ready, you can perform a float test. To do so, fill a small pitcher or cup with cold, clean water. Wet your hands to prevent the leaven from sticking to your fingers. Gently pinch off about 1 Tbsp of the leaven, handling it minimally so as not to deflate the air bubbles, and carefully place it in the water. It should bob or float on the surface, not sink to the bottom. If it hovers or rises slowly, you can still use it, but your bulk fermentation may take a little longer than it would if you used a riper leaven.

Mix the dough.

Pour the water into a large bowl. Add the leaven and stir well to disperse. Add the high-extraction wheat flour, einkorn flour, yogurt, oil, and salt. Mix well with your hands until a cohesive dough forms (it will still feel sticky). Turn the dough in the bowl by gently lifting and stretching up the sides and folding them into the middle. Flour the work surface as needed to prevent sticking. Repeat this action until the dough feels strong and smooth, about 8 minutes. (Alternatively, use a stand mixer fitted with the dough-hook attachment and knead the dough on medium speed until it is stretchy and smooth, 5 to 7 minutes.)

Turn the dough during its bulk fermentation.

Loosely cover the bowl with a clean kitchen towel and let rest in a warm (82° to 85°F), draft-free place for about 3 hours. Every 30 minutes, wet your hands and give the dough several series of turns in the bowl, using the same lifting, stretching, and folding technique you used when mixing the dough. This builds strong gluten bonds in the dough without deflating it. The last turn should be a gentle one, turning the dough just until it has all been gently folded over once; the mass should hold its shape in the bowl. This first rise, also called the bulk fermentation or bulk rise, is a crucial time for the dough to develop strength and depth of flavor.

When the dough has finished rising, it will feel airy and fluffy. You can check the dough's readiness with a float test: If a small piece of dough bobs or floats when gently placed in a pitcher of cool water, your dough is ready for the next stage. If it sinks, the dough needs additional time to bulk ferment.

Shape the dough.

Lightly flour a clean work surface. Transfer the dough to the surface and use a bench knife to cut into twelve equal pieces, each about 80g. Roll each piece into a smooth ball, lightly flour the balls, and let rest on the work surface for 20 minutes or so.

Preheat the oven.

While the dough rests, position an oven rack at the lowest level, place a sheet pan or a 12-inch cast-iron skillet on the rack, and preheat the oven to 475°F. (Alternatively, you can use a baking stone. Make sure to check the manufacturer's instructions and preheat the stone for as long as necessary. Some stones require up to 1 hour of preheating time.)

Roll out and bake the flatbreads.

You'll need the smoothest work surface available for shaping the flatbreads. A marble, polished stone, or other smooth countertop works great; a wooden cutting board with a rough surface won't. Smear 1 Tbsp of the butter onto the clean, smooth work surface, creating a film to which the dough will stick. Use a table knife to continue smearing the butter until it is silky.

Place a dough ball on the buttered surface and flatten it with your hands. Start to stretch it into a thin, very wide circle—as thin as you can make it. Lift and pull the sides away from the middle, using the tackiness of the buttered work surface to stick the dough to the work surface as you stretch it bigger and bigger. It should stretch to 8 to 10 inches in diameter and be paper-thin and translucent. Using about 1 Tbsp butter, spread a thin layer of butter across the surface of the dough. Roll up the dough like a rug, then coil the roll around itself like a snail's shell. Pinch closed the exposed end to the coil to seal it. Using a rolling pin, flatten the coil into a round 6 inches in diameter and about ¼ inch thick. (Adding a thin layer of butter, enclosing it in the dough, and rerolling is called laminating.) Repeat to make one or two more rounds.

Using a bench knife, carefully transfer the rounds, one at a time, to the preheated sheet pan or skillet and bake, turning once, until tawny brown on both sides, 3 to 4 minutes on each side. Repeat to stretch, quick-laminate, roll out, and bake the remaining dough balls. Serve warm from the oven. The flatbreads are best the day they are made but can be stored in a bread box at room temperature for 1 day. To refresh, toast over medium heat in a cast-iron skillet.

Einkorn Pitas

One you've shaped the flatbread dough into balls and the balls have rested for 20 minutes, flour a clean work surface. Using a rolling pin, flatten one ball into a 6-inch round about ¼ inch thick. It is very important that the flattened round has an even thickness, with no rips or tears in the dough. The diameter size of the round doesn't matter as much as its thickness and evenness. This dough can be sticky, so add flour to your work surface as needed while you roll out the rounds. It's okay if the rounds have a little flour on their surface when they go in the oven; it gives them a rustic look when baked. When the disks are uniform, the intense heat of the oven quickly makes its way to the center of the dough, creating a puff of steam that expands the pocket before the dough cooks through and becomes too rigid. Repeat to roll the remaining dough balls into rounds the same way.

Let the rounds rest for 30 minutes, uncovered, in a draft-free place, which gives the gluten time to relax and enables the pitas to open in the middle during baking. Position an oven rack in the middle position, place a baking stone or steel or a sheet pan on the rack, and preheat the oven to 500°F. Alternatively, heat a cast-iron skillet over high heat on the stove top until blazing hot.

Carefully place two or three rounds on the preheated baking surface and bake (or in the skillet and cook) until they puff up, about 3 minutes. (Pitas that do not puff well are still delicious to eat.) Repeat to bake (or cook) the other dough rounds, letting the oven (or skillet) reheat for about 5 minutes between batches. Wrap the pitas in a clean kitchen towel to stay soft. Serve warm. The pitas are best the day they are made but can be stored in a bread box at room temperature for up to 2 days. To refresh, wrap in aluminum foil and warm in a 300°F oven for about 10 minutes.

Green Shakshuka

Shakshuka is a Middle Eastern egg-in-sauce dish that has become popular
in the United States. It is delicious, nutritious, and perfectly suited for any
time of the day. The dish has Tunisian roots, but it is a staple meal in Israel
and, uncoincidentally, California. There are red versions with tomato, and
green versions with a hearty leafy base; but at its heart, shakshuka is a baked
egg dish with saucy seasonal vegetables. Since the combo of eggs, greens,
herbs, and bread never gets old, I humbly submit another iteration.

Makes 4 servings

1 tsp cumin seeds

1 tsp caraway seeds

1 tsp fennel seeds

2 bunches green chard, collard greens, or mustard greens

Fine sea salt

1 bunch flat-leaf parsley, leaves pulled from stems

4 sprigs mint, leaves pulled from stems

4 sprigs cilantro, leaves pulled from stems

2 garlic cloves, finely chopped

2 small spicy green chiles (such as serrano), stemmed and finely chopped (I like to use pickled chiles if I have them)

¼ cup good-quality extra-virgin olive oil, plus more as needed

1 yellow onion, chopped into ½-inch pieces

8 ripe green heirloom tomatoes (such as Green Zebra or Green Giant), cored and halved longitudinally through the stem end

4 eggs

½ lemon

Freshly ground black pepper

2 sprigs flat-leaf parsley, leaves pulled from stems

Einkorn flatbreads (page 170) or einkorn pitas (page 177) for serving

Preheat the oven to 350°F.

In a dry small saucepan over medium heat, toast the cumin seeds and caraway seeds, shaking the pan often, just until fragrant, 1 to 2 minutes. Let cool, then combine with the fennel seeds and finely grind in a spice grinder or with a mortar and pestle.

Set a large, ovenproof skillet over medium-high heat. While the skillet heats, trim, coarsely chop, and rinse half of the chard. Then, when the pan is hot and while the chard is still very wet, add the chard to the skillet and cook until bright green and wilted, 1 to 2 minutes, stirring gently halfway through cooking. You can add a sprinkle of water to the skillet if needed—the idea is to quickly steam the leaves. Lightly season with salt as they are wilting. Set aside to cool.

In a blender, combine the parsley, mint, cilantro, garlic, chiles, and cooled chard and blend until smooth, drizzling in 2 Tbsp of the oil (or as much as needed to create a smooth sauce).

Trim and chop the remaining chard into about ½-inch pieces. Wipe out the skillet, place over medium heat, and warm the remaining 2 Tbsp oil. Add the onion and cook, stirring, until translucent, 3 to 5 minutes. Lightly season the onion with salt, then add the chopped chard to the skillet and cook, stirring occasionally, until the stems are soft and the leaves are wilted, about 7 minutes. Add the green tomatoes and the herb sauce to the skillet and stir to mix well. Using the back of a spoon, create four small, evenly spaced wells in the vegetable mixture. Crack an egg into each well.

Transfer the skillet to the oven and bake until the egg whites are just set, 10 to 15 minutes. Finish with a squeeze of lemon juice, a few grinds of pepper, and the parsley. Serve immediately with the flatbreads on the side for scooping.

Slow-Cooked Lamb Shoulder with Pickled Red Onions, Yogurt-Cucumber-Avocado Salad, and Zhug

I'm always adding herbs and dark greens to whatever I can, from salsa verde, chimichurri, and herb-laced vinaigrettes to aioli. Zhug, an herby sauce, is a Yemeni staple and a favorite of mine. Here it accompanies a lamb dish that goes well with making bread, as it, too, is an extended process in which time and heat do most of the work, punctuated by infrequent attention from the cook. This is a great recipe to make over a long, slow, cozy weekend.

Makes 6 to 8 servings

Pickled Red Onions

1 red onion, cut into ¼-inch-thick slices

1 cup white wine vinegar

1 cup water

1 tsp granulated sugar

Slow-Cooked Lamb

1 (5 to 7-lb) bone-in lamb shoulder

Fine sea salt

1 large yellow onion, cut into ¾-inch dice

Extra-virgin olive oil as needed

4 large carrots, peeled and chopped

1 (750ml) bottle light red wine (such as Beaujolais)

4 stalks celery, chopped

2 ripe heirloom tomatoes, cored and quartered through the stem end

4 cups chicken stock

2 sprigs cilantro, leaves pulled from stems

2 sprigs mint, leaves pulled from stems

Zhug

3 garlic cloves

1 to 2 serrano chiles, stemmed and seeded

1½ cups loosely packed flat-leaf parsley leaves, chopped

2 cups loosely packed fresh cilantro leaves, chopped

1 Tbsp freshly squeezed lemon juice

¾ tsp ground coriander

¾ tsp ground cumin

½ tsp ground turmeric

½ tsp freshly ground black pepper

½ tsp fine sea salt

1 cup good-quality extra-virgin olive oil

Yogurt-Cucumber-Avocado Salad

1 ripe avocado, halved, pitted, peeled, and cut into ½-inch-thick slices

1 Persian cucumber or ½ English cucumber, cut into ½-inch-thick slices

1 cup whole-milk plain yogurt (not Greek yogurt)

2 sprigs mint, leaves pulled from stems

2 sprigs cilantro, leaves pulled from stems

Einkorn flatbreads (page 170) or einkorn pitas (page 177) for serving

CONTINUED

To make the pickled onions: At least 1 day before you plan to serve the meal, place the red onion slices in a 1-qt canning or other heatproof jar, packing them down as needed so they fit. In a small saucepan over medium heat, combine the vinegar, water, and sugar and bring to a simmer. Pour the simmering pickling liquid over the onion slices, immersing them completely. Let sit, uncovered, until completely cool. Cover tightly and store in the refrigerator for at least 24 hours before using. The onions will keep for up to 1 month.

To cook the lamb: Preheat the oven to 275°F. Season the lamb shoulder by rubbing it generously with salt.

Set a Dutch oven or other large, heavy pot over high heat. Place the lamb shoulder in the hot, dry pot and let it cook until a caramelized brown crust has formed on the bottom side. Flip the shoulder as needed to sear it on all sides the same way. Try not to turn the shoulder until a side is well browned, as you want to create a flavorful crust but not begin to cook the lamb through. Transfer the lamb to a plate and set aside.

Turn the heat to medium and add the yellow onion to the pot. There might already be enough lamb fat to cook the onion without any additional oil; it depends on the piece of meat. If the bottom of the pot looks dry, drizzle in a splash of oil. Cook, stirring, until the onion is translucent, 3 to 5 minutes. Add the carrots and, using a wooden spoon, scrape up any bits of lamb stuck to the pot bottom. If they are stubbornly stuck, add a splash of the wine to loosen. Cook the carrots, stirring, until they have caramelized a little around the edges, about 5 minutes.

Add the celery to the pot and cook just until it starts to soften, about 1 minute. Add the tomatoes and stock, stir to mix, and then return the lamb shoulder to the pot. Pour in the wine to come three-quarters of the way up the sides of the meat. You may not need all of it.

Cover the pot and transfer to the oven. Braise until almost all of the liquid has been absorbed and the meat is very tender when a knife tip is inserted, about 5 hours. Remove from the oven and let rest in the pot with the lid askew for 30 minutes to 1 hour before serving.

To make the zhug: While the lamb is cooking, chop the garlic and chiles, then smash them to a paste using a mortar and pestle. Add the parsley and cilantro and crush to incorporate. Transfer the garlic-chile-herb paste to a small bowl and mix in the lemon juice, coriander, cumin, turmeric, pepper, salt, and oil.

To make the salad: Just before serving, in a medium bowl, combine the avocado, cucumber, and yogurt and fold gently to mix. Garnish with the mint and cilantro.

Pull the lamb apart into pieces. Garnish with pickled onions, cilantro, and mint.

Serve the lamb with the onions, zhug, salad, and flatbreads.

Reheat any leftover lamb by warming it in a 275°F oven. Alternatively, you can char large pieces of meat on a grill or in a cast-iron skillet over very high heat.

Einkorn Pita Chips with Dulse

This is an homage to Maine Coast Sea Chips and Have'a Corn Chips—two of my favorite salty-savory snacks. Dulse is a seaweed that grows wild in northern Atlantic and Pacific coastal waters. It has a lovely briny flavor and is chock-full of minerals, like iodine, calcium, and potassium and vitamins A, C, and B12. It usually comes in a partially dried form. I like to toast it very lightly in a low oven (325°F) for 3 to 5 minutes, just until it becomes fragrant. Once it cools, it crisps up and can be very easily crumbled into a fine powder and sprinkled over anything (popcorn is a favorite).

Makes 4 to 6 servings

4 Tbsp unsalted butter

¼ cup good-quality extra-virgin olive oil

⅓ cup good-quality soy sauce (preferably shoyu)

12 einkorn pitas (page 177), at least 2 days old, quartered and triangles separated

¼ cup dulse, lightly toasted and finely crumbled

1 Tbsp sea salt

Preheat the oven to 375°F. Line two sheet pans with parchment paper.

In a small saucepan over low heat, melt the butter. Stir in the oil and soy sauce. In a large bowl, toss the pita triangles with the butter mixture to coat lightly. Sprinkle the dulse and salt over the pita triangles and toss again.

Spread the pita triangles in a single layer on the prepared sheet pans. Bake for 7 minutes, then, using tongs or a spoon, stir the pita triangles so they will toast evenly. Continue to bake until lightly browned, 7 to 10 minutes.

Let the pita chips cool completely on the pans before serving. Store leftover chips in an airtight container at room temperature for up to 1 week.

Burger and Sandwich Buns

Vegetable purees are a clever and easy way to add moisture, sweetness, and nutrients to bread doughs. We've often snuck vegetable purees into various recipes at Tartine—the parsnip ice cream from Bar Tartine was an all-time favorite. Historically, we do not add vegetable puree to our hearth loaves. For those, we generally to stick to grains, water, salt, and leaven. But vegetable purees are a great addition to enriched breads, such as buns or soft pan breads. You knows where future experimentation will lead?

All over the world, bakers add mashed cooked potato to bread. There are robust traditions of potato-enriched breads in Ireland and Scotland but also in Poland, Hungary, Germany, and even Chile. Those breads are typically made with white potatoes and are soft with a tight, tender, almost cakey crumb. Potato flour is often used in recipes for buns. For our version, we chose to use the whole vegetable instead of the more processed cooked, dried, and ground tuber.

Our goal was to make a soft bun, like a Hawaiian-style roll but using whole foods (less processed ingredients), for our breakfast egg sandwiches and burgers. We settled on sweet potato for its complex sweetness and subtle sunset hue. Sweet potatoes also add nutritional value; they are a great source of fiber, vitamins, and minerals and contain high amounts of beta-carotene and other antioxidants. We add buttermilk powder in addition to fresh buttermilk because the concentration of protein and milk sugars in the powder helps the buns' exterior to caramelize during the quick, high-heat baking, giving us the very thin crust and super-soft bun we want. The Edison flour is a perfect medium-soft protein white wheat that is suited to this dough. It retains much of its bran and germ but is naturally a neutral pale color, which lets the orange-yellow hue of the sweet potato come through.

A note about the sweet potato: We use sweet potatoes instead of yams in these buns, and the recipe will work best with sweet potatoes. The two vegetables are unrelated botanically, despite sweet potatoes often being labeled "yams." Sweet potatoes are members of the Ipomoea genus, and they originated in Central and South America. Yams are members of the Dioscorea genus and are native to Africa and Asia. Although some sweet potatoes and yams look and taste similar, true sweet potatoes take less time to cook and retain more moisture once they are cooked. To get the best results from this recipe, look for orange-fleshed sweet potatoes, such as Jewel or Garnet.

Sweet Potato Buns Method

Makes 12 buns

INGREDIENT	QUANTITY	BAKER'S %
Pureed roasted sweet potato	80g	30%
Poolish	67g	25%
Leaven	67g	25%
Egg (about 1)	45g	17%
Cool (70°F) water	45g	17%
Buttermilk, at room temperature	72g	27%
Granulated sugar	13g	5%
High-extraction white wheat flour (such as Edison)	266g	100%
Buttermilk powder	13g	5%
Salt	9g	3.25%
Instant yeast	3g	1%
Unsalted butter, at room temperature	40g	15%

Prepare the sweet potato and the poolish.

The day before you want to mix the dough (or up to 3 days ahead), roast the sweet potato. The sweet potato will lose some weight when roasted, so pick one that weighs at least 100g, or use a couple of small ones. Preheat the oven to 450°F.

Cut the sweet potato (peel left on) into six equal pieces (each about 2 inches) and place in a baking dish. Cover tightly with aluminum foil and bake until the pieces are tender and yield very easily when pierced with a fork, 30 to 35 minutes. Let the potato pieces cool to the touch, then mash well with a fork or blend in a food processor until smooth. (The smoother the sweet potato puree, the more easily you will be able to incorporate it into the dough.) Transfer to an airtight container and store in the refrigerator until your bake day.

The night before you want to mix the dough, prepare an overnight poolish by following the directions on page 59.

Prepare the leaven.

The next morning, prepare the leaven as directed on page 46. This dough requires a young, fresh leaven (but not a booster leaven) for the right flavor and rise. The leaven is ready for bread-making when it looks bubbly and tastes slightly tangy but also slightly creamy (like yogurt). Unready leaven tastes like raw pancake batter. Overripe leaven tastes very sour or boozy.

If you are unsure if your leaven is ready, you can perform a float test. To do so, fill a small pitcher or cup with cold, clean water. Wet your hands to prevent the leaven from sticking to your fingers. Gently pinch off about 1 Tbsp of the leaven, handling it minimally so as not to deflate the air bubbles, and carefully place it in the water. It should bob or float on the surface, not sink to the bottom. If it hovers or rises slowly, you can still use it, but your bulk fermentation may take a little longer than it would if you used a riper leaven.

Pre-mix the dough.

Remove the sweet potato puree from the refrigerator and set aside to come to room temperature.

Place a small bowl on the scale and tare the scale. Crack the egg into the bowl. If there's more egg than you need for this recipe, use a spoon or your fingers to remove enough of the egg white so only 45g remains.

In the bowl of a stand mixer fitted with the dough-hook attachment, combine the water, buttermilk, egg, leaven, poolish, and sugar and gently whisk until mostly combined. In a medium bowl, whisk together the flour and buttermilk powder. On low speed, mix the dry ingredients into the wet ingredients until combined, about 3 minutes. Cover the bowl with a clean kitchen towel and let the dough autolyze (rest) for 20 minutes.

Finish mixing the dough.

Mix the dough on low speed for 3 minutes. Add the salt and yeast and continue to mix on low speed until the dough is smooth, supple, and stretchy, about 5 minutes. With the mixer running, add the butter in three equal additions, mixing in each addition completely before adding the next. When all of the butter has been incorporated, add the sweet potato puree and mix until combined.

Let the dough rise.

Loosely cover the dough and let rest in a warm (82° to 85°F), draft-free spot for 30 minutes. Give the dough a turn by gently lifting and stretching up the sides and folding them into the middle. Re-cover and let rest for another 30 minutes, until doubled in volume.

Shape the buns.

Line two sheet pans with parchment paper. Transfer the dough to a clean, unfloured work surface. Using a bench knife, divide the dough into twelve equal pieces, each about 60g. Using lightly floured hands, shape each piece into a ball. Working with one ball at a time, very gently cup your dominant hand over the dough and press it into the work surface while rotating your hand clockwise in a circular motion. The bottom of the bun should stick to the surface a little, anchoring it. Continue the circular motion until you have a tight, cohesive ball. Repeat to shape the remaining balls, placing them about 3 inches apart on the prepared sheet pans as they are ready.

Let rise before baking.

Cover the sheet pans with a clean kitchen towel and let rise in a warm (82° to 85°F), draft-free spot until the balls have almost doubled in volume, 1 to 2 hours. (The amount of time this takes depends on the proofing environment, thus the wide range.) They will be very large, delicate, and full of air when they are ready.

Bake the buns.

About 15 minutes before the buns have finished rising, preheat the oven to 450°F. Fill a clean, food-grade spray bottle with water (or ready a small bowl of water and a brush).

When the buns are ready to bake, spray or gently brush the tops of the buns with water. Bake for 7 minutes, then switch the pans between the racks and rotate them front to back and continue to bake the buns until they are golden brown, another 7 minutes. Let the buns cool completely on the pans on cooling racks.

Store the buns in a bread box at room temperature for up to 3 days. To dress for sandwiches, using a bread knife, cut the buns in half horizontally. If using on the second or third day after baking, butter the cut sides and toast, cut-side down, in a cast-iron skillet over medium heat until golden, 2 to 3 minutes. To store longer, once the buns have cooled and been split, place in an airtight freezer-proof container and freeze for up to 2 weeks. To refresh, toast directly from the freezer.

MARINATED TOFU SANDWICHES WITH CARROT-KOHLRABI SLAW AND AVOCADO MOUSSE

Marinated Tofu Sandwiches with Carrot-Kohlrabi Slaw and Avocado Mousse

When I apprenticed with Richard Bourdon at his bakery in the Berkshires, there was an excellent smoked fish company in the neighborhood. They smoked fish most days of the week, but on the off days, they smoked tofu. Smoked fish and tofu are still two of my absolute favorite foods. In this sandwich, we approximate the flavor of smoked tofu through marinating, using an ingredient and technique that I've learned from talented chefs I've worked with. The key ingredient in the marinade is shio koji, a salted and hydrated version of koji, which is rice that has been inoculated with *Aspergillus oryzae*, or koji mold, and is the base for many fermented Japanese foods, including soy sauce, sake, and miso. Shio koji has probiotic properties and a mouthwatering sweet-and-salty quality and makes a great marinade for meats, not only for its flavoring but also for its tenderizing properties. It may seem like a specialty ingredient, but that won't be the case for long. Shio koji is becoming more common in American pantries and is easily found at health food stores and Japanese markets and online. It's an ingredient worth seeking out for this recipe. The tofu marinates overnight, so you'll start the prep work a day ahead.

Makes 4 sandwiches

Tare Marinade
⅔ cup soy sauce

½ cup shio koji

¼ cup mirin

¼ cup packed
dark brown sugar

½ tsp black peppercorns

1 tsp peeled and grated
fresh ginger

1 garlic clove, sliced

1 green onion, white and
green parts, chopped

2 (10-oz) blocks firm tofu

Carrot-Kohlrabi Slaw
1 large carrot, peeled and
grated

1 kohlrabi or large turnip,
peeled and grated

1 tsp caraway seeds,
plus more as needed

Sea salt

⅓ cup good-quality extra-virgin olive oil

⅓ cup white wine vinegar

Avocado Mousse
2 ripe avocados, halved, pitted,
and peeled

Juice of 1 lime

2 Tbsp good-quality
extra-virgin olive oil

Sea salt

4 sweet potato buns (page 190)

CONTINUED

To make the marinade: In a small saucepan over medium heat, combine the soy sauce, shio koji, mirin, brown sugar, peppercorns, ginger, garlic, and green onion and bring to a simmer, stirring to dissolve the sugar. Remove from the heat and let cool until slightly thickened, about 10 minutes. Strain through a fine-mesh strainer and discard the solids. The marinade can be used immediately or transferred to an airtight container and refrigerated for up to 2 weeks.

Cut the tofu vertically into ½-inch-thick slices and place them in a single layer in a glass baking dish. Pour the marinade evenly over the tofu, cover the dish tightly, and place in the refrigerator to marinate overnight.

To make the slaw: In a medium bowl, mix together the carrot, kohlrabi, and caraway seeds. Season with salt, let sit for 30 minutes, and then drain off any excess water. In a small bowl, whisk together the oil and vinegar to make a dressing. Drizzle the dressing over the carrot-kohlrabi mixture and toss to coat evenly. Taste and adjust the seasoning with salt and more caraway if needed.

To make the mousse: In a blender, combine the avocados, lime juice, and oil and puree until smooth and airy or mousse-like. Season with salt.

Just before you're ready to assemble the sandwiches, set a large cast-iron skillet over medium-high heat. Remove the tofu from the marinade and pat dry with paper towels. Working in batches, add the tofu in a single layer to the hot pan and sear until golden brown on the first side, 3 to 5 minutes. Flip and sear on the second side, 3 to 5 minutes longer. As the batches are ready, transfer to a large plate.

Place the buns, cut-side up, on a work surface. Spread the top and bottom halves of each bun with the mousse. Arrange a pile of slaw on the bottom half and top with a layer of tofu slices. Close with the bun tops and serve immediately.

Soft-Cooked Egg Sandwiches

This is a popular dish at all of our cafés. It's a filling and comforting way to start your day and is yet another example of the eggs-and-greens theme that just never gets old. At the cafés, we serve these with a side of fermented-chile hot sauce, but you can use any fermented or vinegar-based hot sauce you like. I'm a big fan of Crystal hot sauce. Bacon or breakfast sausage is also a popular add-on. So many nights, I dream of waking up to one of these for breakfast.

Makes 4 sandwiches

Wilted Greens

1 Tbsp unsalted butter

Shallots, sliced

1 cup loosely packed tender green leaves (such as chard, spinach, orach, or dandelion)

Pinch of sea salt

2 Tbsp good-quality extra-virgin olive oil

9 eggs

¼ cup crème fraîche

½ tsp sea salt

4 Tbsp unsalted butter, plus more at room temperature for toasting the buns

1 cup grated sharp white Cheddar cheese

4 sweet potato buns (page 190)

Hot sauce for serving

To make the greens: Set a medium skillet over medium-high heat. Once the pan is warm, add the butter. When it melts, add the shallots and sauté for 2 to 3 minutes, until translucent. Add the greens and salt and then drizzle with the oil. Cook, stirring occasionally, until the greens have wilted and are tender but still bright green, 3 to 5 minutes. Transfer to a plate and set aside.

Place a baking dish in the oven and preheat the oven to the lowest setting—150° to 200°F. Crack the eggs into a medium bowl. Add the crème fraîche and salt and whisk well until combined. Set an 8-inch nonstick skillet over medium-low heat. Add 1 Tbsp of the butter to the warm skillet and let it melt slowly. If it melts right away or starts to turn brown at the edges, lower the heat.

Pour ½ cup of the egg mixture into the pan. Let cook slowly until the bottom and sides are set and only the top is still translucent. Place ¼ cup of the cheese in the middle of the egg and gently fold the top, both sides, and the bottom over the cheese to make a roughly 3-inch square. Transfer the cooked egg square to the baking dish in the oven to keep warm. Repeat with the remaining butter, egg mixture, and cheese to make three more egg squares.

Butter the cut sides of the buns. Set a large cast-iron skillet over medium heat. Working in batches, add the bun halves, cut-side down, to the hot pan and toast until golden, 2 to 3 minutes. Place the buns, cut-side up, on a work surface. Place one egg square on each bun bottom. Top each egg square with one-fourth of the wilted greens and close with the bun tops. Serve immediately, with hot sauce.

Fillet of Fish Sandwiches

Fish fillet sandwiches were a childhood favorite of mine (yes, fish sticks too). Ling cod and albacore tuna work well in this recipe, as does any flaky white fish. There are a few components to prepare from scratch for these sandwiches— bread crumbs for the dredge, aioli for the tartar, fried fish fillets—but the attention to detail in the preparation is what makes them a truly modern interpretation. Bread crumbs and aioli find good use in lots of other recipes and can be made ahead and kept on hand. If Brussels sprouts are not in season, substitute slivered cabbage, collard, or kale.

Makes 4 sandwiches

Brussels Sprouts Slaw

10 brussels sprouts, trimmed, then shaved as finely as possible

1 cup freshly squeezed lime juice

¾ cup granulated sugar

1 cup sambal oelek

½ cup fish sauce

Tartar Sauce

1 cup aioli (page 113) or good-quality mayonnaise

1 large pickle, cut into ¼-inch dice

1 to 2 Tbsp pickle juice

2 sprigs dill, fronds pulled from stems and finely chopped

4 sprigs flat-leaf parsley, leaves pulled from stems and finely chopped

Fish Fillets

½ cup all-purpose flour (Edison or Sequoia works well)

1 egg

1 cup bread crumbs (see page 85)

4 (3-oz) flaky white fish fillets (such as sand dab or black cod)

Vegetable oil (such as avocado or grapeseed) for panfrying

4 sweet potato buns (page 190)

Lacto-fermented bread-and-butter pickle slices

To make the slaw: In a small bowl, combine the brussels sprouts, lime juice, sugar, sambal oelek, and fish sauce and toss to coat evenly. Let sit at room temperature while you prepare the tartar sauce and fish.

To make the tartar sauce: In a medium bowl, whisk together the aioli, pickle, pickle juice, dill, and parsley. Cover and set aside.

To prepare the fish: Place the flour, egg, and bread crumbs in separate shallow bowls. Beat the egg until blended. Dredge a fish fillet in the flour, tapping off the excess, then coat in the egg, allowing the excess to drip off, and then finally dredge in the bread crumbs, again tapping off the excess. Place the prepared fillet on a plate. Repeat with the remaining fillets.

Line a plate with paper towels or a brown paper bag and set near the stove. Set a large cast-iron skillet over high heat. Add a drizzle of oil to the hot skillet and tilt to coat the bottom. When the oil is hot, add two fish fillets to the hot pan and cook until browned on the underside, about 3 minutes. Flip the fillets and fry until the second side is well browned, another 3 minutes. Transfer to the prepared plate and repeat with the remaining two fillets.

Put the buns, cut-side up, on a work surface. Place one fish fillet on each bun bottom half and spread the bun tops with the tartar sauce. Top each fillet with a generous scoop of slaw and pickles and then close the sandwiches with the tops. Serve immediately.

Dinner Rolls

Homemade dinner rolls are often the superstar assist player at holiday dinners—their soft, pillowy sweetness providing the perfect counter to salty gravy and sharp, vinegar-tinged cranberry sauce. Sandwiches made on these rolls with leftovers the next day, strengthen this assertion considerably. These are our version of a Parker House–style roll; we named them after Tartine's beloved home neighborhood in San Francisco.

We use a medium-high gluten flour, such as Sequoia or Yecora Rojo. I want them to be tender but have a good amount of loft. The secret to these is proofing them until they are very large and delicate, like wobbly water balloons, and then baking them with a generous amount of steam in a hot oven.

Parker House–style dinner rolls are made with lots of milk and butter. Here we keep the decadence while using more whole-grain flour (for flavor and fiber) and natural leaven, in addition to the commercial yeast, to add flavor and increase digestibility. What we were going for with this formula is a very soft bread with a thin, deeply caramelized crust. These rolls come out of the oven with a firm yet delicate "shell" that softens as they cool. Once you have your leaven game down, these are one of the most straightforward breads to make, and the results are far superior to the additive-laden commercially produced versions. As with the kids' bread and pizza dough, the goal is to preserve the flavor and texture we all love in these American staples while adding more flavor and nutrition.

Mission
Rolls
Method

Makes 15 rolls

INGREDIENT	QUANTITY	BAKER'S %
Leaven	94g	25%
Egg (about 1)	45g	12%
Whole milk	206g	55%
Sea salt	9g	2.5%
Instant yeast	2g	0.5%
Granulated sugar	19g	5%
High-extraction Sequoia flour	375g	100%
Unsalted butter, at room temperature	75g	20%
Unsalted butter, melted	4 Tbsp for brushing	
Flaky sea salt	for sprinkling on top	

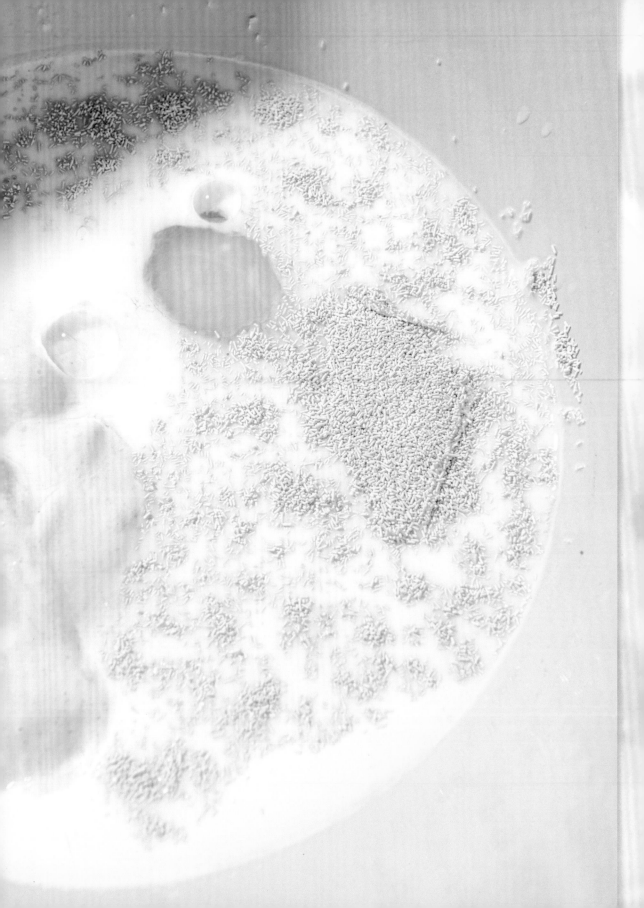

Prepare the leaven.

Prepare the leaven as directed on page 46. This dough requires a peak leaven (but not a booster leaven) for the right flavor and rise. The leaven is ready for bread-making when it looks bubbly and tastes slightly tangy but also slightly creamy (like yogurt). Unready leaven tastes like raw pancake batter. Overripe leaven tastes very sour or boozy.

If you are unsure if your leaven is ready, you can perform a float test. To do so, fill a small pitcher or cup with cold, clean water. Wet your hands to prevent the leaven from sticking to your fingers. Gently pinch off about 1 Tbsp of the leaven, handling it minimally so as not to deflate the air bubbles, and carefully place it in the water. It should bob or float on the surface, not sink to the bottom. If it hovers or rises slowly, you can still use it, but your bulk fermentation may take a little longer than it would if you used a riper leaven.

Warm the egg and milk.

Place the egg in a small bowl of hot (about 120°F) water for 5 minutes. Warm the milk (in a saucepan or in the microwave) until it is about 90°F.

Place a small bowl on the scale and tare the scale. Crack the egg into the bowl. If there's more egg than you need for this recipe, use a spoon or your fingers to remove enough of the egg white so only 45g remains.

Mix the dough.

In the bowl of a stand mixer fitted with the dough-hook attachment, combine the leaven, egg, milk, salt, yeast, and sugar. Mix on medium-low speed until the egg breaks up and the leaven is somewhat distributed. On low speed, add the flour and mix until incorporated. Stop the mixer and scrape the bottom of the bowl and the dough hook with a rubber spatula. Then mix on medium speed until the dough is cohesive and springy, 8 to 10 minutes. With the mixer on medium-low speed, add the room-temperature butter, 1 Tbsp at a time, mixing well after each addition. The dough should be smooth, sticky, and slightly shiny.

Turn the dough during its bulk fermentation.

Transfer the dough to a large, clean bowl. Loosely cover the dough with a clean kitchen towel, and let rest in a warm (82° to 85°F), draft-free place for 1½ hours. Every 30 minutes, wet your hands and give the dough several series of turns in the bowl, gently lifting and stretching the sides of the dough and folding them into the middle to build strong gluten bonds in the dough without deflating it. The last turn should be a gentle one, turning the dough just until it has all been gently folded over once; the mass should hold its shape in the bowl. This first rise, also called the bulk fermentation or bulk rise, is a crucial time for the dough to develop strength and depth of flavor. As the dough rises, it will become puffy and double in volume.

Shape the rolls and let rise.

Generously butter a 9 by 13-inch baking pan. Transfer the dough to a clean, unfloured work surface. Using a bench knife, divide the dough into fifteen equal pieces, each about 55g. Using lightly floured hands, shape each piece into a ball. Working with one ball at a time, very gently cup your dominant hand over the dough and press it into the work surface while rotating your hand clockwise in a circular motion. The bottom of the roll should stick to the surface a little, anchoring it. Continue the circular motion until you have a tight, cohesive ball. Repeat to shape the remaining balls. Gently transfer the rolls to the prepared pan, nestling them together so they are barely touching.

Cover with a clean kitchen towel and let rise in a warm draft-free spot (78° to 82°F) until the rolls have grown in size significantly and a fingertip poked into a roll leaves an impression that bounces back slowly, 45 minutes to 1 hour.

Bake the rolls.

Preheat the oven to 400°F. Fill a clean, food-grade spray bottle with water.

Brush the tops of the rolls with half of the melted butter. Place the pan of rolls in the oven, then spray the sides and bottom of the oven generously with water. Immediately close the oven door. Bake for 7 minutes, rotate the pan front to back, and continue baking until the tops of the rolls are deep golden brown, 7 to 10 minutes.

Remove the rolls from the oven, brush the tops with the remaining melted butter, sprinkle with flaky salt, and serve warm. Store leftover rolls in a bread box at room temperature for up to 1 day. To store longer, once the rolls are cool, place in an airtight freezer-proof container and freeze for up to 2 weeks. To reheat, wrap tightly in aluminum foil and warm in a 250°F oven for 10 to 15 minutes.

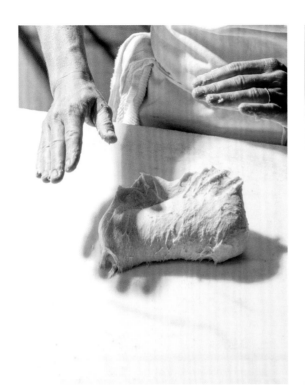

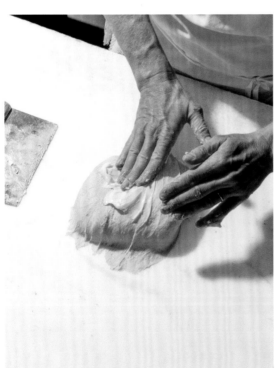

Chipped Ham Sandwiches with Honey-Mustard Butter and Wilted Collard Greens

To me, chipped ham is all of the little shreds left over from carving a whole ham. They tend to be the most flavorful, tender corner bits and take and hold sauce well. My grandmother got a ham for every Easter dinner, and I would always look forward to the sandwiches with the leftover chipped ham. You can ask for very thinly sliced honey ham from your deli counter and get much the same result.

Makes 4 sandwiches

6 Tbsp unsalted butter, at room temperature

3 Tbsp whole-grain mustard

1 Tbsp honey

Fine sea salt

1 bunch collard greens, trimmed and chopped

2 Tbsp good-quality extra-virgin olive oil

½ lemon

4 Mission rolls (page 208), warm from the oven (see Note)

8 oz chipped ham

In a medium bowl, mix together the butter, mustard, and honey until well combined. Season with salt.

In a large skillet over medium-high heat, combine the collard greens and oil and cook, stirring often, until wilted and tender, 10 to 15 minutes. Season with salt and a squeeze of lemon juice.

Split the rolls and arrange them, cut-side up, on a work surface. Spread the honey-mustard butter across the cut side of both halves. Pile the ham on the bottom halves of the rolls and top with the wilted collards. Close the sandwiches with the roll tops and serve immediately.

NOTE: If your rolls aren't warm from the oven, it's best to toast them before assembling the sandwiches. Split them open, butter the cut sides, and toast, cut-side down, in a cast-iron skillet over medium heat until golden, 2 to 3 minutes.

MISSION ROLLS WITH CULTURED BUTTER, CURED SALMON, AND CAVIAR

Mission Rolls with Cultured Butter, Cured Salmon, and Caviar

Cultured butter is churned from cream that is fermented much like yogurt, buttermilk, or crème fraîche. This results in a tangier, more complex flavor. We used to make homemade cultured butter with kefir grains at Bar Tartine, which is still my favorite iteration. For these sandwiches, we use caviar from The Caviar Company, a sustainable, local-to-us, woman-owned business. We are lucky to have a salmon connection through our millers in the Pacific Northwest. Smoking salmon makes it very stable, so if you don't have a good local source, you can order some of the good stuff through the mail and it won't suffer for the trip. It's worth procuring sustainably caught smoked salmon not only for the flavor but also for its positive environmental impact.

Makes 4 servings as a light meal or 8 as a snack or appetizer

Kefir Butter
4 cups heavy cream

1 tsp milk kefir grains (available at specialty grocers and online)

Cured Salmon
1 side skin-on fresh salmon, about 3 lb

½ cup coarse sea salt

¼ cup granulated sugar

¼ cup packed dark brown sugar

¼ cup ground black pepper

Finely grated zest of 2 lemons

8 Mission rolls (page 208), warm from the oven (see Note)

2 to 4 oz caviar

Finely chopped fresh chives for serving (optional)

To make the butter: Pour the cream into a large jar (I use a 1-qt canning jar). Cut a roughly 4-inch square piece of cheesecloth. Place the kefir grains on the cheesecloth, then gather the edges of the cheesecloth and secure with butcher's string to make a little pouch. Place the pouch of grains into the cream and let sit, uncovered, at room temperature for 24 to 48 hours. The cream is ready when it sets to the consistency of sour cream or crème fraîche. Remove the pouch of kefir grains, cover the jar, and place in the refrigerator for at least 24 hours or up to 1 week. (To store the kefir grains, place them in 1 cup cold milk and refrigerate, draining and changing the milk at least once a week until you're ready to use the grains again. The grains can be kept this way indefinitely and, if healthy, will continue to reproduce and create more grains, which you can give to your friends.)

Line a medium bowl with a piece of cheesecloth, allowing the cloth to overlap the sides by a few inches. Transfer the thoroughly chilled cream to the bowl of a stand mixer fitted with the paddle

CONTINUED

attachment and mix on high speed until the butter separates from the buttermilk. It will become whipped cream first, so keep whipping past that stage. Once the butter separates, transfer the butter mixture to the cheesecloth-lined bowl, then gather the edges of the cheesecloth and twist together to squeeze out the buttermilk into the bowl. Shape the butter mass however you like: in a stick or a patty or pressed into a decorative butter mold. Store both the butter and the buttermilk in tightly covered containers in the refrigerator for up to 5 days.

To prepare the cured salmon: Remove any pin bones and trim away any tough sinews from the salmon. Place the fish, skin-side down, in a glass baking dish. In a small bowl, stir together the salt, both sugars, pepper, and lemon zest, mixing well. Generously cover the salmon with the salt-sugar mixture, using all of it. Place a piece of wax paper over the fish and set a weight on top; a heavy plate or bowl works well. The weight will help some of the juices express to give you a proper cure. Refrigerate the salmon for 5 days, turning the fish after 2 ½ days into the curing process.

Remove the fish from the cure and express the juices. Pat the fish with a paper towel to remove the excess juices from the surface. Using a sharp knife, slice the salmon very thinly. (I like to include the skin but you can trim it off if that's more to your taste.) Arrange the slices on parchment paper.

Split the rolls and arrange them, cut-side up, on a platter alongside the caviar, salmon, kefir butter, and chives, if desired, for your guests to assemble their sandwiches at the table.

Leftover cured salmon can be stored in an airtight container in the refrigerator for up to 4 weeks.

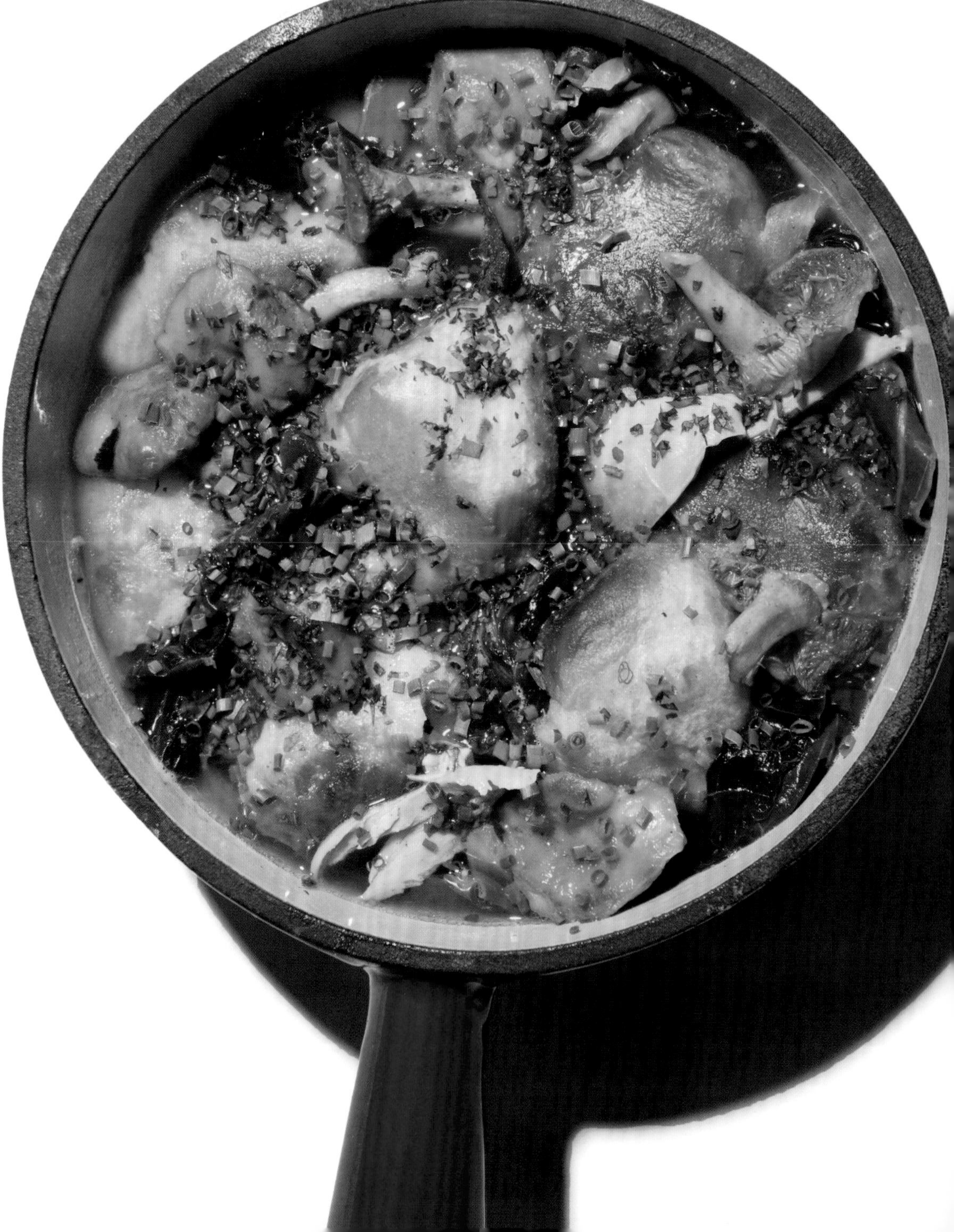

Chicken and Dumplings
Mushroom Kombu Soup

Sincere thanks to my mom for making chicken and dumpling soup when I was a kid. I still love it. Here is a mash-up version that incorporates some of my favorite kombu dashi–based soup techniques from Nick Balla and Courtney Burns when they were the chefs at Bar Tartine on Valencia Street in San Francisco. Searing the yeasted roll dough in a hot pan results in tender savory dumplings with caramelized notes. I love boiled gnocchi, but their cousin, the pan-fried gnudi, properly brought to America by indefatigable chef April Bloomfield, led me to this alternate dumpling universe. We all thank you, Chef!

Makes 4 servings

1 recipe Mission rolls dough (page 208)

4 qt water

2 (3 by 6-inch) pieces dried kombu

1 cup dried shiitake mushrooms

2 to 3 Tbsp cold-pressed sesame oil, or as needed

½ chicken, cut into four pieces (1 leg, 1 thigh, 1 breast, 1 wing)

8 oz fresh maitake (hen-of-the-woods) or other wild mushrooms, trimmed of any woody stems

1 bunch collard greens, trimmed and chopped into ½-inch pieces

2 Tbsp unsalted butter

6 sprigs flat-leaf parsley, leaves pulled from stems and chopped

1 small bunch chives, finely chopped

Sea salt and freshly ground black pepper

Mix the dough and set aside to proof for 1½ hours as directed. Lightly flour a sheet pan.

While the dough is proofing, add the water to a stockpot and place over medium heat. Use kitchen scissors to snip small slits in the kombu to help release its flavor and then slip the kombu into the water. Bring to a rolling simmer, turn down the heat until the water is barely simmering, and simmer for 20 minutes. Add the shiitake and continue to barely simmer for another 30 minutes. Remove from the heat, strain the liquid through a fine-mesh strainer, and discard the kombu and shiitake. Set this dashi aside.

Check the dough. If it has doubled in volume, cut it into 1-inch square pieces and place on the prepared sheet pan. Cover lightly and place in the refrigerator until ready to use.

Line a second sheet pan with a brown paper bag or paper towels. Set a 6-qt Dutch oven or other heavy pot over medium-high heat. When the pot is warm, add the sesame oil. When the oil is shimmering, add two pieces of the chicken and cook, turning once, until browned on both sides, 3 to 5 minutes on each side. As the pieces are ready, transfer them to the second prepared sheet pan.

CONTINUED

Repeat with the remaining two pieces. Some of the browning will occur on the skin and some on the meat, which is fine.

With the pot still over medium-high heat, add a little more oil if needed to coat the bottom. Working in batches, add the maitake mushrooms in a single layer and cook, turning once, until well browned on both sides, 2 to 3 minutes on each side. Transfer them to the sheet pan with the chicken. Repeat until all the mushrooms are browned.

Once the chicken and mushrooms are browned, add the dashi to the pot and bring to a slow simmer over low heat. Add the chicken pieces and mushrooms and, keeping the soup at a low simmer, cook until the chicken is falling off the bones, 40 to 60 minutes. Using tongs and a fork, remove and discard the bones and shred the chicken into the soup. Add the collard greens and simmer on low heat until they wilt, 1 to 2 minutes.

When the soup is almost done, set a cast-iron skillet over medium-high heat. Remove the dumplings from the refrigerator. Melt the butter in the warm skillet and place the dumplings in the butter. Let them cook in the skillet until one side is browned, about 3 minutes. Turn them and brown the next side. Continue until all the sides are browned and they are cooked through.

Ladle the soup and dumplings into individual bowls and garnish with the parsley and chives. Season with salt and pepper and serve immediately.

Rye
Bread

This bread was born from a conversation I had with our head baker, Jen Latham, after I returned from a bread research trip in Germany. While traveling, I was directed by a friend and colleague to hop on a train and visit "free baker" Arnd Erbel's twelfth-generation mountain bakery, Backstube Erbel, in the northern Bavaria town of Dachsbach, where I first tasted this classic southern German style of bread. Those huge, burnished, enchanting loaves stayed with me. As I listed off the flavors of that bread for Jen one day—whole wheat, spelt, rye, caraway, anise, and orange—her face lit up with joyful recognition. Jen spent some of her childhood in Germany and has many fond bread memories from her time there. She knew exactly where I was coming from. The next day she pulled these fragrant, hearty rye loaves out of the oven—having created a bread that is now one of my all-time favorites.

In America, most people eat rye bread only with specific ingredients, such as pastrami or smoked salmon. And American versions are typically made with very little rye flour but lots of caramel coloring to make them look like dark whole-grain breads. In Germany, rye breads are much more versatile and eaten throughout the day, topped with all sorts of foods. This hearty and healthy spiced rye is especially nice for breakfast paired with hard cheese, jam, soft-boiled eggs, and cured meats.

You can also use it to make classic sandwiches, such as egg salad, turkey, BLTs, or even just open-faced avocado toast. It'll give you a whole new flavor experience and perspective. In my kitchen, the rye bread version of these standards are is the new classics.

Spiced Scalded Rye Bread Method

Makes two 1kg loaves

INGREDIENT	QUANTITY	BAKER'S %
Leaven	102g	12%
Scalded whole-grain rye flour	340g	40%
High-extraction red wheat flour (such as Yecora Rojo)	340g	40%
Whole-wheat flour	340g	40%
Whole-grain spelt flour	170g	20%
Warm (85° to 90°F) water	636g	75%
Sea salt	23g	2.75%
Toasted caraway seeds	5g	0.05%
Fennel seeds	5g	0.05%
Orange zest, finely grated	6g	5%
Room-temperature (72° to 75°F) bassinage	42g	5%
White rice flour	for dusting the baskets	

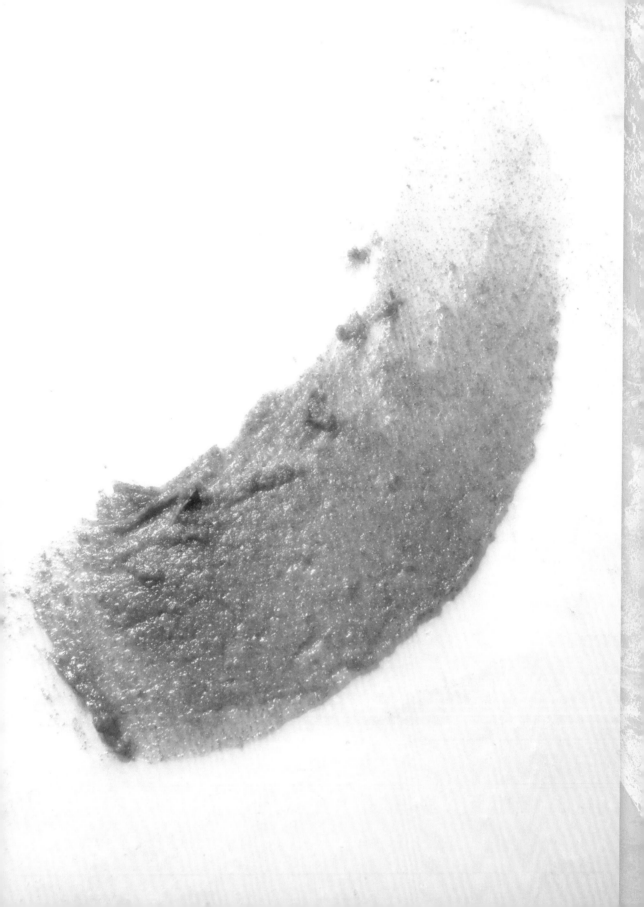

Prepare the leaven.

Prepare the leaven as directed on page 46. The leaven is ready for bread-making when it looks bubbly and tastes slightly tangy but also slightly creamy (like yogurt). Unready leaven tastes like raw pancake batter. Overripe leaven tastes very sour or boozy.

If you are unsure if your leaven is ready, you can perform a float test. To do so, fill a small pitcher or cup with cold, clean water. Wet your hands to prevent the leaven from sticking to your fingers. Gently pinch off about 1 Tbsp of the leaven, handling it minimally so as not to deflate the air bubbles, and carefully place it in the water. It should bob or float on the surface, not sink to the bottom. If it hovers or rises slowly, you can still use it, but your bulk fermentation may take a little longer than it would if you used a riper leaven.

Scald the rye flour.

Once the leaven passes the float test, it's time to scald the rye flour. Measure 375g cold water and 125g rye flour into a medium saucepan and whisk until well mixed. (This will yield a little more than the required 340g for the recipe, but some will inevitably get stuck to the spatula and pan.) Place the slurry over medium heat and cook, whisking constantly, until the mixture starts to thicken, then switch to a heat-resistant rubber spatula and stir continuously until it darkens and becomes a stiff paste, 3 to 5 minutes total (it should register at least 160°F on a kitchen thermometer). Transfer the gelatinized flour to a sheet pan and spread it out to cool until just warm to the touch (85°F) while you start mixing the dough. (For more on scalding flour, see page 44.)

Pre-mix the dough.

In a large bowl, combine the leaven, high-extraction flour, whole-wheat flour, spelt flour, and warm water. Mix with your hand until all the ingredients are well combined and no dry clumps remain, about 3 minutes. Cover the bowl with a clean kitchen towel and let the dough autolyze (rest) for 30 minutes.

Finish mixing the dough.

To develop some strength in the dough, mix it with your hands in the bowl by gently lifting and stretching up the sides and folding them into the middle. Repeat this action for about 3 minutes. Let rest for 3 minutes, then lift, stretch, and fold again for another 3 minutes. Let rest again for 3 minutes. Add the salt and mix again the same way for 1 minute. Then add the scalded flour, caraway seeds, fennel seeds, and orange zest and mix with your hands until fully incorporated. You may need to squeeze in the scalded flour, which will break up the dough somewhat. Don't worry, as the dough will come back together as you continue to mix. At this point, you can mix in up to the full 42g of the bassinage to achieve a strong but stretchy dough.

Turn the dough during its bulk fermentation.

Loosely cover the dough with a clean kitchen towel and let rest in a warm (82° to 85°F), draft-free place for about 1½ hours. Every 30 minutes, wet your hands and give the dough several series of turns in the bowl, using the same gentle lifting, stretching, and folding technique you used when mixing the dough. This builds strong gluten bonds in the dough without deflating it. As the dough rises, it will become puffy and increase in volume. The last turn should be a gentle one, turning the dough just until it has all been gently folded over once; the mass should hold its shape in the bowl. This first rise, also called the bulk fermentation or bulk rise, is a crucial time for the dough to develop strength and depth of flavor.

When the dough has finished rising, it will feel airy and light and should be starting to develop bubbles. You can check the dough's readiness with a float test: If a small piece of dough bobs or floats when gently placed in a pitcher of cool water, your dough is ready for the next stage. If it sinks, the dough needs additional time to bulk ferment.

Pre-shape the dough.

Transfer the dough to a clean, unfloured work surface. Lightly flour the top of the dough and use a bench knife to cut into two equal pieces. The dough should sit on the work surface, sticking to it, with the lightly floured side on top. Using barely floured hands and the bench knife, work each piece of dough into a round shape, creating some taut tension on the surface without causing any rips. Use as little flour as possible—just enough so that you can handle the dough. Using too much flour will prevent the loaf from holding its shape as you build tension. Use decisive yet gentle force when handling the dough and *try to shape it in as few movements as possible*.

Let the rounds rest, uncovered and about 4 inches apart, on the work surface for 20 to 30 minutes. During this stage, called the bench rest, the dough will relax and spread into a thick mound. At the end of this rest, the dough edge should look plump, not tapered. If the edge is tapered or the dough flattens too fast or too much, the dough did not develop enough strength during the first rise. You can correct this by shaping each round a second time and letting them rest on the work surface for another 20 to 30 minutes. The second pre-shape is essentially an extra turn, like you would do in the bowl.

Finish shaping the loaves.

Generously flour the top of the dough rounds. Gently flip the first one over, taking care to maintain the round shape and all the aeration. The floured side is now on the bottom, and the top now, facing up, is unfloured. To form the final loaf shape, start by folding the third of the dough closest to you up and over the middle third of the round. Then use your right hand to gently stretch out the dough on the right side and fold it over the center. Use your left hand to do the same stretch-and-fold action with the left side. Finally, stretch out the third of the dough farthest from you and fold this flap toward the center, over the previous folds, creating a neat rectangular package, with the edges at the top and bottom being slightly narrower than the length of the sides. Using just the tips of your fingers and grabbing the thinnest portion of dough possible, stitch the edges of the sides together in a few places to make your rectangle a little more oblong and to create an even, strong tension along the sides of the loaf. Grabbing the top edge very gently, roll the whole package lengthwise toward you until the seam is on the bottom. Cup your hands around the dough and round it against the work surface to tighten the tension. Let the shaped loaf rest while you repeat the shaping with the second round.

Let rise before baking.

Line two proofing baskets or medium bowls with clean kitchen towels and lightly flour the towels with rice flour. Using your bench knife as an extension of your dominant hand, and working quickly so the dough doesn't stick to your hands, transfer each shaped loaf to a basket, placing it smooth-side down and seam facing up (the bottom of the loaf is now on top and will become the bottom again when you tip it out to bake). Cover with a clean kitchen towel and let rest in a warm (82° to 85°F), draft-free place for about 3 hours. Alternatively, you can choose to delay the final rise by placing the dough loaves in their baskets, covered with a kitchen towel to keep the tops from drying out, in the refrigerator for up to 12 hours. The cool environment will slow the fermentation and create more complex and mildly acidic flavors in the dough.

Bake the loaves.

About 40 minutes before you are ready to bake, place a cast-iron double Dutch oven in the oven and preheat the oven to 500°F. If you do not have a double Dutch oven, see page 23 for an alternative.

If you are baking the loaves after they have risen in the refrigerator, there's no need to let them come to room temperature before baking; they can go straight from refrigerator to preheated oven. However, if they look a little smaller in the baskets than you hoped they would, you can take them out when you preheat the oven and let them rise a bit more before baking.

Dust the top surface of one of the loaves with flour. Put on oven mitts and, using extreme caution, very carefully remove the shallow lid of the preheated Dutch oven and place it, upside down, on the stove top. Leave the deep pot in the oven. Invert the loaf in one basket onto the upside-down lid. Don't worry if the dough sticks to the kitchen towel; just gently separate them and remember to use a little more flour next time.

Use a lame, razor blade, or sharp scissors to score the top of the loaf, being careful not to burn your forearms. I suggest a simple square pattern of four cuts.

Put on oven mitts again and carefully remove the deep pot from the oven, invert, and place it over the loaf and lid. You now have an upside-down Dutch oven with the loaf inside—a tiny bread oven that will go inside your oven. Return the Dutch oven to the oven. Immediately decrease the oven temperature to 450°F. Bake the loaf for 20 minutes.

Remove the cast-iron bread oven from the oven. Carefully remove the top part of the Dutch oven (the pot piece, which you are using as a lid), opening it away from you and releasing a cloud of very hot steam. Return the lid with the loaf in it to the oven and continue baking, uncovered, until the crust is a burnished, dark golden brown, 20 to 25 minutes. Don't be afraid to continue baking the loaf until it reaches a dark, rich color. The bread is done baking when it has a deeply caramelized, crackling crust. The edges of the ears might even be nearly black. The loaf should feel light for its size and will sound hollow when tapped on the bottom.

Transfer the bread to a cooling rack to cool. (If you don't have a cooling rack, prop up the bread on its side so air can circulate around the bottom.) To bake the second loaf, increase the oven temperature to 500°F. Wipe out the lid and pot with a dry kitchen towel, close up, and return to the oven to reheat for 10 minutes. Then repeat the scoring and baking process with the second loaf.

Let the loaves cool to room temperature before slicing. Using a bread knife, slice the bread with a gentle sawing motion. Store in a bread box at room temperature for up to 3 days. To store longer, slice the bread once it has cooled, place in an airtight freezer-proof container, and freeze for up to 2 weeks. To refresh, toast directly from the freezer.

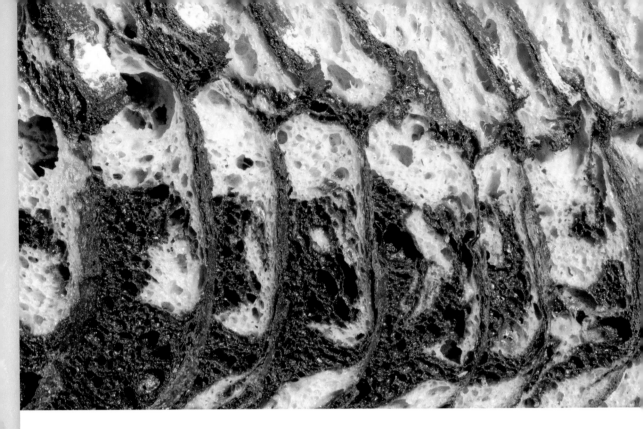

Marbled Rye

For this version of a true marbled rye, we use 100 percent freshly milled dark northern rye flour and black barley malt powder (available at specialty baking or brewing stores). Using this bread for classic marbled rye sandwiches—with deli spreads and dips and smoked fish—is a game changer. To make a marbled rye, divide the spiced scalded rye dough in half immediately after mixing in the salt and scalded flour. Place the two portions of dough in separate bowls. In another bowl, stir together 4g black barley malt powder and 40g very hot (160°F or hotter) water to form a paste. Let the paste cool and then fold it into one portion of the dough, mixing it in well. The dough will turn a very dark brown. Proceed as directed, turning both doughs at the same time. When it is time to divide the dough, divide the light dough into two equal pieces and the dark dough into six equal pieces. Gently place three of the dark dough pieces on top of the two light dough pieces. Pre-shape the dough as directed. As you round the dough into a loaf shape, it will combine and swirl the light and dark doughs. The swirls will become more extensive during the final shaping step. Continue as directed for spiced scalded rye to shape and bake the loaves.

SPICED SCALDED RYE BREAD

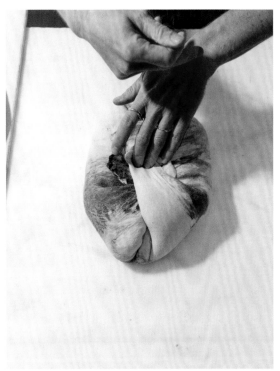

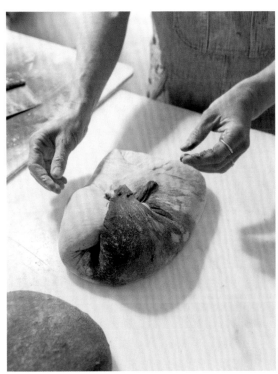

236

German
Breakfast Spread

A traditional breakfast in Germany is perfectly suited to a day of hiking through the Alps. It's a hearty, stick-to-your-ribs kind of affair centered around rye bread and soft-cooked eggs. It features cheese, honey, and jam prominently. It's one of the best ways to start an outdoorsy day.

Grilled Cheese Sandwiches with Pickles on Spiced Rye

Grilled cheese is one of our most popular orders at Tartine, and we've done countless variations over the years. This version is one of my favorites— preferably with beer. At home, I like to use two cast-iron skillets, one large and one medium, to mimic our sandwich press at the café.

Makes 2 sandwiches

2 Tbsp unsalted butter

4 (¾-inch-thick) slices spiced scalded rye bread (regular, page 226, or marbled, page 234)

4 oz Cowgirl Creamery Wagon Wheel cheese (or other semifirm, buttery cow's milk cheese), shredded

2 spicy fermented pickles, cut lengthwise into medium-thick slices

Place an 8-inch cast-iron skillet in the oven and preheat the oven to 450°F for about 20 minutes.

On the stove top, set a 10-inch cast-iron skillet over medium-high heat for 2 to 3 minutes. Add 1 Tbsp of the butter to the warm skillet, and when it melts, place two of the bread slices in the hot pan. Griddle until browned on the underside, about 3 minutes. Flip the slices so the browned side is on top. Distribute half of the cheese evenly over one toasted bread slice. Arrange half of the pickle slices over the cheese. Place the second bread slice, toasted-side down, over the pickles.

Carefully remove the 8-inch skillet from the oven and set it on top of the sandwich. The residual heat and weight will toast the top of the sandwich. Let toast until the sandwich is browned and the cheese is melted, 3 to 5 minutes.

Return the 8-inch skillet to the oven to reheat. Transfer the sandwich to a plate. Repeat with the remaining butter, bread slices, cheese, and pickles to make a second sandwich. Serve immediately.

Braised-Brisket Sandwiches with Sauerkraut and Russian Dressing

Brisket takes me back to my childhood in Texas. Nick Balla and Courtney Burns made a great version at Bar Tartine, and the instructions for a two-day brine and twelve-hour smoke over a charcoal grill are laid out in their book. Here, I've included a recipe for a brined brisket that is braised slowly in the oven over five hours that will give you salty, savory slices perfect for tucking into a sandwich. You have to plan ahead to make this one: The sauerkraut takes up to 1 ½ months to ferment and the brisket requires three days. It's all worth it.

Makes 4 sandwiches

Sauerkraut

5 lb cabbage (any sturdy cabbage of any color will do)

7 Tbsp sea salt

Braised Brisket

2 sweet onions, cut into chunks

1 bunch flat-leaf parsley, coarsely chopped

14 cups cold water

1 ¼ cups kosher salt

4 lb beef brisket

2 Tbsp olive oil

1 ½ cups dry, light white wine

6 garlic cloves

1 large yellow onion, cut into ½-inch dice

2 Tbsp black peppercorns

Russian Dressing

½ cup aioli (page 113) or good-quality mayonnaise

1 Tbsp tomato paste

1 Tbsp prepared horseradish

Pickle spears and slices

1 Tbsp Worcestershire sauce

½ tsp sweet paprika

1 dill pickle, cut into ¼-inch dice

8 (¾-inch-thick) slices spiced scalded rye bread (regular, page 226, or marbled, page 234)

To make the sauerkraut: Core the cabbage and then slice into ribbons. Pile the cabbage into a large bowl, strew the salt over the top, and then, using your hands, massage the salt into the cabbage until evenly coated. Pack the cabbage into a 1-qt canning jar or crock. Set the uncovered container on a countertop for a few hours until the cabbage has expressed much of its liquid. Then press down on the cabbage, submerging it completely in its liquid, and place a clean weight on top of it. Seal the container with a lid outfitted with an airlock if you have one. If you don't, seal it with a tight-fitting lid and open the container once a day to release trapped gas. Keep the container in a cool, dark place until the sauerkraut has soured to your taste, 3 to 6 weeks. Once the taste is to your liking, the sauerkraut will keep in the refrigerator for up to 1 year.

To prepare the brisket: In a blender, combine the sweet onions, parsley, and 8 cups of the water and process until smooth. Transfer to a 2-gallon container or large bowl that will hold the brisket snugly and keep it submerged in the brine, add the remaining 6 cups water and the salt, and stir until this brine is well mixed.

Pat the brisket dry and then prick it all over with fork tines at regular 1- to 1½-inch intervals. Put the brisket into the brine, and then cover tightly. Refrigerate the brisket in the brine for 48 hours.

Remove the brisket from the brine, discarding the brine. Let the brisket come to room temperature. Preheat the oven to 275°F.

Set a large Dutch oven over medium-high heat. When the Dutch oven is warm, add the oil, and when the oil is hot, place the brisket, fat cap up, in the pot. Sear the bottom, sides, and ends until well browned. Sear the fat cap last, then turn so the fat cap is facing up.

Remove the pot from the heat. Pour the wine over the brisket and add the garlic, yellow onion, and peppercorns. Place the lid on the Dutch oven slightly askew. Place the pot in the oven and braise until the meat is very tender (but not falling apart) and the liquid has reduced significantly, about 4 hours.

Remove the Dutch oven from the oven and let the brisket rest in the covered pot for at least 20 minutes. It should absorb some of the remaining liquid while it rests and cools. This step is very important to getting the proper tender texture.

To make the dressing: In a small bowl, whisk together the aioli, tomato paste, horseradish, Worcestershire, paprika, and pickle. Set aside.

Transfer the brisket to a cutting board and slice enough ⅓-inch-thick slices for the sandwiches. (Store the remaining brisket in the refrigerator for up to 3 days.)

Arrange the bread slices on a work surface. Top four of the slices with a layer of brisket. Top the brisket with a generous layer of sauerkraut. Cover with the sliced pickles. Spread the remaining four bread slices with a generous amount of the dressing and place the slices, dressing-side down, over the sauerkraut. Serve immediately with the pickle spears on the side.

Vegan
Bread

This is a vegan variation on our popular seeded-sprouted rye bread. We use buttermilk in that bread, which is based on a traditional Scandinavian recipe. In this recipe, we've used cashew milk yogurt, which offers a similar texture and flavor without the dairy.

Much of our bread is vegan by happenstance—flour, water, and salt can (and do) go a long way toward creating delicious breads. But fats add softness and flavor to dough, and the first fats a baker reaches for are often in the form of dairy, whether butter, milk, or buttermilk. We wanted to think outside the dairy box for this dough to create a formula that garners flavor and texture from a nondairy source.

This loaf also calls for teff and barley, a couple of underutilized grains that deserve more attention, both of which happen to be gluten-free. The Sonora flour is a low-gluten variety from northern Mexico that not only gives the bread a tender crumb but also makes it easily digestible. This bread is even better the day after it is baked.

Seeded-Sprouted Barley Vegan Bread Method

Makes two 1.2kg loaves

INGREDIENT	QUANTITY	BAKER'S %
Whole-grain Sonora wheat flour	425g	80%
Whole-grain teff flour	106g	20%
Pumpkin seeds	48g	9%
Sesame seeds	112g	21%
Brown flaxseeds	159g	30%
Sunflower seeds	48g	9%
Flax meal	58g	11%
Warm (85° to 90°F) water	351g	66%
Leaven	330g	62%
Amber beer, at room temperature	213g	40%
Barley malt syrup	21g	4%
Unsweetened cashew milk yogurt	191g	36%
Sea salt	19g	3.5%
Sprouted barley	319g	60%

Sprout the barley.

About 24 hours before you want to make this bread, prepare the sprouted barley. You must use whole-grain barley for sprouts, as only the tough outer hull is removed in processing. (The hull, bran, and germ are removed in the processing for pearled barley, so it will not sprout.) Use 300g dry barley, which will yield a bit more than the 319g sprouted barley required for the bread, as the grains gain water weight when soaked. Starting with 300g ensures you'll have enough. Store any extra sprouts in an airtight container in the refrigerator for up to 2 days and use to garnish soups or salads.

Rinse the barley well, then put it into a 1-qt canning jar and add cold water to cover by several inches. Let soak at room temperature for 12 hours. After 12 hours, drain the barley and rinse well again, rinsing until the water runs clear. Cover the mouth of the canning jar with cheesecloth and secure with a rubber band. Place the jar upside down on a cooling rack set over a sheet pan so the barley continues to drain and has good air circulation as the grains sprout. Let sprout at room temperature for 12 hours. After 12 hours, the sprouts can be used immediately, or they can be stored in the jar in the refrigerator for up to 2 days.

Prepare the leaven.

The day before you plan to mix your dough, prepare the leaven as directed on page 46. This dough requires a young, fresh leaven (but not a booster leaven) for the right flavor and rise. The leaven is ready for bread-making when it looks bubbly and tastes slightly tangy but also slightly creamy (like yogurt). Unready leaven tastes like raw pancake batter. Overripe leaven tastes very sour or boozy.

If you are unsure if your leaven is ready, you can perform a float test. To do so, fill a small pitcher or cup with cold, clean water. Wet your hands to prevent the leaven from sticking to your fingers. Gently pinch off about 1 Tbsp of the leaven, handling it minimally so as not to deflate the air bubbles, and carefully place it in the water. It should bob or float on the surface, not sink to the bottom. If it hovers or rises slowly, you can still use it, but your bulk fermentation may take a little longer than it would if you used a riper leaven.

Mix the dough.

In a medium bowl, stir together the Sonora flour, teff flour, sunflower seeds, pumpkin seeds, sesame seeds, flaxseeds, and flax meal.

In the bowl of a stand mixer fitted with the dough-hook attachment, combine the water, leaven, beer, barley malt syrup, yogurt, salt, and barley sprouts and mix on low speed until well mixed, about 1 minutes. Add the flour-seed mixture to the wet ingredients and mix on low speed, stopping the machine to scrape down the sides of the bowl with a rubber spatula as needed, until all of ingredients are well incorporated, 3 to 5 minutes. (Alternatively, in a large bowl, mix together the liquids and sprouts by hand. Add the flour-seed mixture to the wet ingredients and mix by hand until all of the ingredients are well incorporated.)

Ferment the dough.

Loosely cover the dough with a clean kitchen towel and set in a warm (80° to 85°F) draft-free place, to bulk ferment for about 1 hour. Oil two 9 by 5 by 3-inch loaf pans with vegetable oil.

After 1 hour of bulk fermentation, transfer the dough to a clean, unfloured work surface. Using a bench knife, divide the dough in half in the bowl and transfer half to each prepared pan. Using damp fingertips, pat the dough firmly into the pans, leveling and smoothing the tops.

Let the dough ferment until the loaves have risen somewhat and their tops are domed, 2 to 3 hours.

Cover the loaves with a clean kitchen towel and place in the refrigerator to ferment slowly overnight.

Bake the loaves.

Preheat the oven to 450°F. Fill a clean, food-grade spray bottle with water.

When you are ready to bake, lightly dock the tops of the loaves with a fork. Place the loaves in the oven and spray the sides and bottom of the oven with water, then quickly close the oven door. Bake the loaves, rotating them front to back about halfway through baking, until dark caramel brown and an instant-read thermometer inserted into the center of a loaf registers 210°F, about 1 hour.

Let the loaves cool in the pans on cooling racks for about 3 minutes. Run a knife blade around the inside of one pan, then invert the pan, gently releasing the loaf, and place the loaf right-side up on the cooling rack. Repeat with the other loaf. Let the loaves cool completely before slicing.

Using a bread knife, slice the bread with a gentle sawing motion. Store in a bread box at room temperature for up to 4 days. To store longer, slice the bread once it has cooled, place in an airtight freezer-proof container, and freeze for up to 2 weeks. To refresh, toast directly from the freezer.

Seeded-Sprouted Barley Vegan Tartines with Coconut Milk Yogurt and Plum Jam

Coconut milk can be cultured with the same bacterias we use to culture dairy milk. The result is a creamy, naturally sweet treat that is full of probiotics. The jam here is a quick jam—not intended for preserving but cooked to concentrate and highlight the flavor of the fruit, using just enough sugar to hold the expressed juices together. Because it is not made for long keeping, it doesn't need to reach a certain jell point during cooking. You can use almost any fruit to make the jam, but I like the way the plum complements the yogurt and barley bread. These open-faced sandwiches are good as a snack or as part of a breakfast spread.

Makes 6 tartines

Coconut Milk Yogurt

2 cups full-fat coconut milk, with or without guar gum

1 Tbsp cornstarch (if using coconut milk without guar gum)

1 tsp powdered yogurt starter culture, or 2 Tbsp unpasteurized cultured yogurt (dairy or coconut)

Quick Plum Jam

1 lb plums, pitted and cut into 1-inch chunks

½ cup raw sugar (such as Demerara or turbinado)

Finely grated zest and juice of 1 lemon

1 Tbsp coconut oil

6 (⅓-inch-thick) slices seeded-sprouted barley vegan bread (page 248)

Organic edible flowers for garnish (optional)

To make the yogurt: Pour the coconut milk into an enameled cast-iron Dutch oven or other nonmetallic pot (metal can interfere with the inoculation) and place over medium heat. If using coconut milk without guar gum, stir in the cornstarch with a wooden spoon. Heat the milk, stirring occasionally, until it reaches 180°F on an instant-read thermometer. Remove the milk from the heat and let cool until it registers 108°F on the thermometer.

If using the yogurt starter, transfer 1 Tbsp of the coconut milk to a small bowl, add the yogurt starter, and stir to mix well. Add the starter–coconut milk mix to the pot with the coconut milk and stir together, mixing well. If using live-culture yogurt from a previous batch, stir the yogurt directly into the warm coconut milk, mixing well.

Pour the coconut milk into a 1-qt canning jar. The milk will need to maintain a temperature of about 108°F to culture properly. You can use a yogurt maker, a home dehydrator, an Instant Pot on the yogurt setting, or an oven preheated to 150°F and then turned off to achieve this.

CONTINUED

After 12 hours, the yogurt will have thickened. Cover the jar with a lid and refrigerate the yogurt to thicken further, at least 6 hours. The yogurt can be kept in the refrigerator for up to 1 week. Don't worry if a little separation occurs; just stir well before using.

To make the jam: In a medium bowl, combine the plums and sugar and stir well. Let macerate at room temperature for 1 hour. Stir together the fruit and its juices and pour into a wide, shallow pot. Place over medium heat and cook, stirring occasionally. The mixture will bubble a lot at first. Once the bubbles start to slow and the mixture thickens and looks glossy, after about 15 minutes (the timing can vary a lot for this, depending on the moisture in your fruit, add the lemon zest and juice. Continue to cook, stirring occasionally, until the juice has cooked down, 2 to 3 minutes.

Remove the pot from the heat and set the jam aside to cool completely. Transfer to a jar with a tight-fitting lid and refrigerate for up to 1 week.

Set a large cast-iron skillet over high heat, then add the oil. When the oil melts, working in batches, place the bread slices in the hot pan and toast until browned on the underside, 3 to 5 minutes. Flip the slices and toast until browned on the second side, another 3 to 5 minutes. Transfer the toasts to a large platter or individual plates.

Spoon a generous dollop of coconut yogurt onto each bread slice. Press the back of the spoon into the middle of each dollop to make a well. Fill the wells with plum jam. Garnish with the flowers, if desired, and serve immediately.

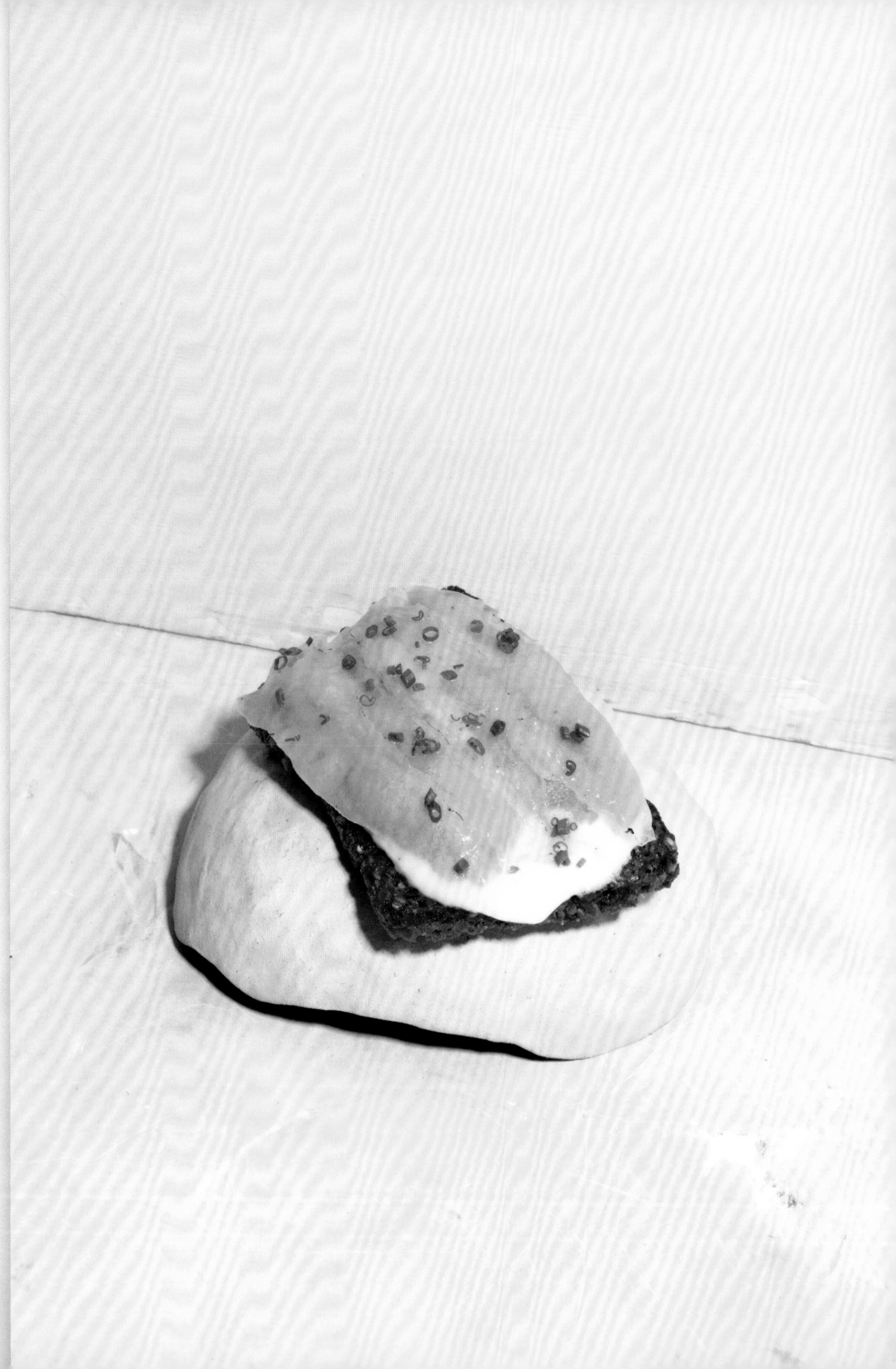

Uni and Lardo on Seeded-Sprouted Barley Vegan Toasts

Uni is the briny edible part of a sea urchin. It's common in Japanese cuisine and is a favorite of mine. Here, we've dressed it with rich lardo for a sort of surf 'n' turf toast.

Makes 4 toasts

1 Tbsp unsalted butter

4 (⅓-inch-thick) slices seeded–sprouted barley vegan bread (page 248)

½ cup crème fraîche

8 pieces uni (available at specialty fish markets and Japanese grocers)

2 oz lardo (available at butcher shops and specialty grocers), sliced paper-thin

Finely chopped fresh chives for garnish

Set a large cast-iron skillet over high heat. When the skillet is warm, add the butter. After the butter melts, place the bread slices in the hot pan and toast until browned on the underside, 3 to 5 minutes. Flip the slices and toast until browned on the second side, another 3 to 5 minutes. Transfer the toasts to a platter or individual plates.

Spread 2 Tbsp crème fraîche on each piece of toast. Carefully place two pieces of uni on each toast. Top with a few curls of lardo and garnish with the chives. Serve immediately.

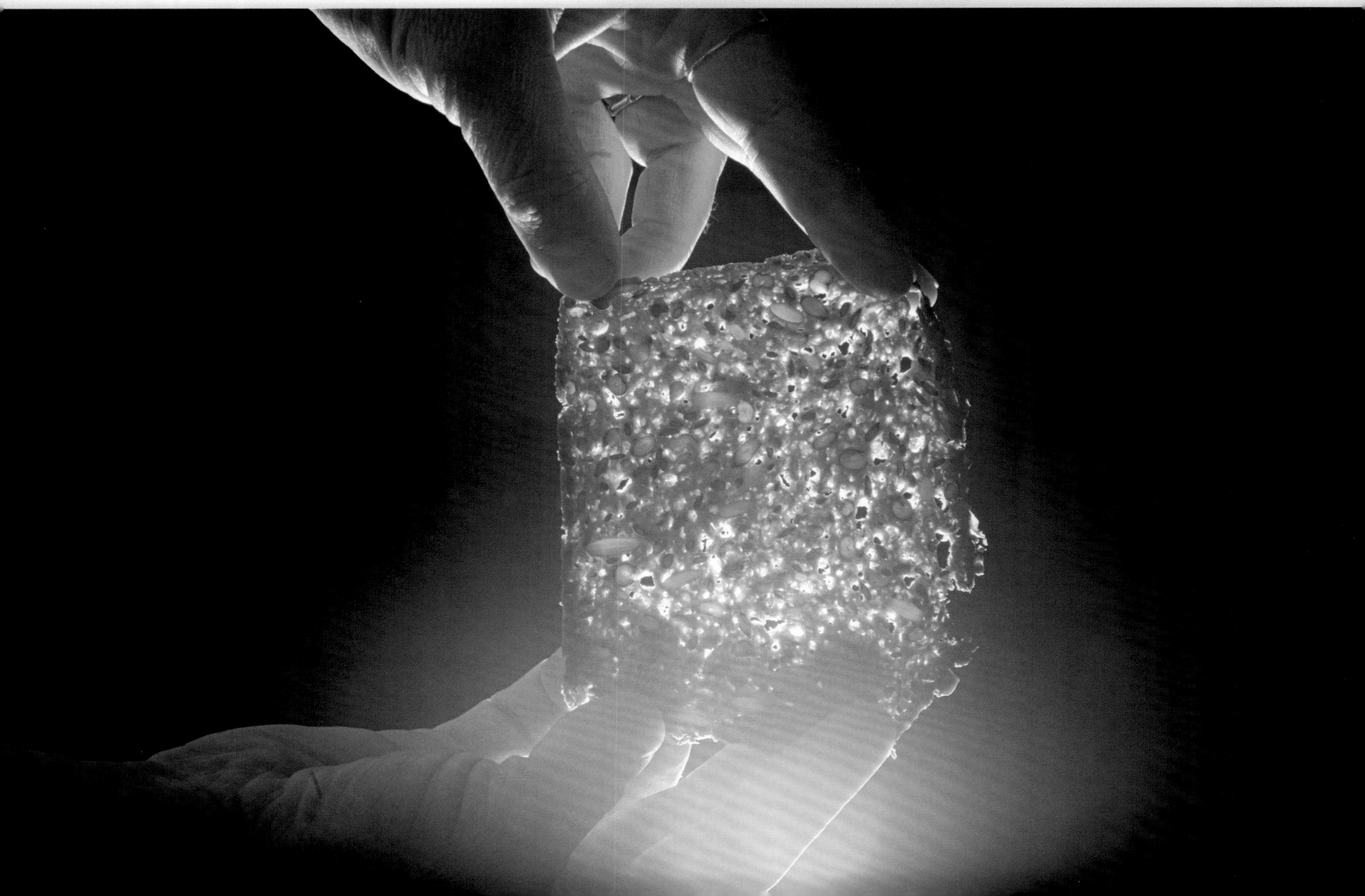

Seeded-Sprouted Barley Vegan Crackers

The vegan bread can be turned into crackers by slicing it very thinly, brushing the slices with oil, and toasting them. It's a great way to bring new life to bread that's a few days old. The crackers are great for scooping up dips or holding cheese, and they also make a tasty, crunchy garnish crumbled over soups or salads.

Makes 20 crackers

1 loaf seeded–sprouted barley
vegan bread (page 248)

6 Tbsp sunflower oil

Sea salt

Preheat the oven to 500°F.

Cut part of the bread loaf into twenty very thin slices—as thin as possible. (At the restaurant, we freeze the whole loaf, then slice it on a meat slicer to get paper-thin slices. You probably won't have a meat slicer at home, so just cut the bread as thinly as you can with a bread knife or a very sharp chef's knife.)

Place the slices in a single layer on a sheet pan. Lightly brush the top of each slice with the oil, then sprinkle lightly with salt. Bake for 5 minutes. Using tongs, very carefully flip all the pieces and continue to bake until they are toasted, 5 to 10 minutes longer. The bake time can vary dramatically depending on how thin the slices are, so just keep an eye on them. When they are well browned, they are done.

Transfer the crackers to cooling racks to cool completely and crisp up. Store in an airtight container at room temperature for up to 1 week.

Gluten-Free Bread

For Tartine, making gluten-free baked goods is more about celebrating different grains than about avoiding wheat. I love wheat, and since we started Tartine, we have always gone to great lengths to make wheat more digestible through grain selection, milling techniques, ample hydration, and long natural fermentation. But I also love teff, buckwheat, amaranth, and many other gluten-free grains and I welcome the challenge of making a bread that can be substituted for glutenous wheat bread for most uses.

We have been making some gluten-free pastries for a while (often an easier endeavor than bread), but this is my first attempt at gluten-free bread. I admire and appreciate bakers who are able to make a wheat-free loaf that looks like a wheat bread, but that isn't what I was going for with this dough.

The bread that I eat most these days is our Danish-style sprouted rye, which we developed years ago to make it a bit more digestible—in a move of California innovation—by sprouting the grains. It's a dense bread in stark contrast to our generously open-crumb wheat breads, and I like to slice it very thinly. For the gluten-free loaf, which is a similarly dense loaf, we use buckwheat, brown rice, and teff flours, plus pulverized oats, as the grains, with the addition of seeds, olive oil, and maple syrup for flavor. Like all of our breads, this dough is amply hydrated and long fermented, using a natural (gluten-free) leaven. The structure is aided by flax, chia, and psyllium, which lend binding vegetable gums to the mix.

Seeded Multigrain Gluten-Free Bread Method

Makes two 1.1kg loaves

INGREDIENT	QUANTITY	BAKER'S %
Teff-brown rice leaven	338g	60%
Bloomed flaxseeds, chia seeds, and psyllium (in 733g water)	873g	155%
Whole-grain buckwheat flour	56g	10%
Brown rice flour	282g	50%
Teff flour	226g	40%
Pulverized rolled oats	169g	30%
Sunflower seeds	28g	5%
Pumpkin seeds	28g	5%
Sesame seeds	28g	5%
Salt	28g	5%
Olive oil	85g	15%
Maple syrup	85g	15%
Honey	28g	5%
Room-temperature (72° to 75°F) bassinage	28g	5%
Mixed seeds or rolled oats	for topping loaves	

Prepare the teff–brown rice leaven.

Prepare the gluten-free leaven, using a gluten-free starter, as directed on page 54. This dough requires a young, fresh gluten-free leaven (but not a booster leaven) for the right flavor and rise. The leaven is ready for bread-making when it has doubled in volume and smells very fruity, yeasty, and almost beerlike. The float test isn't used for this dough because it doesn't hold together in water.

Bloom the flaxseeds, chia seeds, and psyllium in water.

Place 56g flaxseeds, 56g chia seeds, and 28g psyllium in a large bowl and pour 733g very hot (160°F or hotter) water over them. Stir to make sure the seeds and psyllium are evenly hydrated. Set aside to cool. The mixture will become very gelatinous as it sets; stir it regularly as it cools to keep it from getting clumpy. Let cool to warm to the touch (85°F) before mixing the dough.

Mix the dough.

In a large bowl, combine the buckwheat flour, brown rice flour, teff flour, pulverized oats, sunflower seeds, pumpkin seeds, sesame seeds, and salt and stir briefly to mix.

In the bowl of a stand mixer fitted with the paddle attachment, add the bloomed flax-chia-psyllium mixture, leaven, oil, maple syrup, and honey and mix on low speed until just combined.

Add the flour mixture to the wet ingredients and mix on medium speed until all the ingredients are fully incorporated, about 3 minutes. The dough should feel a little sticky—if it feels smooth and dry, add some or all of the bassinage and mix for another minute or two until combined.

Loosely cover the dough with a clean kitchen towel and set in a warm (80° to 85°F), draft-free place to bulk ferment for 30 minutes.

Divide and let rise.

Oil two 9 by 5 by 3-inch loaf pans with olive oil and dust with teff flour. Transfer to a clean work surface dusted with brown rice flour. Using a bench knife, divide the dough in half. Using a gentle kneading motion, shape each portion of dough into a ball. Roll one ball back and forth a few times on the work surface so that it becomes a log shape. Lightly roll the log in a dusting of brown rice flour, then gently transfer it to the pan. Repeat with the other portion. Scatter the mixed seeds or crushed oats over the tops.

Cover the loaves with a clean kitchen towel and let rest in a warm (80° to 85°F) place until the tops are higher and domed, 3 to 4 hours. Make sure these loaves stay warm during this rising; the gluten-free leaven is especially sensitive to cool temperatures. You can bake this bread the same day or let it ferment longer in the refrigerator overnight (to develop a little more flavor and a lighter crumb). If you would like to bake it on the same day that you mix it, let it rise for another hour or so (for a total rise of 5 hours). If you would like to bake it the next day, cover the pans loosely with a tightly woven cloth or other nonpermeable wrap and place in the refrigerator.

Bake the loaves.

About 30 minutes before you are ready to bake, preheat the oven to 400°F. Fill a clean, food-grade spray bottle with water.

When you are ready to bake, lightly dock the tops of the loaves with a fork or lightly score with a lame. Place the loaves in the oven and spray the sides and bottom of the oven with water, then quickly close the oven door. Bake the loaves, rotating them front to back about halfway through baking, until the tops are medium-dark brown and an instant-read thermometer inserted into the center of a loaf registers 210°F, about 1 hour. (The thermometer—or a cake tester—should come out clean, without any traces of dough.)

Let the loaves cool in the pans on cooling racks for about 10 minutes. Run a knife blade around the inside of one pan, then invert the pan, gently releasing the loaf, and place the loaf right-side up on the cooling rack. Repeat with the other loaf. Let the loaves cool completely before slicing.

This bread can be sliced and eaten as soon as it is cool. It should not be eaten while warm, as it will be gummy. Using a bread knife, slice the bread with a gentle sawing motion. Store in a bread box at room temperature for up to 3 days. The flavor and texture of these loaves gets even better over these few days. To store longer, slice the bread once it has cooled, place in an airtight freezer-proof container, and freeze for up to 2 weeks. To refresh, toast directly from the freezer.

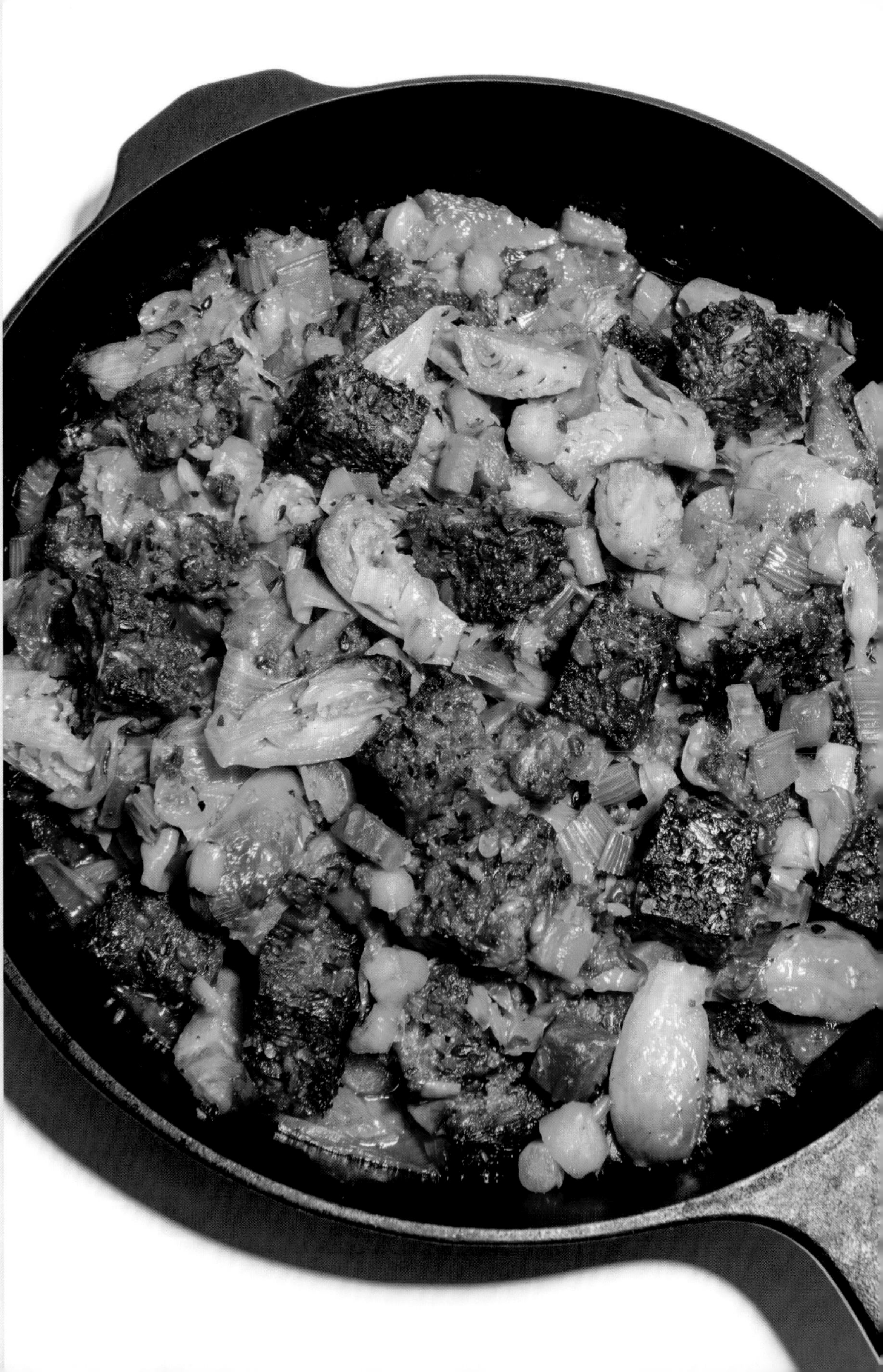

Seeded Multigrain Gluten-Free Stuffing

Stuffing is usually one of the best parts of a holiday meal. I began making mine with our seeded sprouted rye bread a few years ago and never looked back. It absorbs the broth beautifully, and the seeds and sprouts add a tremendous amount of flavor, texture, and nutrition to the dish. It works just as beautifully with this seeded gluten-free loaf. You can make this stuffing a day ahead by preparing it up to the final browning step. Then, about 25 minutes before you're ready to serve the stuffing, place it in a 500°F oven to warm and brown the top. Cover the stuffing for the first 20 minutes and uncover for the final 5 minutes to brown.

Makes 6 to 8 servings

1 loaf seeded multigrain gluten-free bread (page 264), cut into 1-inch cubes

½ cup unsalted butter

2 Tbsp good-quality extra-virgin olive oil

4 leeks, white part only, cut into ⅓-inch-thick slices

Sea salt

6 shallots, quartered

6 rainbow carrots, peeled and cut into ½-inch pieces

4 stalks celery, cut into ½-inch pieces

8 oz brussels sprouts, trimmed and halved lengthwise

½ cup dry white wine

2 cups chicken bone broth or vegetable stock

Preheat the oven to 300°F.

Spread the bread cubes in an even layer on a sheet pan and toast in the oven, stirring occasionally, until lightly browned, 20 to 30 minutes. Remove from the oven and set aside. Turn up the oven temperature to 375°F.

Set a 6-qt Dutch oven or other heavy pot over medium heat and add 2 Tbsp of the butter and the oil. When the butter melts, add the leeks and a light sprinkle of salt and cook, stirring occasionally, until softened, about 10 minutes. Add the shallots and cook for 2 to 3 minutes. Add the carrots and another pinch of salt and cook, stirring occasionally, until they start to soften, about 5 minutes. Add the celery and brussels sprouts and another pinch of salt and cook, stirring occasionally, until the brussels sprouts are bright green, about 5 minutes longer.

Pour the wine over the vegetables and bring to a simmer. Then pour in the broth and, as soon as it starts to simmer, stir in the toasted bread. Slice the remaining 6 Tbsp butter into pats and dot over the top. Cover the pot, place in the oven, and bake for 25 minutes.

Remove the pot from the oven and turn up the oven temperature to 500°F. When the oven has reached temperature, after about 15 minutes, remove the lid and return the pot to the oven. Bake until the top of the stuffing is nicely browned, about 5 minutes. Serve immediately.

Avocado Toasts on Seeded Multigrain Gluten-Free Bread

We have made dozens of variations on this very Californian (or Australian, depending on who you ask) recipe. This one highlights perfectly ripe avocado with a vegan salsa seca (dry salsa) and dukkah (from Egypt) mash-up made of toasted nuts, seeds, and spices with some nutritional yeast, fresh bean sprouts, and cilantro to bring the California vibes home.

Makes 4 servings

1 cup dry mung beans (optional)

1 cup dry raw buckwheat groats (optional)

Salsa Seca

¾ cup cashews, crushed

½ cup pumpkin seeds

½ cup sunflower seeds

¼ cup flax seeds

¼ cup sesame seeds

1 Tbsp nigella seeds

2 Tbsp avocado oil

8 tsp crushed red pepper flakes

1½ tsp ground cumin

1½ tsp ground smoked paprika

5 Tbsp nutritional yeast

½ tsp salt

¼ tsp citric acid

2 Tbsp coconut oil

4 slices seeded multigrain gluten-free bread (page 264)

2 large ripe avocados

1 small bunch cilantro

1 small bunch garlic chive blossoms

Two to three days before you want to prepare the dish, sprout the mung beans and buckwheat groats, if using. Rinse the mung beans well, then place them in a 1-qt canning jar and add cold water to cover by several inches. Let soak for 12 hours.

After 12 hours, drain the mung beans and rinse well again, rinsing until the water runs clear. Return the beans to the canning jar and cover the mouth of the jar with cheesecloth and secure with a rubber band. Place the jar upside down on a cooling rack set over a sheet pan so the mung beans continue to drain and have good air circulation as they sprout.

Rinse the buckwheat groats well, until the water runs clear, then place in a 1-qt canning jar and add cold water to cover by several inches. Let soak for 30 minutes. Buckwheat groats are unique in that they require only 30 minutes of soaking. They also release a lot of vegetable gums and enzymes, which can inhibit sprouting, so be extra careful to rinse them well.

After 30 minutes, drain the groats and rinse well again until the water runs clear. Return them to the canning jar, cover the mouth of the jar with cheesecloth, and secure with a rubber band. Place the jar upside down on the cooling rack set over the sheet pan so the groats continue to drain and have good air circulation as they sprout.

CONTINUED

Let the mung beans and groats sprout at room temperature for 12 hours. After 12 hours, the sprouts can be used immediately, or they can be stored in the jar in the refrigerator for up to 2 days.

To make the salsa: Preheat the oven to 350°F. Place the cashews and pumpkin, sunflower, flax, sesame, and nigella seeds on a sheet pan and toast for 7 to 10 minutes, until golden and fragrant. In a medium skillet over medium-low heat, warm the oil. Add the pepper flakes and cook about 1 minute, until fragrant. Add the nuts and seeds to the pan and stir to combine well. Stir in the cumin and paprika and cook for 2 minutes, again until fragrant. Remove the pan from the heat and add the nutritional yeast, salt, and citric acid. Set aside to cool completely.

Set a 10-inch cast-iron skillet over high heat. When the skillet is hot, add 1 Tbsp of the oil. After the oil melts, place two slices of bread in the hot pan and toast until browned on the underside, about 3 minutes. Flip the slices and toast until browned on the second side, about 3 minutes. Transfer the toasts to a platter or individual plates and cut in half. Repeat with the remaining oil and bread.

Cut the avocados in half and remove the pits. Cupping an avocado half in your nondominant hand, use a butter knife to cut the flesh lengthwise into slices without cutting through the skin. Using a spoon, scoop the slices out of the skin and onto one toast, mashing the slices with the back of the spoon. Repeat with the remaining avocado halves and toasts. Top each toast with about 2 Tbsp each of the mung bean and buckwheat groat sprouts. Spoon about 2 Tbsp of the salsa over the sprouts and garnish with the cilantro leaves and chive blossoms. Serve immediately.

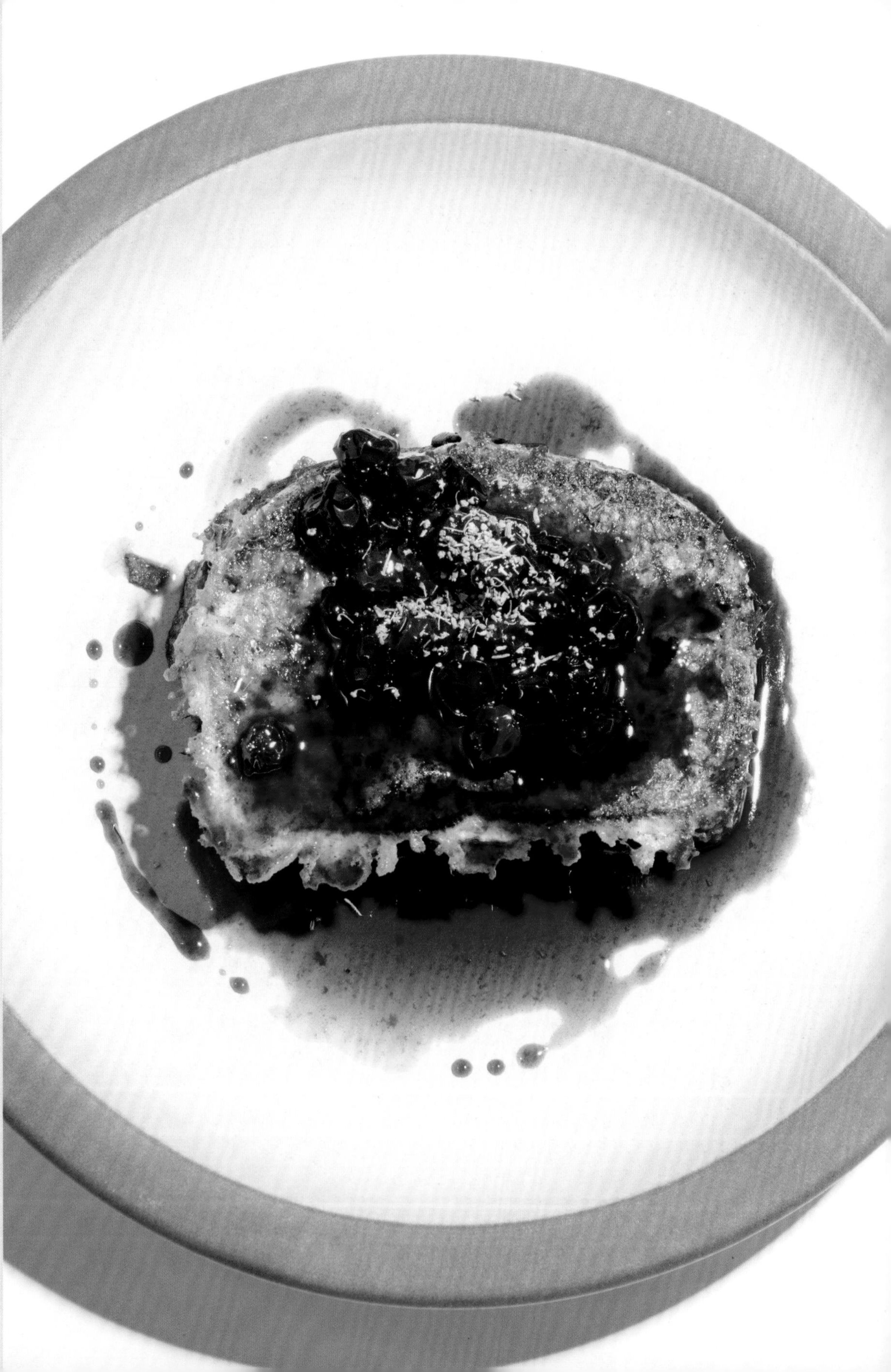

Seeded Multigrain Gluten-Free French Toast

The gluten-free loaf makes a great, hearty French toast. Its density requires an overnight soak to absorb enough egg, but that makes for an easy breakfast, with all the prep done the night before and only the cooking left to do in the morning.

Makes 4 servings

6 eggs

½ cup heavy cream

Pinch of sea salt

2 Tbsp ground cinnamon

1 tsp ground cardamom

Finely grated zest of 2 oranges

1 vanilla bean, split lengthwise

8 (¾-inch-thick) slices seeded multigrain gluten-free bread (page 264)

½ cup unsalted butter

Fruit, maple syrup, jam, and/or confectioners' sugar for serving

The night before you want to serve the toast, in a medium bowl, whisk together the eggs, cream, salt, cinnamon, cardamom, and orange zest. Using the tip of a paring knife, scrape the seeds from the vanilla bean pod and whisk them into the mixture.

Arrange the bread slices in a single layer in the bottom of a large baking dish (use two dishes if you don't have one large enough). Pour the egg mixture evenly over the bread and place in the refrigerator for 30 minutes. Remove the dish from the refrigerator and turn the slices so they are thoroughly coated with the egg mixture. Re-cover the dish, return it to the refrigerator, and leave overnight.

When you are ready to cook, remove the baking dish from the refrigerator. Place a sheet pan in the oven and preheat to the lowest setting (150° to 200°F).

Place a large cast-iron skillet over medium heat. Add 2 Tbsp of the butter, and when it melts, place two bread slices in the hot pan and cook until browned on the underside, 5 to 7 minutes. Flip the slices and cook until browned on the second side, another 5 to 7 minutes. Transfer the toasts to the sheet pan in the oven to keep warm. Repeat with the remaining butter and bread slices. Serve immediately with fruit, maple syrup, jam, and/or confectioners' sugar for adding at the table.

Crispbreads

While it's no secret that I'm partial to super-hydrated, very open-crumb styles of bread, I am also a huge cracker (aka crispbread) fan. (I'm not much of a fan of the stuff in between.) My favorite crackers, which I eat almost daily, are Finn Crisp— it's no surprise they are whole-grain, dark rye, and oat flour, and fermented with natural sourdough. They are thin and very crisp. If someone leaves the box open and it's humid, they soften just slightly. When this happens, I toast them to restore their crispness.

Crispbreads are just as delicious topped with smoked fish, mustard, and strong cheese as they are with jam and ricotta. And they're equally suitable for topping or serving with all sorts of dips, savory and sweet. You can finish them simply with salt and/or brush them with water or flavorful oil and coat in seeds and spices. Just make sure they are super-crisp whenever you serve them.

Rye
Crispbreads
Method

Makes twelve 7-inch round crispbreads

INGREDIENT	QUANTITY	BAKER'S %
Discard leaven	111g	30%
Pulverized rolled oats	74g	20%
Whole milk, warmed to 80°F	222g	60%
Barley malt syrup	7g	2%
Whole-grain rye flour	185g	50%
High-extraction wheat flour	111g	30%
Salt	11g	3%
Flaky sea salt, sesame seeds, and/or crushed anise or other seeds or spices (optional)	for sprinkling on top	

Make the dough.

The leaven in this recipe is not primarily for leavening, so you can use discard leaven (see page 55) that is not at its peak. If not using discard leaven, prepare the leaven as directed on page 46.

Using a blender, blitz 80g rolled oats in a series of 5-second pulses until they break down a little. (Some of the oats will inevitably remain at the bottom of the blender, so you start with more to yield the 74g needed.)

In a large bowl, combine the leaven, milk, and barley malt syrup. Stir gently with your hand, then add the oats, rye flour, wheat flour, and salt. Mix until the flour is almost fully hydrated.

Turn the dough out onto a clean, unfloured work surface. Knead with your hands until the dough is stiff, smooth, and strong, about 10 minutes.

Let the dough rest.

Wrap the dough in plastic wrap and let it rest in a warm (82° to 85°F), draft-free place for 3 hours. Transfer the dough to the refrigerator to rest overnight.

Roll out the dough.

The next day, place a baking stone or steel or a sheet pan on the middle rack of the oven and preheat the oven to 425°F.

Remove the dough from the refrigerator. Lightly flour a work surface and transfer the dough to it. Using a bench knife, divide into twelve equal pieces, each about 60g. Using a cupped hand, roll each piece into a ball about the size of a golf ball. Let the dough balls rest on the work surface for 10 minutes.

Lightly flour the work surface a second time. Using a rolling pin, roll out each dough ball into a very thin circle about ⅛ inch thick. Prick the surface all over with fork tines or use a stippled rolling pin to mark the top. You can bake the crispbreads plain or add one or more toppings. To add toppings, lightly spray or brush the top of each round with water and sprinkle with sea salt, sesame seeds, and/or crushed anise or other seeds or spices.

283

Bake the crispbreads.

Lightly flour a baker's peel. Carefully transfer one round at a time to the peel by gently grasping it with your fingertips and scooting it onto the peel. Then slide the round off the peel onto the preheated baking surface. Depending on the size of your baking surface, you might be able to bake two crackers at a time. Bake until lightly browned with darker brown speckling where bubbles have textured the surface, about 7 minutes. Use a spatula to lift the cracker to check the underside for doneness. The underside should also be lightly browned with darker brown speckling where bubbles have textured the surface. Do not bake until the bubbles have darkened. Transfer the cracker to a cooling rack to cool. Don't worry if it is not perfectly crisp, as it will crisp a little more as it cools.

Repeat to bake the other crispbreads. After you've baked all of them, turn down the oven temperature to 200°F. Once the crackers are cooled, stack on a sheet pan in two stacks of six. When the oven has reached temperature, return the crackers to the oven for 20 minutes to 1 hour for a final, slow caramelization. Use your nose as your guide. When the crackers smell nice and toasty, they are done. This second toasting is optional, but it does result in a tastier cracker.

Let the crackers cool completely on cooling racks before serving. Store leftover crackers in an airtight container at room temperature for up to 1 week.

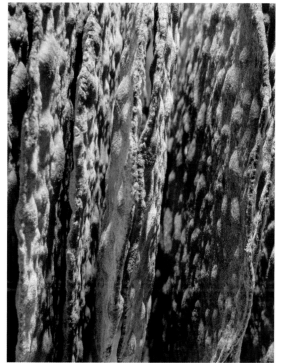

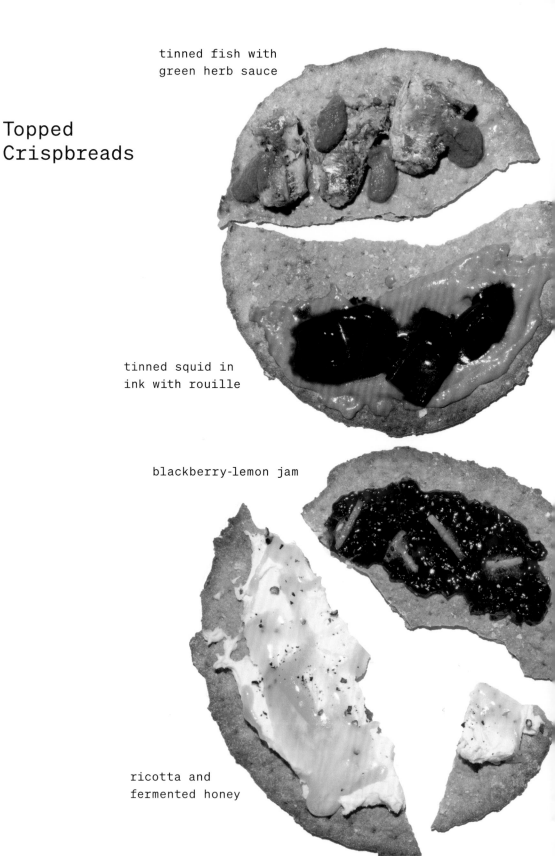

tinned fish with
green herb sauce

Topped
Crispbreads

tinned squid in
ink with rouille

blackberry-lemon jam

ricotta and
fermented honey

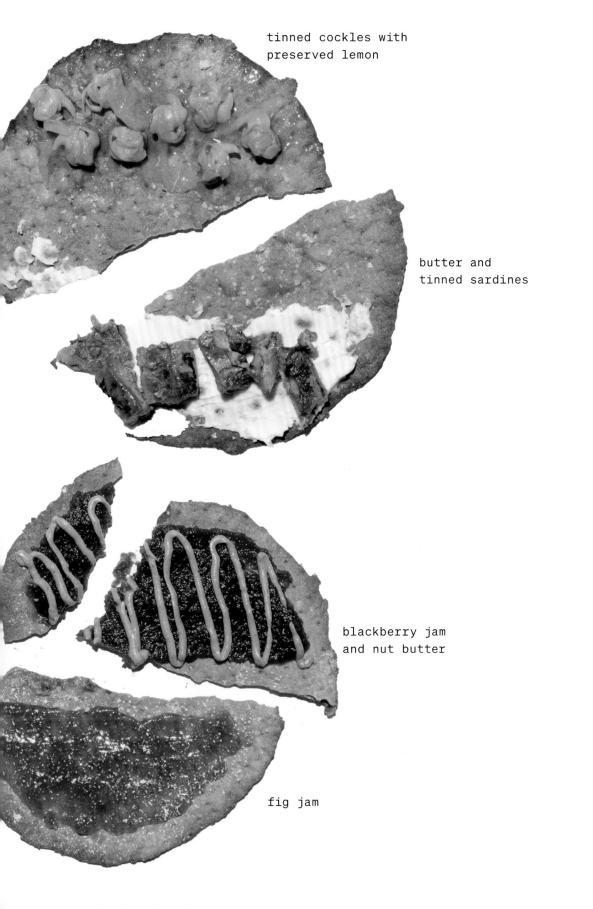

tinned cockles with
preserved lemon

butter and
tinned sardines

blackberry jam
and nut butter

fig jam

Tortillas

We appreciate a perfectly made corn masa tortilla. But when I was growing up in Texas, a handmade flour tortilla was one of the most comforting foods. So often the tortilla is just a vehicle for a filling, but a just-made hot tortilla needs nothing else to be delicious. As a kid, the best treat I could hope for after school was a fresh tortilla slathered in butter and cinnamon sugar.

Modern tortillas, both wheat and corn, use commercially produced industrial flour. And in the case of wheat, they use highly processed, refined, and bleached flour much the same as other popular and staple grain-based foods do, such as pasta, pizza, and pastry. Commercial flour tortillas are similar to soft, white supermarket bread: they don't have much flavor except for what you put inside or on top of them. And tortillas are not fermented, so you're essentially eating highly refined, unfermented white flour. Yes, I have lots of fond childhood memories of eating commercial flour tortillas and foamlike soft white bread, but neither was doing any good in my gut.

For our tortillas, we use a beautiful high-extraction Sonora wheat flour and ferment the dough with our natural leaven. Just as when I first tasted long-fermented whole-grain bread, upon tasting tortillas made the same way, my flour tortilla experience was bifurcated into *before* and *after*. I loved the ones I grew up eating, but these long-fermented tortillas, using freshly milled high-extraction flour from a wheat variety native to northern Mexico, took them to a higher level in flavor, nutrition, and digestibility.

We also use lard (rendered pig fat) in the tortilla dough. Lard swiftly fell out of favor along with butter and suet (rendered beef fat, which produced arguably the best McDonald's fries) after vegetable shortening was heavily promoted in the 1950s for its shelf-stable and perceived healthful advantages. I guess "vegetable" just sounds healthier than pork or beef fat (and generally could be). But after four decades, when the ill effects of hydrogenated fats (aka trans fats) were discovered and documented by the medical community, vegetable shortening fell out of favor and butter made a comeback along with, to a lesser degree, lard and suet. Lard has a neutral flavor, with no trans fats and less saturated fat and cholesterol than butter.

Nowadays, some good vegan butter products are available with increasing quality and in greater quantity. The vegan diet and lifestyle is steadily growing in popularity as more and more of us seek to decrease our impact on climate change and increase sustainability in our daily lives and in how we affect others—both animal and plant.

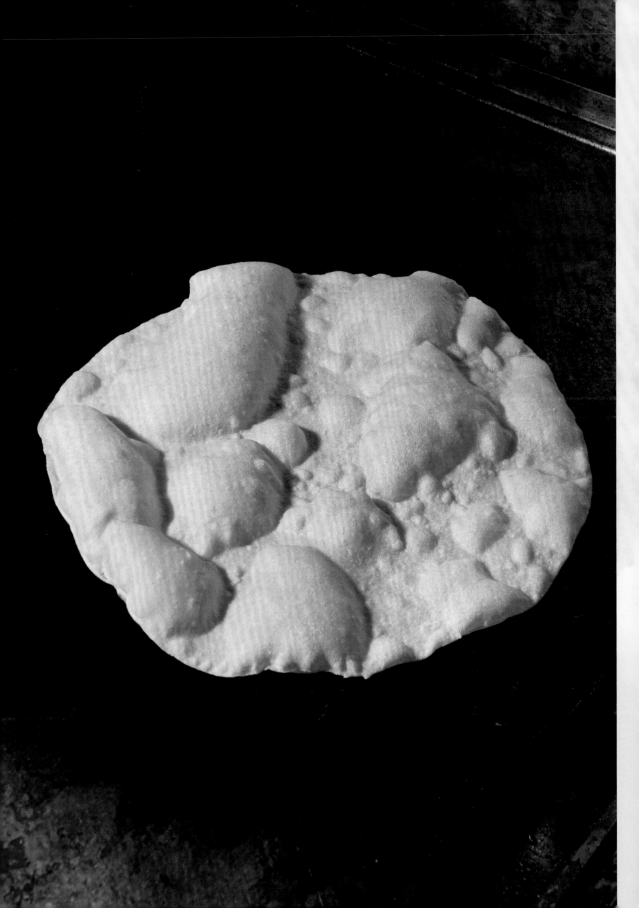

Sonora
Flour
Tortillas
Method

Makes twelve 7-inch tortillas

INGREDIENT	QUANTITY	BAKER'S %
Discard leaven	75g	15%
Very cold (40°F) water	249g	50%
Salt	15g	3%
High-extraction Sonora wheat flour	497g	100%
Lard, cut into ¼-inch cubes and chilled	124g	25%
Vegetable oil (such as canola, safflower, or grapeseed)	for cooking the tortillas	

Prepare the leaven.

The leaven in this recipe is not used primarily for leavening, so you can use discard leaven (see page 55) that is not at its peak.

Mix the dough.

In a large bowl, stir together the water, leaven, and salt.

In another large bowl, combine the flour and lard. Use your fingertips to rub the cubes of lard into the flour until the mixture has a pebbly texture and no lard pieces larger than a pea remain. Dump the flour mixture into the water mixture and stir with your hand until just combined.

Turn the dough out onto a clean, unfloured work surface and knead briefly to bring the dough together into a cohesive ball. Do not knead the dough too much; those little bits of lard will make the tortillas tender and flaky.

Chill and develop the dough.

Wrap the dough in plastic wrap and place in the refrigerator for at least 4 hours or up to overnight. Chilling overnight is best because the longer the dough rests, the more time the leaven has to work and the flavors have to develop.

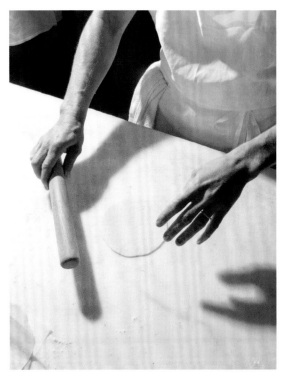

Shape the tortillas.

Remove the dough from the refrigerator and place on a clean, unfloured work surface. Using a bench knife, cut the dough into twelve equal pieces, each about 80g. Shape each piece into a ball, dusting with flour as necessary to keep it from sticking, then cover all the balls with a clean kitchen towel and let rest for 20 minutes. (This short rest will make it easier to roll the balls into thin tortillas.)

Using a tortilla press or a rolling pin, flatten each ball into a very thin tortilla about 7 inches in diameter.

Cook the tortillas.

Set a large cast-iron skillet over high heat for 2 minutes. Lightly oil the skillet. Place one tortilla in the skillet and cook until dark brown and blistered in a few places on the first side, about 1 minute. Flip the tortilla and cook on the second side for 1 minute. The tortilla may puff up a little while it cooks, but it will flatten out when removed from the heat. Transfer the tortilla to a clean kitchen towel and wrap to keep warm. Repeat to cook the other tortillas the same way, adding a little more oil to the skillet when needed.

Serve the tortillas warm. These are best eaten right away, but you can store them in an airtight container in the refrigerator for a few days. Reheat quickly in a skillet before serving.

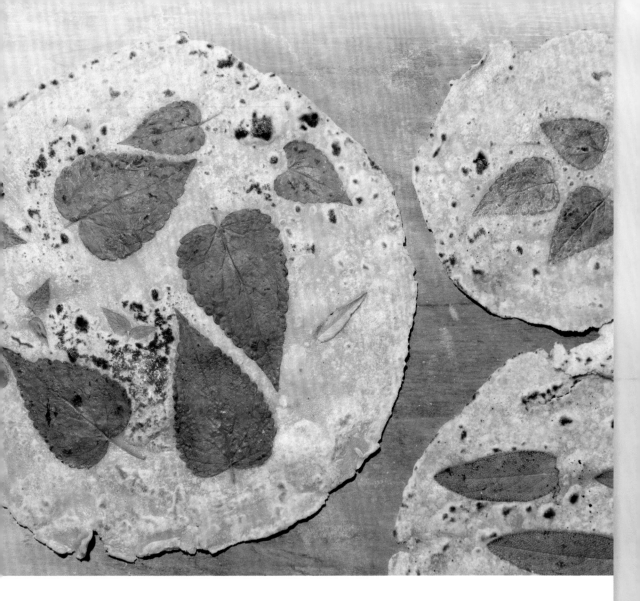

Pressed-Herb Tortillas

We like to layer herbs and flowers into thin crispbreads. It dresses
up a simple staple and adds color and flavor. The same technique
is easily applied to tortillas, which I first saw at Atla in New York
City when Daniela Soto-Innes was at the helm. When the tortilla
is almost rolled out, dampen an epazote leaf (epazote is a bright,
piquant Mexican herb) and press it into the raw tortilla with your
fingertips. Finish rolling the tortilla to seal the leaf into the dough,
then griddle the tortilla as directed in the tortilla method. In the
absence of epazote, I've used purple shiso, sage, or orach. This is a
fun way to experiment with different flavors and decorative styles.

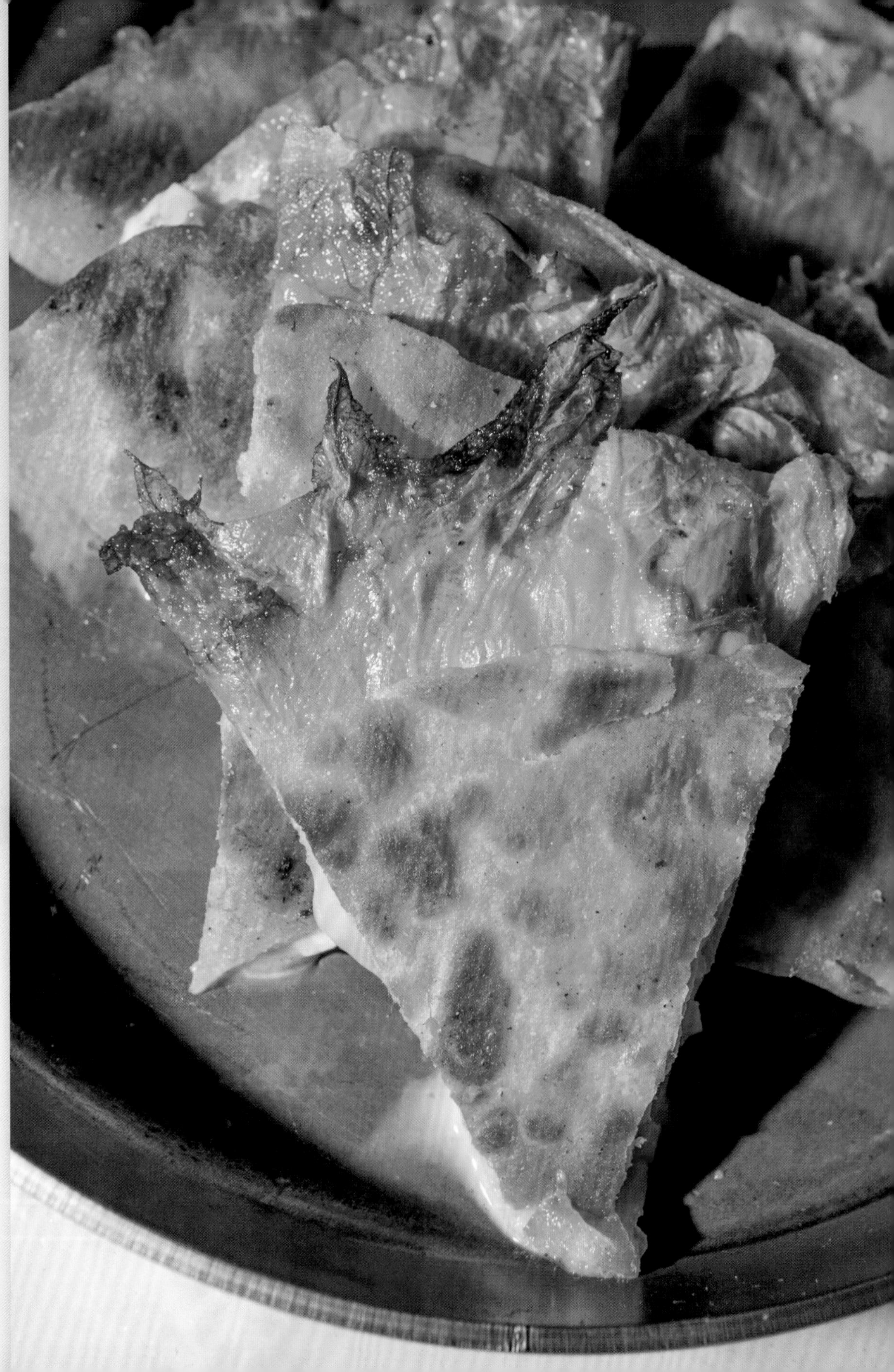

Squash Blossom Quesadillas

The quesadilla is a perennial crowd- and kid-pleaser. It's the Mexican equivalent of a grilled cheese sandwich, and when done well, it's one of the most transcendent things you will ever eat. My first excursion into Baja California was with my dear friend, collaborator, and surf mentor Eric Wolfinger. We had epic intentions. We didn't find much surf that week, but Eric made squash blossom quesadillas for dinner over the fire as we camped on a beach far from civilization. We made a solid book together that same season that I'm very proud of. And a decade later, our head baker, Jen, made these tortillas, which took Eric's version to the next level. This is for you, brother—abrazo grande.

Makes 4 servings

4 Sonora flour tortillas (page 296), preferably still warm

2 cups grated flavorful melting cheese (such as Oaxaca, mozzarella, fontal, Cowgirl Creamery Wagon Wheel, or a combination)

12 squash blossoms

4 sprigs epazote, leaves pulled from stems and finely chopped

Hot sauce for serving (optional)

Set a large cast-iron skillet or griddle over high heat.

While the skillet is heating, lay a tortilla flat on a work surface in front of you. Imagine a line down the middle of the tortilla that divides it into halves. Cover one-half of the tortilla amply with about ½ cup of the cheese. Arrange three squash blossoms in a flat layer over the cheese. Sprinkle one-fourth of epazote over the top. Fold the uncovered half of the tortilla over the filling, covering the filling completely.

Place the quesadilla in the hot skillet and press on it with a spatula to keep it closed. Cook until the underside browns and the cheese melts, about 2 minutes. Flip the quesadilla and cook until the second side browns, about 1 minute longer.

Transfer the cooked quesadilla to a cutting board, cut into four equal wedges, and serve immediately with hot sauce, if desired. Repeat to assemble and cook the remaining three quesadillas.

Brothy Beans with
Sonora Flour Tortillas

Beans in broth is one of my all-time favorite things to eat. I can think of few dishes that leave me feeling more nourished and satisfied. You can use almost any type of dried bean here. The cooking time will vary widely depending on the size and age of the beans. Fresher and smaller beans will take much less time to cook. There is a lot of literature out there about the relative merits of soaking beans overnight, soaking them for a short time, or not soaking them at all before cooking. I try to use heirloom beans that I know will be fresh and then I just skip the soak. If you prefer to soak them, you can certainly add that step. The most important thing is to keep an eye on them as they cook and to pull them from the heat at the moment their texture becomes creamy. One easy and very practical way to hedge your bets is to use an Instant Pot (or a slow cooker) and cook on very low heat (sub-simmer) overnight. I like to use nutrient-dense bone broth to cook the beans for its flavor and health benefits. You could also use vegetable stock or even water, as lots of beans make their own lovely broth as they cook in water. Tortillas are a practical and delicious edible utensil for this dish. Plus, whole grains and beans together contain all nine amino acids to form a complete protein, which is an added dietary benefit.

Makes 4 servings

2 Tbsp good-quality
extra-virgin olive oil

1 small white onion, chopped into
½-inch pieces

1 lb medium-size dried beans
(such as ayacote morado,
cranberry, or Anasazi)

8 cups bone broth, vegetable
stock, or water

6 sprigs epazote or oregano:
4 whole sprigs, and leaves pulled
from 2 sprigs and chopped

Sea salt

12 Sonora flour tortillas
(page 296), warmed

Zhug (page 181)

Bread crumbs (page 77), toasted

Set a Dutch oven or other large, heavy
pot over medium heat. When the pot is
warm, add the oil and onion and cook,
stirring occasionally, until the onion is
translucent, about 5 minutes.

Add the beans, broth, and the whole
epazote sprigs to the pot and bring to
a boil. Turn down the heat to low, cover
partially, and cook at a gentle simmer,
stirring and adding water or broth to
the pot as needed to keep the beans
covered by about 2 inches of liquid, until
the beans are tender, 45 minutes to
2 hours, depending on the type of beans.
After about 45 minutes of cooking time,
check the beans every 15 minutes or so
for doneness by scooping out a bean,
letting it cool slightly, and biting into it.
It should be soft and yielding and not
chalky at all but also not mushy. Once the
beans are cooked, season them with salt.

Ladle the beans and broth into individual
bowls and garnish each bowl with
spoonfuls of Zhug and a healthy sprinkling
of bread crumbs. Serve the tortillas on
the side. Store any leftover beans in a
covered container in the refrigerator for
up to 3 days. Reheat gently over low heat.

brothy beans with
cracked pepper

brothy beans with
roasted lacto-fermented
Jimmy Nardello peppers,
corn, and onion

SOFT SCRAMBLE WITH JIMMY NARDELLO PEPPERS AND SONORA FLOUR TORTILLAS

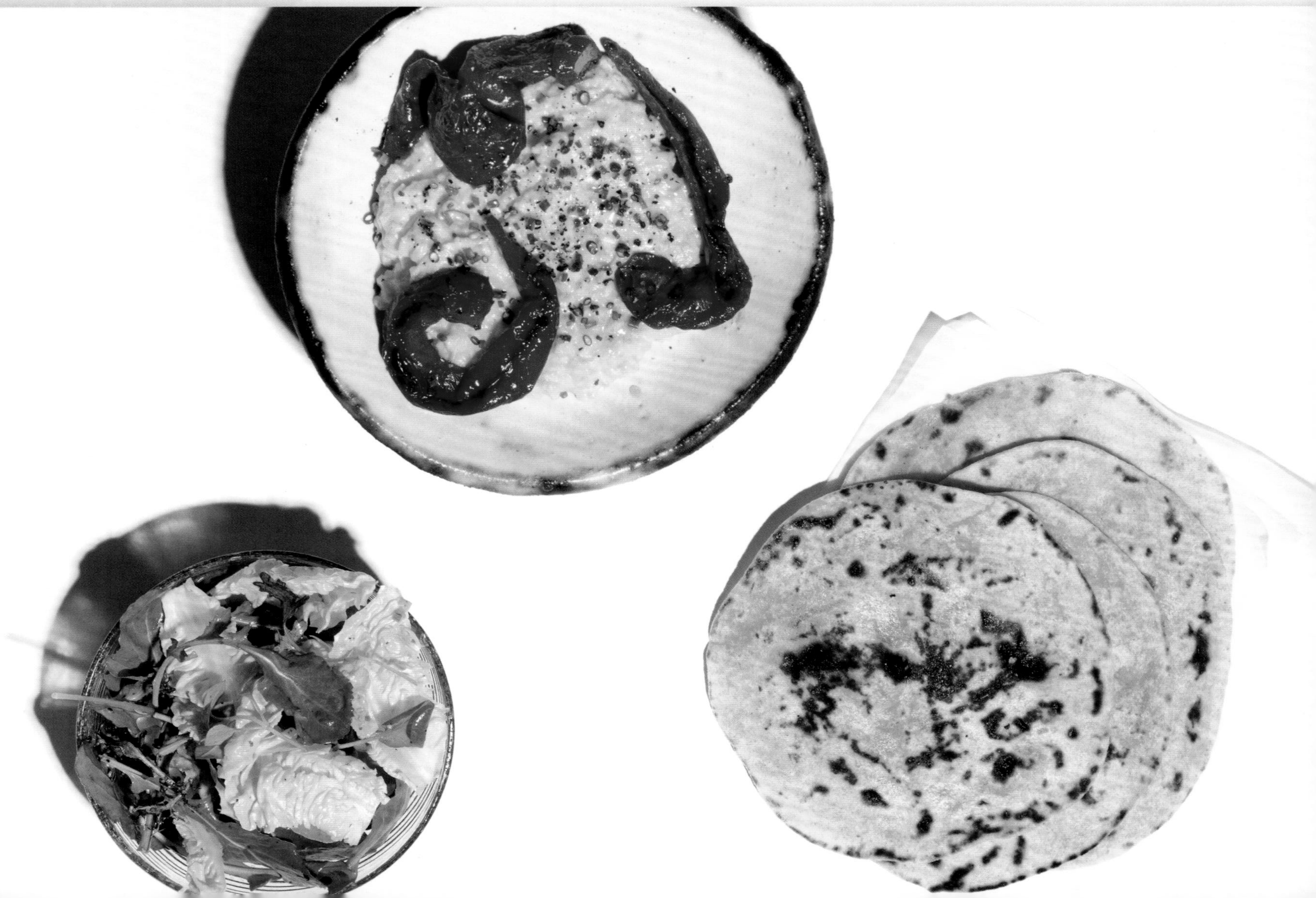

Soft Scramble with Jimmy Nardello Peppers and Sonora Flour Tortillas

This is so easy and so good, for breakfast, lunch, or dinner. Just start with the best ingredients and careful technique and you can't go wrong. You can make egg-and-pepper tacos or simply use the tortillas as an edible implement for scooping them up.

Makes 4 to 6 servings

12 Jimmy Nardello peppers (or other sweet peppers, such as Lipstick or Cornito)

Good-quality extra-virgin olive oil for drizzling

Fine sea salt

12 eggs

5 Tbsp crème fraîche or dashi

Freshly ground black pepper

½ bunch chives, finely chopped

8 Sonora flour tortillas (page 296), warmed

Preheat the oven to 375°F.

Trim off the stem from each pepper, then arrange the peppers in a single layer on a sheet pan. Drizzle oil over them and sprinkle lightly with salt. Roast until the skins are wrinkled and starting to blister, 20 to 30 minutes.

Crack the eggs into a large bowl. Add the crème fraîche and ½ tsp salt and, using a fork, mix together. Stir to break up the eggs but try to avoid incorporating too much air.

Set a large nonstick skillet over medium heat. Drizzle in enough oil to thinly coat the pan bottom, then tilt the pan to coat evenly. Pour the egg mixture into the pan and cook without stirring for 1 minute. Gently drag a heat-resistant rubber spatula through the eggs a few times in different directions, then let cook undisturbed again for about 15 seconds. Gently drag the spatula through the eggs the same way again, then let cook undisturbed again for about 15 seconds. Repeat this gentle stirring and cooking process until the eggs are very softly cooked and holding together in thick curds but are still shiny, about 7 minutes total.

Transfer the eggs to a serving bowl and garnish with several grinds of black pepper and the chives. Serve the eggs alongside the roasted peppers and tortillas and invite your guests to help themselves.

Pizza Dough

Our sourdough pizza recipe was published in my first bread book over a decade ago. As in most bakeries these days, pizza has been a longtime staff family meal and favorite baker's snack. We have made our pizza from country bread dough for as long as we've been open. When we opened the Manufactory in 2016, it included a Roman pizza oven so we could finally make the pizza for our guests that we had been making for ourselves for years.

This recipe is the result of many conversations with friends and bakers over the years, coupled with Tartine's trademark porridge and whole-grain doughs. This version adds to the pizza universe in a way I'm proud of. It's largely whole-grain, super-light, and open-textured—the perfect base for all sorts of healthy toppings, whether vegetable or nonvegetable. Pizza is literally 50 percent of lots of kids' dietary intake. Let's try to make it work harder.

When we make pizza from our country bread dough, we divide it into 250g balls at the dividing stage instead of the 1kg portions for our country loaves. Then we round it and rest it overnight in the retarding box at 48°F. The next day, we shape and bake it. This makes a delicious pizza, but the dough is wet enough that it is finicky to shape and handle. To solve for that here, we decreased the hydration a little and mixed it more to build some gluten strength. We also added spelt for extensibility and whole-wheat flour for flavor and texture. The scalded flour adds flavor and moisture and helps the pizza stay fresh longer and reheat better.

Pizza
Dough
Method

Makes four 12-inch pizza crusts

INGREDIENT	QUANTITY	BAKER'S %
Leaven	101g	20%
Scalded whole-grain durum flour	25g	5%
Warm (85° to 90°F) water	354g	70%
High-extraction wheat flour	430g	85%
Whole-wheat flour	51g	10%
Whole-grain spelt flour	25g	5%
Salt	13g	2.5%
Semolina flour	for dusting the peel	

Prepare the leaven.

Prepare the leaven as directed on page 46. This dough requires a peak leaven (but not a booster leaven) for the right flavor and rise. The leaven is ready for bread-making when it looks bubbly and tastes slightly tangy but also slightly creamy (like yogurt). Unready leaven tastes like raw pancake batter. Overripe leaven tastes very sour or boozy. For this recipe, the leaven needs to be in peak form, just as it does for the country dough. A spent or discard leaven will be too acidic and will degrade the structure of the dough, making it hard to shape and compromising the rise on the crust.

If you are unsure if your leaven is ready, you can perform a float test. To do so, fill a small pitcher or cup with cold, clean water. Wet your hands to prevent the leaven from sticking to your fingers. Gently pinch off about 1 Tbsp of the leaven, handling it minimally so as not to deflate the air bubbles, and carefully place it in the water. It should bob or float on the surface, not sink to the bottom. If it hovers or rises slowly, you can still use it, but your bulk fermentation may take a little longer than it would if you used a riper leaven.

Scald the durum flour.

Once the leaven passes the float test, it's time to scald the durum flour. Measure 40g cold water and 20g whole-grain durum flour into a small saucepan and whisk until well mixed. (This will yield a little more than the required 25g for the recipe, but some will inevitably get stuck to the spatula and pan.) Place the slurry over medium heat and cook, whisking constantly, until the mixture starts to thicken, then switch to a heat-resistant rubber spatula and stir continuously until it darkens and becomes a stiff paste, 3 to 5 minutes total (it should register at least 160°F on a kitchen thermometer). Transfer the gelatinized flour to a sheet pan and spread it out to cool until just warm to the touch (85°F) while you start mixing the dough. (For more on scalding flour, see page 44. You may want to make extra batches of scalded flour so you have it on hand for regular pizza-dough making.)

Pre-mix the dough.

In the bowl of a stand mixer fitted with the dough-hook attachment, combine the water, leaven, high-extraction wheat flour, whole-wheat flour, and spelt flour. Mix on low speed until

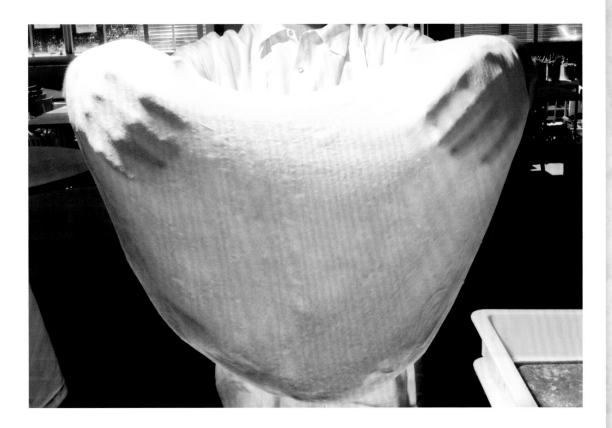

fully incorporated, about 3 minutes. Cover the bowl with a clean kitchen towel and let the dough autolyze (rest) for 30 minutes.

Finish mixing the dough.

After the resting period, mix the dough on low speed for 4 minutes, then let rest for 3 minutes. Add the salt and scalded flour and mix again on low speed for 4 minutes, then let rest for 3 minutes. Mix once again on low speed for 4 minutes.

Check the dough temperature.

The dough should be warm to the touch but not hot (85°F is ideal). If it needs to cool down, place it somewhere cooler. If it needs to warm up, place it on a heating pad turned to low or in an oven preheated to the lowest setting (150° to 200°F) and then turned off.

Turn the dough during its bulk fermentation.

Loosely cover the dough with a clean kitchen towel and rest in a warm (82° to 85°F), draft-free place for about 2 hours. Every 30 minutes, wet your hands and give the dough several series of turns in the bowl, gently lifting and stretching the sides and folding them into the middle to build strong gluten bonds in the dough without deflating it. The last turn should be a gentle one, turning the dough just until it has all been gently folded over once; the mass should hold its shape in the bowl. This first rise, also called the bulk fermentation or bulk rise, is a crucial time for the dough to develop strength and depth of flavor.

When the dough has finished rising, it will feel airy and fluffy. You can check the dough's readiness with a float test: If a small piece of dough bobs or floats when gently placed in a pitcher of cool water, your dough is ready for the next stage. If it sinks, the dough needs additional time to bulk ferment.

Pre-shape the dough and let rest.

Line a sheet pan with parchment paper. Lightly flour a work surface and transfer the dough to it. Using a bench knife, divide the dough into four equal pieces, each about 250g. Working with one piece at a time, place the dough on the work surface in front of you. Cup your hand around the dough and pull it counterclockwise in a small continuous circle. Use the stickiness of the dough on the work surface to build tension across the top of the dough ball. The finished dough ball should feel firm and even. Repeat to shape the other dough balls. Place the balls on the prepared pan, very lightly flour them, and cover loosely with a clean kitchen towel. Place in the refrigerator for at least 12 hours or up to 48 hours.

Preheat the oven and prepare the pizza toppings.

About 2 hours before you want to bake the pizzas, remove the dough from the refrigerator and let warm up to room temperature.

About 1 hour before baking, place a baking stone or steel on the middle rack of the oven and preheat the oven to 550°F (or as high as it will go).

While the oven heats up, prepare the pizza toppings. (See pages 318 to 319 for a few ideas.) Cook anything that needs to be cooked. Trim, clean, and chop whatever needs to be prepped. Once you're ready to bake, you'll want to stretch, top, and cook the pizzas in rapid succession.

Finish shaping the dough.

Lightly dust a pizza peel with semolina flour and set it aside. Dust some high-extraction wheat flour on a work surface and gently set one dough ball on it. Using your fingertips, pat and flatten the ball into a thick disk. Pick up the disk and drape it over the back of both hands. Gently stretch the dough by spreading your hands apart slowly. Rotate the dough over your knuckles and continue stretching the dough into a 12-inch circle. Place the stretched dough on the prepared peel.

Bake the pizzas.

Top the pizza dough with your desired toppings. Open the oven and slide the pizza from the peel onto the preheated baking surface. Bake until the crust is lightly browned with some very dark blistered spots and the toppings are hot, 5 to 8 minutes. Remove the pizza from the oven using the peel and slide it onto a cutting board. Immediately slide the next pizza into the oven. Repeat to bake the remaining pizzas. Cut into wedges and serve.

Lemon Pie

Using a mandoline or a very sharp knife, cut 1 lemon crosswise as thinly as possible. Soak the lemon slices in cold water to cover at room temperature for at least 2 hours or up to overnight. Drain the lemon slices, pat dry, and arrange on top of the stretched pizza dough. Dollop 1 cup whole-milk ricotta cheese on top of the lemon slices and then lightly drizzle the pie with good-quality extra-virgin olive oil. Bake the pizza as directed, then remove from the oven and, using a fine-rasp grater, grate ½ oz bottarga evenly over the top. Garnish with mixed chopped fresh herbs (such as flat-leaf parsley, mint, and oregano), cut into wedges, and serve immediately.

Lemony Red Pie

Using a mandoline or a very sharp knife, cut one lemon crosswise as thinly as possible. Soak the lemon slices in cold water to cover at room temperature for at least two hours or up to overnight. Spread tomato paste over the stretched pizza dough. Drain the lemon slices, pat dry, and arrange on top of the tomato paste, then lightly drizzle the pie with good-quality extra-virgin olive oil. Bake the pizza as directed, cut into wedges, and serve immediately.

Spicy Dungeness Crab Pie

Spread Calabrian chile–spiked pizza sauce over the stretched pizza dough. Dollop 1 cup whole-milk ricotta cheese on top and then lightly drizzle the pie with good-quality extra-virgin olive oil. Bake the pizza as directed, then remove from the oven and top with hunks of cooked crabmeat. Cut into wedges and serve immediately.

Pepperoni Pie

Spread pizza sauce over the stretched pizza dough. Dollop 1 cup whole-milk ricotta cheese on top and then lightly drizzle the pie with good-quality extra-virgin olive oil. Top with pepperoni slices. Bake the pizza as directed, then cut into wedges, and serve immediately.

Potato-Lardo Pie

Top the stretched pizza dough with shredded fontina. Mince the leaves of a few rosemary sprigs and sprinkle over the fontina. Slice one yellow potato and one purple potato paper-thin and place over the cheese. Lightly drizzle the pie with good-quality extra-virgin olive oil. Bake the pizza as directed. Drape slices of lardo over the top. Cut into wedges and serve immediate

Green Garlic and Nettles Pie

Very thinly slice a few bulbs of green garlic and distribute over the stretched pizza dough. Top with a generous handful of nettles. Cover with shredded mozzarella. Lightly drizzle the pie with good-quality extra-virgin olive oil. Bake the pizza as directed, then cut into wedges and serve immediately.

spicy dungeness crab pie

potato-lardo pie

green garlic and
nettles pie

Fermented
Pasta

My first trip to Rome kicked off an exploratory weeklong journey with friend and chef Christian Puglisi and his team, who were researching recipes and ingredients before Christian opened his first "Italian" restaurant, Baest, in Copenhagen. Christian was born and raised in southern Italy but moved to Denmark when he was a teenager. His and his colleagues' cooking in Denmark at Noma (where he ran the kitchen for years) came to define the new Nordic style of cuisine in its own distinctive way more than a decade ago. Next, he was ready to make Italian food with the best Scandinavian ingredients and invited me to come along on the inspiration trip, starting in Rome and then moving south through Campania to Naples.

Our first meal was a standing lunch at Pizzarium Bonci, where we had dozens of mind-bending bites of groundbreaking pizza. For dinner we had cacio e pepe at a place famous for the storied Roman pasta preparation—also amazing. We made our way south, stopping every half day to eat, explore, and rest. All we ate were pasta, pizza, salumi, and freshly made mozzarella (the ingredients that Christian intended to focus on producing at his new restaurant). Aside from a wonderful adventure eating a week's worth of excellent Italian classics with an inspiring group of chefs, the main thing I remember is that, by the end of the trip, my digestion had almost completely stopped— something that had never happened to me before in all my years of professional cooking. I felt like I was moving through a fog with my legs stuck in quicksand; I was so groggy that I could barely keep my eyes open. The culprit, of course, was my steady diet of mostly refined white flour in the form of pizza and pasta. The pizza was fermented with yeast though not commonly with sourdough cultures, so it wasn't highly digestible. In the case of the pasta, it was not fermented at all, was generally made from highly refined flour, and, when in Rome, was hardly cooked—

extra al dente being the local custom. (More fully cooked pasta would have at least helped aid digestibility.)

Considering the extreme popularity of both pasta and pizza around the world, and knowing how much of the US diet comprises these foods (especially among kids), I decided it was time to make pizza and pasta more nutrient dense and digestible. Sure, the toppings on pizza and the vegetables, meat, seafood, and cheese in many popular pasta dishes can add lots of flavor, nutrition, and fiber, but the base doughs invited reinvention. I would make them lacto-fermented—not so much to add sour flavor (it's very subtle if at all detectable) but rather to add depth of flavor and increase digestibility. For starters, we used high-extraction flours (75% to 85% of the 100% in the formula), including durum, which is the hard wheat traditionally used in Italy to make many classic pastas, while also incorporating more diverse flours, such as rye and buckwheat. Again, in the spirit of *Tartine Book No. 3*, we were using different flours in ways that hadn't seen much use in the past, starting with a traditional technique and bringing in new variables to see where they took us.

Here we are working with two very broad categories of noodles: egg noodles and eggless noodles, drawing heavily from the past but with wide-open eyes looking forward. Eggless noodles are made with only flour and water. Both types of noodles can be fermented with sourdough starter for a more complex flavor and increased digestibility. Pasta, as we are reimagining it, is a very dry bread dough. At its core, it's also the basis for a grain bowl when you employ key preparations to make it a foundation for building healthy, vegetable-forward meals.

There is a trick to fermenting pasta dough: you want it to ferment long enough to get some of the flavor benefits but not so long that bubbles form, which will weaken the dough and make it difficult to roll out and shape. It helps to use a starter that is a little more sour than you would use for country bread. This is a good use for starter that has not been fed frequently or for discard leaven. The best way that I have found to ensure good flavor without overfermentation is to let the dough sit out for about an hour at room temperature and then overnight in the fridge. The next day, the dough is still plenty strong and supple enough to roll out and shape but has developed some flavor from the leaven. Then, as you roll, cut, and shape the dough, it continues to warm and develop flavor.

Pasta is a great way to use flours that are not perfectly suited to country bread and other hearth loaves. This simple format is one of the best ways to explore or showcase the unique flavors and characters of different grains. I think of our pasta dishes as grain bowls: we use the most flavorful whole grains available and ferment them to develop even more flavor, then build dishes with copious amounts of vegetables and other whole foods. This is by no means anyone's nonna's pasta, but it is how I like to eat it.

Durum is the classic flour for pasta, and it is a perfect fit. It has a high proportion of glutenin to gliadin (the two proteins that combine to form gluten; see About Grain and Flour, page 29), which makes it more plastic than elastic, giving pasta its characteristic toothiness. Durum is also very high in overall protein, which makes it one of the strongest types of wheat flour. The evolution of pasta in Italy, where durum wheat grows especially well, is a beautiful example of a cuisine evolving over time to dovetail with the best use for the local grain. That said, today some of the finest durum in the world is grown in Arizona and shipped to Italy, where it's milled and made into pasta. The pasta is then dried, packaged, and shipped back to America.

The combination of sourdough fermentation and whole-grain durum in the pappardelle formula has a striking synergy: when boiled in salted water for just a few minutes and eaten unadorned, the noodles taste like they have already been sauced with butter.

If you experiment with other flours, such as khorasan or emmer, for the pappardelle, you'll need to make some adjustments to the flour-to-egg ratio. Some will require a little more or less flour than the recipe for durum given here. It's a good idea when experimenting to hold back a little flour at first and add it as needed, and also to have a little more than the recipe calls for on hand, in case you need to add more. The main thing is that the dough should feel very smooth and stiff and not at all sticky after it has been kneaded well. Kneading by hand on a countertop lets you feel the dough as you are mixing it and add flour if needed as you go.

While durum and other hard wheats are great for pasta, softer grains, such as rye and buckwheat, are delicious and surprising ways to make pasta more than just a vehicle for the sauce. Since those flours are weaker, you will want to blend them in with another strong flour, such as durum. Using 20 to 30 percent buckwheat or rye flour is plenty to flavor the pasta but won't make the dough too weak to hold together. These pastas will be a little stickier and softer—I recommend practicing with durum first.

There are myriad ways to shape fresh egg pasta dough (some people spend their entire lives studying regional pasta shapes in Italy), so you can really have fun with it and try anything you dream up. I'm giving a very versatile one here: pappardelle are wide noodles that let you really get the flavor and the bite of the noodle. You could cut the noodles narrower for tagliatelle, if you like. This dough is also suitable for stuffed pastas, such as tortelli, ravioli, and agnolotti.

Eggless pasta doughs can be shaped by hand or with a machine called an extruder. An extruder applies pressure to a very dry dough to squeeze it out through a die. Different-shaped dies produce different-shaped pastas. This is how most dried pastas, such as spaghetti and linguine, are made. The dough for extruded pasta is extremely dry—so dry it barely forms a cohesive ball and only truly comes together under the pressure of the extruder.

Hand-shaped doughs, like orecchiette and cavatelli, are usually made by rolling a long rope of dough, cutting it into small pieces, and shaping those individual pieces. The eggless buccatini dough in this chapter is great for someone who doesn't have an extruder but still wants to shape eggless pasta at home. It's my favorite eggless pasta. It uses a blend of durum flour and buckwheat flour, so you get the strength from the durum and the flavor of the buckwheat.

Whole-Grain Durum Pappardelle Method

Makes (600g) 4 servings

INGREDIENT	QUANTITY	BAKER'S %
Discard leaven	68g	20%
Eggs (about 4)	191g	56%
Whole-grain durum flour	341g	100%
Semolina flour	for dusting the pasta	

Make the dough.

The leaven in this recipe is not primarily for leavening, so you can use discard leaven (see page 55) that is not at its peak (one that has become sour and started to fall). If not using discard leaven, prepare the leaven as directed on page 46.

Place a medium bowl on the scale and tare the scale. Crack the eggs into the bowl. If there's more egg than you need for this recipe, use a spoon or your fingers to remove enough of the egg white so only 191g remains. Add the leaven to the bowl and mix with a fork until well mixed.

Measure the flour into a large bowl. Make a well in the center of the flour large enough to hold the egg mixture. Pour the egg mixture into the well and start beating the egg with a fork, pulling small amounts of flour from the sides of the well into the egg mixture. Continue to beat the egg mixture, slowly drawing more flour into it, until the eggs and flour become a paste that has the consistency of pancake batter.

Turn the dough out on to a work surface (preferably wooden but any countertop with sufficient space to mix and knead will do). Using your fingertips and a bench knife, toss the remainder of the flour into the egg mixture, scraping, mixing, and squeezing until it starts to come together. It will seem very dry at first; just keep working it. It will come together once the flour starts to absorb the egg mixture. Incorporate any bits of dough from the fork, bench knife, and your hands.

Knead the dough.

Knead the dough for 3 to 5 minutes, using the palm of your dominant hand to press the dough into the work surface and away from you. Use your nondominant hand to rotate the dough a quarter turn. Using the heel of your dominant hand, pull the top of the dough toward you and then press it into the middle and away from you. Your dominant hand will be making a continuous circular motion perpendicular to your body while your nondominant hand continues to rotate the dough a quarter turn with each stroke of your dominant hand. You can almost imagine that you are looking at a Ferris wheel coming toward you as it crests the top of the circle and moving away from you at the bottom.

At this point, if there are any dry bits of flour left on the work surface, clear them away. The dough should feel slightly tacky but not be sticking to your hands or the work surface. Continue to knead the dough until it feels very smooth, stiff, and strong, another 3 to 5 minutes. If the dough feels soft and sticky and has absorbed all of the flour, you can dust some additional flour on the work surface as you knead, but you'll want to knead for at least 3 minutes after the last of the dry flour is added to ensure proper gluten development. If the dough feels too dry and will not come together in a ball, you can wet your hands with water and the dough will absorb the additional water as you knead it.

Let the dough ferment.

Shape the dough into a 1-inch-thick disk, wrap tightly in plastic wrap, and let it rest at room temperature for 2 to 3 hours.

Place the wrapped dough in the refrigerator to ferment overnight.

Roll the dough.

The next day, remove the dough from the refrigerator about 1 hour before you plan to roll it.

Set up your pasta rolling machine. Unwrap the dough and place it on a clean, unfloured work surface. Tap the edge against the work surface until you have a flat side, then rotate it a quarter turn, tapping to create another flat side, and so on until you have a rough square. You can press the dough flat with your fingertips if it becomes too squat. Keep tapping, flattening, and pressing the dough until you have an approximately 6-inch square about 1 inch thick.

Using a bench knife, cut the square into four equal pieces. Work with one piece at a time and place the other three under a clean kitchen towel so they don't dry out. Using a rolling pin, flatten the piece into a rough square about ¼ inch thick. Open the roller on your pasta machine to its widest setting. Slip the edge of the flattened dough between the rollers and roll it through. Fold the rolled dough into thirds (like a business letter), stretching the corners as needed so the edges are neat. Turn the dough so you are feeding the narrower end through the rollers first.

With the machine still on the widest setting, roll the folded dough through again. Fold into thirds again. The wide end should now be about the same width as the machine. Turn the dough so you are putting the wide, folded side through the machine first and roll the dough through once more. (It's okay to fold and press the dough a little to make it wider or narrower to fit your machine.)

Narrow the width of the roller by one notch and roll the dough through. Narrow the width of the roller by another notch and roll the dough through again. Repeat until you reach the third narrowest setting. Roll the dough through that setting twice. At this point, your dough may be thin enough. You want it to be about the thickness of a paper envelope—thin enough to be pleasantly delicate to eat but not so thin that it falls apart when you add ingredients to the cooked pasta. If needed, you can roll it through the second narrowest setting. Place the rolled pasta sheet on the work surface, flipping it after a few minutes so it air-dries a bit on both sides, while you roll the remaining dough pieces.

Cut the noodles.

After air-drying, the dough sheets will feel almost leathery but not dried out to the point that the edges are cracking. Working with one sheet at a time (and keeping the others covered with a clean kitchen towel if they are already sufficiently air-dried), generously dust the pasta with semolina flour. Fold it in half crosswise, then in half again, and then in half again. You should have a six-layered folded sheet of dough. Orient the dough on the work surface in front of you so the folded edge is toward you and the open edge is farthest from you. Using a very sharp knife, cut the folded sheet into ½-inch-wide strips. Use your fingertips to pick up all the strips, unfolding the dough into long noodles. Let the noodles air-dry a little further while you cut the remaining dough sheets. Finally, dust the air-dried noodles generously with semolina flour and coil them into nests on a sheet pan. It's best to cook this pasta about 1 hour after the noodles are cut.

Buckwheat Bucatini Method

Makes (600g) 4 servings

INGREDIENT	QUANTITY	BAKER'S %
Cool (70°F) water	197g	45%
Discard leaven	110g	25%
Buckwheat flour	130g	30%
Whole-grain durum flour	308g	70%
Semolina flour	for dusting the pasta	

Make the dough.

The leaven in this recipe is not primarily for leavening, so you can use discard leaven (see page 55) that is not at its peak (one that has become sour and started to fall). If not using discard leaven, prepare the leaven as directed on page 46.

Pour the water into a large bowl. Add the leaven and mix well with your hand to break it up. Add the buckwheat and durum flours and combine until a stiff dough forms.

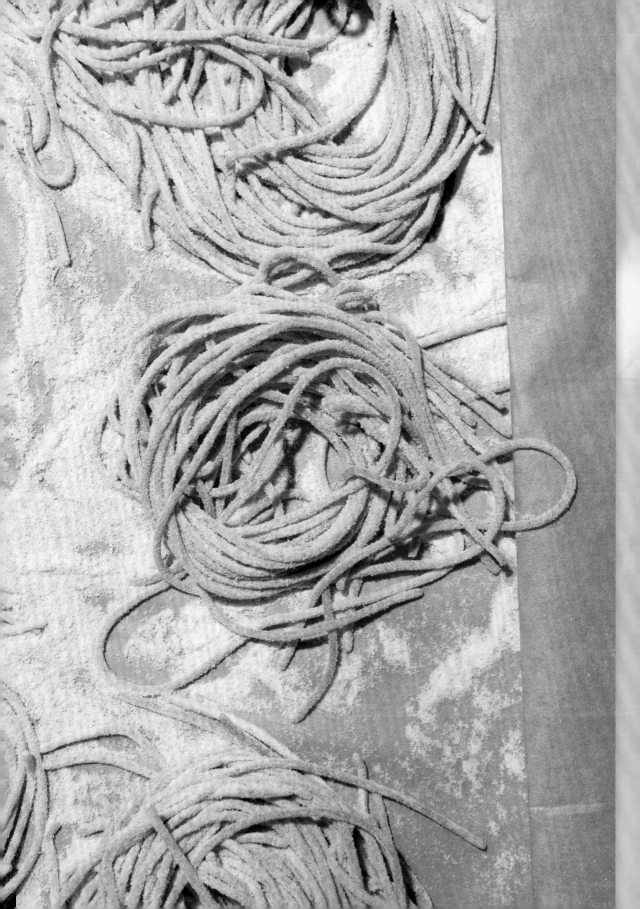

Knead the dough.

Turn the dough out onto a clean, unfloured work surface and knead it until it feels smooth and strong, about 8 minutes, using the palm of your dominant hand to press the dough into the work surface and away from you. Use your nondominant hand to rotate the dough a quarter turn. Using the heel of your dominant hand, pull the top of the dough toward you and then press it into the middle and away from you. Your dominant hand will be making a continuous circular motion perpendicular to your body while your nondominant hand continues to rotate the dough a quarter turn with each stroke of your dominant hand. You can almost imagine that you are looking at a Ferris wheel coming toward you as it crests the top of the circle and moving away from you at the bottom. The dough will be quite dry. If the dough sticks to the work surface at all, dust it with durum flour and continue kneading. If the dough feels too dry and will not come together in a ball, you can wet your hands with water and the dough will absorb the additional water as you knead.

Let the dough ferment.

Shape the dough into a 1-inch-thick disk. Wrap tightly in plastic wrap and let it rest at room temperature for 2 to 3 hours. Place the wrapped dough in the refrigerator to ferment overnight.

Extrude the noodles.

Set up your pasta extruder and fit it with the bucatini die. Following the manufacturer's instructions, process the dough through the extruder. Toss the shaped noodles in semolina flour to prevent them from sticking together and lay them flat and straight on a clean sheet pan. You can cook the fresh pasta right away, keep it covered on the countertop at room temperature for several hours, or store it in an airtight container in the refrigerator for up to 72 hours.

Rye Cavatelli and Orecchiette Method

Makes (600g) 4 servings

INGREDIENT	QUANTITY	BAKER'S %
Discard leaven	88g	20%
Whole-grain rye flour	106g	30%
Whole-grain durum flour	247g	70%
Room-temperature (72° to 75°F) water	159g	45%
Semolina flour	for dusting the pan and pasta	

Make the dough.

The leaven in this recipe is not primarily for leavening, so you can use discard leaven (see page 55) that is not at its peak (one that has become sour and started to fall). If not using discard leaven, prepare the leaven as directed on page 46.

In a large bowl, stir together the rye and durum flours. Make a well in the center of the flour mixture and pour in the water. Add the leaven to the well and, using your hand, stir to break it up. Then mix everything in the bowl together until a stiff dough forms.

Knead the dough.

Turn the dough out onto a clean, unfloured work surface and knead it until it feels smooth and strong, about 8 minutes, using the palm of your dominant hand to press the dough into the work surface and away from you. Use your nondominant hand to rotate the dough a quarter turn. Using the heel of your dominant hand, pull the top of the dough toward you and then press it into the middle and away from you. Your dominant hand will be making a continuous circular motion perpendicular to your body while your nondominant hand continues to rotate the dough a quarter turn with each stroke of your dominant hand. You can almost imagine that you are looking at a Ferris wheel coming toward you as it crests the top of the circle and moving away from you at the bottom. The dough will be quite dry. If it sticks to the work surface at all, dust the surface with durum flour and continue kneading. If the dough feels too dry and will not come together in a ball, you can wet your hands with water and the dough will absorb the additional water as you knead.

Let the dough ferment.

Shape the dough into a 1-inch-thick disk. Wrap tightly in plastic wrap and let it rest at room temperature for 2 to 3 hours. Place the wrapped dough in the refrigerator to ferment overnight.

Hand-shape the dough.

The next day, remove the dough from the refrigerator about 1 hour before you plan to shape it. Dust a sheet pan with semolina flour and set it aside.

Unwrap the dough and place it on a clean, unfloured work surface. Using a bench knife, cut into four equal pieces. Work with one piece at a time and place the other three under a clean kitchen towel so they don't dry out. Using the palms of your hands and working from the center outward, roll the first piece of dough against the work surface into a long rope about ½ inch in diameter. Using the bench knife or a sharp knife, cut the rope into ¾-inch segments.

Using the rounded tip of a butter knife, press a dough segment and rock in a circular motion, which will result in a shape that is round through the middle with a lip around the edge. Continue this way to make cavatelli. To make orecchiette, turn the shapes inside out. *Orecchiette* means "little ears" in Italian because that's exactly what they resemble.

After shaping the pasta, place it on the prepared pan. Keep the pieces in a single layer and well dusted with semolina so they don't stick to one another. Repeat with the remaining three dough pieces. Shaping cavatelli and orecchiette will seem laborious at first, but keep at it. Once you get the hang of it, you can move along at a good pace. When all of the pieces are shaped, toss them with a little semolina flour to prevent sticking and let them dry at room temperature in a single layer on a clean sheet pan.

Cook the pasta the same day that you shape them. You can leave them at room temperature or refrigerate them in an airtight container for up to a few hours. If you leave them any longer, whether at room temperature or in the refrigerator, they will continue to ferment and will eventually become too sour and gooey from the acid by-products of fermentation.

Whole-Grain Durum Pappardelle with Wild Mushrooms and Dandelion Greens

Think of this pasta as a grain bowl: fermented whole-grain durum loaded with mushrooms, bitter greens, and herbs. As I think about what I enjoy eating, I'm always asking myself, Could I live (well) on this? I consider what anthropologists found in the stomach of a caveman discovered frozen in the tundra: einkorn wheat; dark, leafy green fern; and dried meat of some sort. With this in mind, a new perspective on the paleo diet—one with properly fermented grains as a base—starts to make a lot more sense than the meat-based program.

Makes 4 servings

1 lb wild mushrooms (such as chanterelles, oyster mushrooms, black trumpets, porcini, or a combination)

4 Tbsp unsalted butter

½ cup dry white wine

Sea salt

½ cup coarsely chopped dandelion greens

1 batch whole-grain durum pappardelle (page 328)

½ cup finely chopped fresh flat-leaf parsley leaves

¼ cup finely chopped fresh mint leaves

2 Tbsp finely chopped fresh thyme leaves

Finely grated zest of 1 lemon

Use a clean, dry pastry brush to brush any debris off the mushrooms. Trim any woody stems.

In a large skillet over medium heat, melt the butter. Pour in the wine and bring to a simmer. Add the mushrooms, season lightly with salt, and cook, stirring occasionally, until the mushrooms have released their juices and have shrunk slightly, 5 to 10 minutes.

Meanwhile, bring a large pot of generously salted water to a boil. It should taste briny like the sea.

Add the dandelion greens to the mushrooms and cook, stirring, until the greens are wilted and tender, about 5 minutes. Then continue cooking, stirring periodically, until the sauce has reduced in volume and thickened slightly, about 5 minutes longer. Remove the pan from the heat.

Add the pappardelle to the boiling water, give them a good stir, and cook until tender but not at all mushy, 1 to 3 minutes. Test for doneness by removing a noodle from the water, letting it cool for a moment, and then biting into it. It should be yielding but firm. Drain the noodles and transfer them to the pan of mushrooms and greens.

Return the skillet to medium heat and cook, stirring constantly, until the noodles absorb almost all of the sauce, 1 to 2 minutes. Stir in the parsley, mint, and thyme. Portion the pasta onto plates, garnish with the lemon zest, and serve immediately.

Buckwheat Bucatini with Cranberry Beans, Nettles, Goat Cheese, and Herby Bread Crumbs

Bucatini are extruded tubular spaghetti with a hollow center. That's already hitting a lot of high notes, style-wise, for me. I first made this dish for a fun collaborative chef dinner hosted by San Francisco chef Corey Lee at Benu, one of the most innovative chefs and restaurants anywhere. It's another example of combining beans, grains, greens, and bread to make a dish that's more than the sum of its parts. At the Benu event, we finished the plates with finely grated soy sauce–cured egg yolk, which is a rustic way to add umami and protein to many dishes. Nettles are one of our most intensely healthful foods. We get them farmed or foraged wild here in Northern California. They are covered in fine hairs, which can sting or cause a rash, so use gloves or tongs when handling them raw.

Makes 4 servings

Herby Bread Crumbs

½ loaf country bread (page 74), ideally 2 days to 1 week old, cut or torn into 1-inch pieces

¼ cup loosely packed flat-leaf parsley leaves

6 sprigs thyme, leaves pulled from stems

¼ cup loosely packed oregano leaves, finely chopped

¼ cup loosely packed basil leaves, finely chopped

1 batch buckwheat bucatini (page 336)

2 Tbsp good-quality extra-virgin olive oil, plus more for drizzling

6 oz nettle leaves, picked from the stems using gloves or tongs and scissors

Sea salt

2 Tbsp fresh goat cheese

1 cup drained cooked cranberry beans

Finely grated zest and juice of 1 lemon

Freshly ground black pepper

1 lemon, cut into wedges

CONTINUED

To make the herby bread crumbs: Preheat the oven to 450°F. Spread the bread pieces on a sheet pan in an even layer and toast in the oven until browned and fragrant, about 7 minutes, stirring once or twice for even toasting. Turn down the oven temperature to 300°F and continue toasting until there are no soft pieces, 10 to 15 minutes longer. Let cool completely.

In a food processor, combine the toasted bread, parsley, and thyme and pulse until the bread is reduced to fine bread crumbs. (If there are large pieces that are too soft and won't crumble completely, you can return them to the oven to toast longer and then process them again.) Transfer the bread crumbs to a bowl and stir in the oregano and basil. Set aside.

Bring a large pot of generously salted water to a boil. It should taste briny like the sea. Add the buccatini to the boiling water, give them a good stir, and cook until tender but not at all mushy, 2 to 5 minutes. Test for doneness by removing a noodle from the water, letting it cool for a moment, and then biting into it. It should be yielding but firm. Scoop out and reserve ½ cup of the pasta cooking water, then drain the noodles. Set the noodles aside.

Pour the reserved cooking water into a large skillet over medium heat, add the oil, and bring to a simmer. Add the nettles, sprinkle lightly with salt, and cook, stirring, until wilted, about 1 minute. Stir in the goat cheese, cranberry beans, cooked noodles, and lemon zest and juice and cook until the beans and noodles are evenly coated, about 2 minutes. Finish with a drizzle of oil and a few grinds of pepper. Scatter the bread crumbs over the top and serve immediately straight from the skillet.

Rye Orecchiette with Flowering Broccoli Rabe, Preserved Lemon, and Garden Greens

This pasta is inspired by Jen's garden in late spring and early summer. She loves to grow edible flowers, tons of herbs, and leafy greens and uses them daily in the kitchen during that time of the year. Orach is one of her favorite leaves to eat, and since it is hard to find in stores, she always grows it so she has some on hand. It is a tall, handsome plant with triangular leaves ranging in color from light green to deep purple. It has a briny, delicate flavor and is a nutrient powerhouse—full of calcium, minerals, and anthocyanins. Nasturtium grows rampant in Northern California and has a lovely, peppery, delicately bitter flavor. The preserved lemons for this recipe can be purchased at grocery stores that sell foods from North Africa, where they are a staple. They are also easy to prepare at home and make a piquant garnish for salads, grain bowls, and pasta and seafood dishes. Use Eureka lemons or another sour, thick-skinned variety; sweeter, thinner-skinned Meyer lemons are not ideal for preserving.

Makes 4 servings

Preserved Lemons

5 to 6 Eureka lemons, scrubbed

1 cup kosher or sea salt

1 large bunch flowering broccoli rabe, trimmed and coarsely chopped

3 Tbsp good-quality extra-virgin olive oil

½ cup loosely packed nasturtium leaves

½ cup loosely packed nasturtium flowers

1 cup loosely packed orach leaves (or dandelion greens or another dark, leafy green), coarsely chopped

1 batch rye orecchiette (page 340)

2 oz firm sheep's milk cheese (such as canestrato or pecorino), shaved into broad, thin slices with a vegetable peeler

To make the preserved lemons: Cut each lemon lengthwise into quarters. Pack one layer of lemon quarters onto the bottom of a 1-qt canning or other glass jar. Sprinkle generously with some of the salt and press down on the fruit to compact it. Pack another layer of lemon quarters on top of the first one. Salt this layer and again press down. Repeat the layering process until all of the lemon quarters are in the jar, are well salted, and are packed very tightly. Cover the jar with its lid and set aside at room temperature for 30 minutes. During this time, the salt will draw out juice from the lemons and there will be enough juice in the jar to cover the fruit completely. Every so often, invert the jar and gently shake it to dissolve all the salt.

CONTINUED

Place the jar in a cool, dark place until the lemons become soft and translucent, about 3 weeks. They are then ready to use. The lemons will keep in the jar in the refrigerator for up to 6 months.

When ready to use preserved lemon in a recipe, remove a lemon piece from the jar and mince or very thinly slice it. (Some people prefer to rinse the lemon before cutting it, but I really like the saltiness and flavor in all its intensity.)

Prepare a large bowl of ice water and set it near the stove. Bring a large pot of generously salted water to a boil. It should taste briny like the sea. Add the broccoli rabe to the boiling water and cook until bright green, about 30 seconds. Using tongs, transfer the broccoli rabe to the ice water to halt the cooking. Keep the pot of boiling water on the stove top.

In a large skillet over medium-low heat, warm the oil. Thinly slice one or two quarters of preserved lemon. Add the lemon, nasturtium leaves, nasturtium flowers, and orach and cook, stirring, until just wilted, about 3 minutes. Drain the broccoli rabe, stir it into the nasturtium and orach, and remove the pan from the heat.

Bring the cooking water to a rapid boil again. Add the orecchiette, give them a good stir, and cook until tender but not at all mushy, 3 to 5 minutes. Test for doneness by removing one from the water, letting it cool for a moment, and then biting into it. It should be yielding but firm. Drain the pasta.

Return the skillet to medium heat and stir in the orecchiette. Garnish with the cheese and serve immediately straight from the skillet.

cavatelli

orecchiette

Acknowledgments

Many thanks to Jen Latham, my coauthor and dear friend, surf pal, and head of bread for the past several years at Tartine, who did much of the heavy lifting to get all these ideas into book form and was a true gem to work with outside of the bread room.

—Chad Robertson

I'm deeply grateful to Jay, without whom none of this would have happened. And to Mom and Dad for being epic parents and grands. Thank you to Chad, for every opportunity and for always believing in me. Your friendship and mentorship mean the world to me.

—Jennifer Latham

Heartfelt thanks to:

Liz Barclay, photographer and creative collaborator, who shot the book over this last challenging and strange year, between San Francisco and Los Angeles, shining her light all along the way.

Katherine Cowles, friend, advisor, and literary agent, for her continued steadfast support in both talking me up and talking me down.

Lorena Jones, longtime editor and de facto director of book operations, without whom none of the last few books would have ever been finished.

Juliette Cezzar, longtime designer and collaborator who filters and focuses the crazy ideas in the beginning and makes the really hard parts at the end actually fun.

Maria Ziska, recipe tester and writer, master of the thoughtful and thorough details of the style sheet.

Nidia Cueva, for her wonderful work on prop selection and styling.

The Tartine bakers who make the bread happen every day no matter what else is going on, and especially to managers Meg Fisher, Lisa Chun, Veronica Cates, and Michael Rogers, who each performed many unparalleled feats of bread heroism during the making of this book.

Chef collaborators Nico Pena, Jordan Whittrock, Max Blachman Gentile, DK Kollender, and their teams in San Francisco and Los Angeles, for making lots of simple, healthy, and beautiful food.

Kevin Morse and his team at Cairnspring Mills along with Tom and Sue Hunton at Camas Country Mill, for pioneering a new way of building a sustainable, regional grain model for all of us.

—Chad Robertson and Jennifer Latham

Index

Published in the United States by Lorena Jones Books,
an imprint of Random House, a division of Penguin
Random House LLC, New York.
www.tenspeed.com

Lorena Jones Books and the Lorena Jones Books
colophon are registered trademarks of Penguin Random
House LLC.

Library of Congress Cataloging-in-Publication
Data is on file with the publisher.

Library of Congress Control Number: 2021933063

Hardcover ISBN: 978-0-399-57884-7
eBook ISBN: 978-0-399-57885-4

Printed in China

Editor: Lorena Jones
Production editor: Doug Ogan
Designers: Juliette Cezzar and Kelly Booth
Production designers: Mari Gill and Mara Gendell
Production manager: Serena Sigona
Prop stylist: Nidia Cueva
Copyeditor: Sharon Silva
Proofreader: Rachel Markowitz
Indexer: Ken DellaPenta
Publicist: Kristin Casemore
Marketer: Allison Renzulli

10 9 8 7 6 5 4 3 2 1

First Edition